STUDIES IN BAPTIST HISTORY AND THOUGHT
VOLUME 28

# Pulpit and People

## Studies in Eighteenth Century Baptist Life and Thought

STUDIES IN BAPTIST HISTORY AND THOUGHT
VOLUME 28

# Pulpit and People

## Studies in Eighteenth Century Baptist Life and Thought

Edited by
John H. Y. Briggs

WIPF & STOCK · Eugene, Oregon

Wipf and Stock Publishers
199 W 8th Ave, Suite 3
Eugene, OR 97401

Pulpit and People
Studies in Eighteenth-Century Baptist Life and Thought
By Briggs, John H. Y.
Copyright©2009 Paternoster
ISBN 13: 978-1-60899-164-8
Publication date 10/6/2009
Previously published by Paternoster, 2009

This Edition published by Wipf and Stock Publishers by arrangement with Paternoster

STUDIES IN BAPTIST HISTORY AND THOUGHT

# Series Preface

Baptists form one of the largest Christian communities in the world, and while they hold the historic faith in common with other mainstream Christian traditions, they nevertheless have important insights which they can offer to the worldwide church. *Studies in Baptist History and Thought* will be one means towards this end. It is an international series of academic studies which includes original monographs, revised dissertations, collections of essays and conference papers, and aims to cover any aspect of Baptist history and thought. While not all the authors are themselves Baptists, they nevertheless share an interest in relating Baptist history and thought to the other branches of the Christian church and to the wider life of the world.

The series includes studies in various aspects of Baptist history from the seventeenth century down to the present day, including biographical works, and Baptist thought is understood as covering the subject-matter of theology (including interdisciplinary studies embracing biblical studies, philosophy, sociology, practical theology, liturgy and women's studies). The diverse streams of Baptist life throughout the world are all within the scope of these volumes.

The series editors and consultants believe that the academic disciplines of history and theology are of vital importance to the spiritual vitality of the churches of the Baptist faith and order. The series sets out to discuss, examine and explore the many dimensions of their tradition and so to contribute to their on-going intellectual vigour.

A brief word of explanation is due for the series identifier on the front cover. The fountains, taken from heraldry, represent the Baptist distinctive of believer's baptism and, at the same time, the source of the water of life. There are three of them because they symbolize the Trinitarian basis of Baptist life and faith. Those who are redeemed by the Lamb, the book of Revelation reminds us, will be led to 'fountains of living waters' (Rev. 7.17).

## Series Editors

Anthony R. Cross, Fellow of the Centre for Baptist History and Heritage, Regent's Park College, Oxford, UK

Curtis W. Freeman, Research Professor of Theology and Director of the Baptist House of Studies, Duke University, North Carolina, USA

Stephen R. Holmes, Lecturer in Theology, University of St Andrews, Scotland, UK

Elizabeth Newman, Professor of Theology and Ethics, Baptist Theological Seminary at Richmond, Virginia, USA

Philip E. Thompson, Assistant Professor of Systematic Theology and Christian Heritage, North American Baptist Seminary, Sioux Falls, South Dakota, USA

## Series Consultant Editors

David Bebbington, Professor of History, University of Stirling, Scotland, UK

Paul S. Fiddes, Professor of Systematic Theology, University of Oxford, and Principal of Regent's Park College, Oxford, UK

Ken R. Manley, Distinguished Professor of Church History, Whitley College, The University of Melbourne, Australia

Stanley E. Porter, President and Professor of New Testament, McMaster Divinity College, Hamilton, Ontario, Canada

# Contents

**Contributors**     ix

**Foreword**
D. Densil Morgan     xi

**Chapter 1**
**The Changing Pattern of Baptist Life in the Eighteenth Century**
John H. Y. Briggs     1

**Chapter 2**
**Benjamin Keach (1640-1704): Tailor Turned Preacher**
Austin Walker     25

**Chapter 3**
**Stogdon, Foster, and Bulkeley: Variations on an Eighteenth-Century Theme**
Stephen Copson     43

**Chapter 4**
**James Fanch (1704-1767): The Spiritual Counsel of an Eighteenth-Century Baptist Pastor**
Karen E. Smith     58

**Chapter 5**
**Gilbert Boyce: General Baptist Messenger and Opponent of John Wesley**
Clive Jarvis     75

**Chapter 6**
**Benjamin Beddome (1717-1795): His Life and His Hymns**
Michael Haykin     93

**Chapter 7**
**Daniel Turner and a Theology of the Church Universal**
Paul S. Fiddes                                                            112

**Chapter 8**
**Andrew Fuller and** *The Gospel Worthy of All Acceptation*
P. J. Morden                                                              128

**Chapter 9**
**Caleb Evans and the Anti-Slavery Question**
Roger Hayden                                                              152

**Chapter 10**
**Martha Gurney and William Fox: Baptist Printer
and Radical Reformer, 1791-1794**
Timothy Whelan                                                            165

**Index**                                                                 203

# Contributors

**John H. Y. Briggs**, Director of the Baptist History and Heritage Centre, Regent's Park College, University of Oxford and Visiting Research Professor, the International Baptist Theological Seminary, Prague

**Austin Walker**, Pastor of Maidenbower Baptist Church, Crawley, Sussex

**Stephen Copson**, Secretary the Baptist Historical Society and Regional Minister, Central Baptist Association, The Baptist Union of Great Britain

**Karen E. Smith**, Tutor, South Wales Baptist College, Cardiff and Minister, Orchard Place Baptist Church, Neath, Wales

**Clive Jarvis**, Minister, Seaford Baptist Church

**Michael Haykin**, Professor of Church History, The Southern Baptist Theological Seminary, Louisville, Kentucky, USA

**Paul S. Fiddes**, Professor of Systematic Theology, The University of Oxford, sometime Principal of Regent's Park College

**P. J. Morden**, Tutor in Church History, Spurgeon's College, London

**Roger Hayden**, Honorary Research Fellow, and Archivist, Bristol Baptist College

**Tim Whelan**, Professor, Department of Philosophy and Literature, Georgia Southern University, Statesboro, Georgia, USA

# Foreword

As the second decade of the twenty first century approaches, the study of Baptist history is in a flourishing state. A stream of excellent dissertations, many of the best of which have been published in Paternoster's 'Studies in Baptist History' series, to say nothing of the fresh research which appears regularly in *The Baptist Quarterly* and other outlets, gives evidence of a vibrancy which would, perhaps, be unexpected in a so-called 'post-Christian' world. There is no doubt that a new generation is engaging intelligently and insightfully into the Christian past. In order to dialogue with that past we first need to understand it and to understand researchers need to be involved in the painstaking task of uncovering it. That there is a commitment to doing this in what many regard as an epoch in which immediacy is valued above all else, with the past, in a globalized world, being dispatched to the realms of irrelevance, gives pause for thought. When denominationalism is rejected (even when it has been hardly understood) and even ecumenism is being superseded, the vitality of Baptist studies is quite remarkable.

The remarkable nature of this contemporary ebullience is compounded by the fact that Baptists, of all Christians, are thought to be the least enamoured of the concept of tradition. 'The Bible and the Bible alone is the religion of Protestants', an adage which was deeply misleading even when it was first coined, is thought best to describe the Baptist attitude to tradition. But, as Keith Clements has written: 'Baptists have now been in existence for nearly four centuries, more than long enough to have acquired a distinctive history to own and cherish (the "heritage"), an identity shaped by struggle and circumstance over the generations; in short, a tradition, and one which moreover is virtually as old as the Anglican settlement'. Biblicism is not a straightforward concept, while the very nature of biblical religion demands an understanding of history and the dynamics of God's involvement with his people from one generation to the next. Understanding the implications of the *paradosis* or 'handing on', in which the gospel message is perpetuated within a specific culture, is something which has always engaged the skills and abilities of Baptist historians from Joseph Ivimey (and Joshua Thomas) to the present time.

John Briggs's volume *Pulpit and People: Studies in Eighteenth Century Baptist Life and Thought* is the latest example of this long engagement: it is also one of the best. The editor's opening chapter sets the scene with clarity and perceptiveness: the intertwining of social factors with doctrinal concerns among both the Particular and the General Baptists; the impact of the Evangelical Revival undoubtedly for good though, perhaps, in the realm of ecclesiology at least, for bad with the dissipation of a covenant or communal faith in favour of a vibrant individualism; a renewal of the association ideal; an energetic and immensely confident and creative world-wide missionary endeavour and much else beside. The subsequent chapters provide fascinating detail, historical acumen and not infrequently sharp insight into the way in which specific religious convictions were worked out in the context of the complexities and variety of eighteenth century life. There is also much which can be applied to the witness of our Baptist churches in a very different age. The abiding impression of the state of pulpit and people among eighteenth century Baptists is one of energy and inventiveness grounded in a belief in the power of the gospel and its potential for creating something new though rooted in the given-ness of a faith once delivered to the saints.

There is no doubt that Baptist historiography and the dissenting tradition, constantly being renewed in the face of fresh challenges, have much to offer contemporary British Christianity still. The present volume, replete with an impeccable scholarship, witnesses eloquently to that fact.

D. Densil Morgan
*School of Theology and Religious Studies*
*Bangor University*
*Wales*

CHAPTER 1

# The Changing Pattern of Baptist Life in the Eighteenth Century

John H. Y. Briggs

The larger part of the eighteenth century is often treated as something of a Baptist wilderness with extremes of hyper-Calvinism emerging among the Particular Baptists, and Christological aberrations amid the General Baptists, savaging the denomination's evangelical usefulness in many parts of the country. The third strand in Baptist life was that of the Seventh Day Baptists, a dwindling cause as the century progressed, representing further divisiveness in the Baptist body, though some important families like the Chamberlains, the Bampfields and the Stennetts had their roots among them. The irony of all this is that the churches had been stronger in those years of persecution which followed the restoration of the monarchy in 1662 than in the years of limited toleration brought in by the Act of Toleration in 1689, or put differently internal division proved more inhibiting than external persecution. Of themselves those two dates indicate that the lives of the churches were politically conditioned by the outlook of the secular authorities of the times.

In seeking to unravel the history of the century it is worth underlining that there is a bias in the record towards the literate rather than the illiterate, the male rather than the female, the leaders rather than the led, though clearly Baptist congregations, in which women were nearly always in the majority, contained many unable to read, who were heavily dependent on the leadership for the forming of their Christian lives, though a 'heard' rather than a 'read' theology might prove more enduring in times of difficulty. The congregations that have left the best records tend to be urban rather than rural, the successful rather than the weak and failing, the metropolitan rather than the provincial, though there are important exceptions to this pattern. Thus there is a built-in 'Whig' bias in the surviving records, and conscious effort has to be made to recreate that much more fragile world of the little Bethel, meagrely financed, often living with an uncertain future, prone to division and schism, which is also part of the experience of the people called Baptists.

## Limited Toleration and Social Violence

Only slowly did the state come to understand that tender consciences could not be coerced by force into conformity with Canterbury, and that the state had nothing to fear, and much to gain, by allowing them a measure of freedom. In this way Britain came to pioneer within the nations of Christendom, a recognition of Christian, if not religious, pluralism, even if only within the very prescribed form of toleration secured in 1689. Beyond that there was not only legislative status to be secured, but a social acceptance to be attained. In the early eighteenth century dissenting meeting houses were vulnerable to civil riot, especially in the Sacheverell riots of 1715, and even at the end of the century, the Baptists of King's Heath, Birmingham suffered from an overflow of the venom against the Unitarian, Joseph Priestly, in the Church and King Riots of 1791. This was a movement which continued into the early nineteenth century when, for example, landlord, parson and magistrate combined against village preaching in Wickham Market, failing to give the preachers the protection which they could properly expect from the law.[1]

Rural dissenters suffered more than their urban counterparts, for in towns and cities, dissenters were soon taking a leading part in trade, manufacture and, legal restraints notwithstanding, in civic life. Indeed it has been argued that the very exclusion from political office in the earlier part of the period encouraged the concentration of their efforts in commercial and industrial endeavour. It was here that, with an ethic which encouraged conscientious labour, but which put restrictions on those patterns of ostentatious consumption associated with the aristocracy, that puritan, indeed puritanical, dissenters came to accumulate large amounts of capital, which was available for both philanthropic and larger commercial-industrial purposes. Amongst the most successful were the Hollis family whose wealth initially derived from the cutlery trade in Sheffield but who seem to have become master drapers shortly after their removal to Lon-

---

[1] D. Lovegrove, *Established Church, Sectarian People: Itinerancy and the Transformation of English Dissent, 1780-1830* (Cambridge: Cambridge University Press, 1988), p. 211, n. 42, provides a list of the cases of disturbance of worship that the Dissenting Deputies dealt with between 1740 and 1825; J.H.Y. Briggs, 'Oxford and the Meeting House Riots of 1715', in R. Chadwick (ed.), *A Protestant Catholic Church of Christ: Essays on the History and Life of New Road Baptist Church, Oxford* (Oxford: New Road Baptist Church, 2003), pp. 35-64; L. Kreitzer, '"A Famous Prank" in Oxford: the Jacobite Riots of 1715 and the Charge of Sexual Scandal', *Baptist Quarterly*, 42.1 (2007), pp. 33-52; A.S. Langley, *Birmingham Baptists Past and Present* (London: Kingsgate Press, 1939), pp. 129-30. [I think the house where the blind John Harwood resided and which he had licensed for worship is to be identified with the Baptist Chapel at King's Heath which David Wykes (in 'A finished monster of the true Birmingham breed', in A.P.F. Sell (ed.), *Protestant Nonconformists and the West Midlands of England* (Keele: Keele University Press, 1996)) says was ransacked.] M. Thorp, '"No Pogroms Here": The Wickham Market Riots, 1810', *Baptist Quarterly*, 40.5 (2004), pp. 284-301.

don, playing an important part in the Drapers' Company. Profits from the business coupled with the shrewd handling of property and wise financial investments led to a considerable fortune, part of which was given to the founding of the Particular Baptist Fund in 1717, of which Thomas Hollis [III] became a Treasurer/Trustee. The Fund might have received more, but his fellow trustees refused to accept gifts from the Pinners' Hall congregation because it practised open membership, though it did not stop them receiving money from Thomas who was a member there. Much of his subsequent philanthropy was devoted to funding chairs and scholarships at the infant Harvard.[2]

## Of High and Hyper Calvinism

Much debate has turned round the extensiveness of hyper-Calvinism among eighteenth-century Particular Baptists, as indeed about the nature of that hyper-Calvinism. Roger Hayden has argued that such an emphasis was essentially a London phenomenon and that provincial Baptist life was not so much influenced by this, especially where that life was nourished by traditions of Evangelical Calvinism propagated by Bristol College.[3] The Bristol influence was more a matter of connexion than geography, for as close as Bath, high if not hyper, Calvinist forces were influential.[4]

The extreme Calvinists seemed to have derived their particular interpretation of Calvinism from the writings of Dr Tobias Crisp [1600-43], a Wiltshire rector, whose writings, popular in certain dissenting circles, were republished by his son in 1690. The second major influence was that of Joseph Hussey [1660-1726], minister of Hogg Hill Independent Church in Cambridge Such background is important as indicating that the controversy was far from being an exclusively Baptist squabble. One of Hussey's converts, though the language is, of course, most improper, was John Skepp [c1670-1721], who for the last ten years of his life was pastor of the Baptist church which met at the Curriers' Hall. He has been credited as the first Baptist minister to question the right of preachers to invite their hearers to put their trust in Christ, action which he described as 'a piece of robbery against the Holy Spirit'.[5]

---

[2] R.E. Davies, 'Thomas Hollis and Family: Baptist Benefactors', *Baptist Quarterly* 42.3 (2007), pp. 234-44.

[3] R. Hayden, *Continuity and Change: Evangelical Calvinism among Eighteenth-Century Baptist Ministers Trained at Bristol Academy, 1660-1791* (Chipping Norton: Nigel Lynn for Roger Hayden and the Baptist Historical Society, 2006), especially Part III.

[4] Kerry J. Birch, 'The Contribution of the Baptists of Bath to the Religious and Social History of the City [1774-1837], with Special Reference to Somerset Street and Twerton Baptist Churches' (MLitt thesis, University of Bristol, 2008).

[5] R. Brown, *English Baptists of the Eighteenth Century* (London: Baptist Historical Society, 1986), pp. 72-74; P. Naylor, *Calvinism, Communion and the Baptists: A Study of English Calvinistic Baptists from the Late 1600s to the Early 1800s* (Carlisle; Waynesboro, GA: Paternoster, 2003), pp. 172-78.

Skepp's books on Hebrew and rabbinics were purchased by John Gill [1697-1771] in whose ordination service he participated, whilst his successor at Curriers' Hall was John Brine [c1703-1765]. Both Gill and Brine, who were commanding figures amongst the London Particular Baptists in the mid eighteenth century, nurtured a high Calvinist understanding of soteriology; neither of them however should properly be called antinomian, an all too frequently used term of abuse for those of thorough-going Calvinist persuasion. Whilst Gill's soteriology might appear to limit the number of those who would be saved, his eschatology seemed to anticipate widespread missionary activity. Both Gill and Brine were brought up in, and called to the ministry by, the Kettering congregation, that same congregation which would later call Andrew Fuller to be their pastor. Both by pen and action Fuller sought to restate an inherited Calvinist theology in terms that, influenced by Jonathan Edwards, released new and vital energies of outreach and missionary endeavour.

### General Baptist Difficulties

The decline of the General Baptists was the child not only of heterodoxy but of a form of internal sectarianism that could make a practice such as the laying on of hands the occasion of one church dis-fellowshipping another. General Baptists at the end of the seventeenth century also suffered significant losses to the Quakers The expansion of the denomination was also heavily inhibited by rules about young people 'marrying out' of the narrow tradition in which they had been nurtured. Only with difficulty was the matter of congregational singing negotiated without causing division. As Raymond Brown argues, 'A literal interpretation of biblical passages often forced them into controversy and division on what appear to us to be marginal issues.'[6] The discernment of doctrine in scripture was of crucial concern, but there was little attempt to read the Bible within the fellowship of the whole church, past and present, that is to say to read it within a tradition of Reformed doctrine, let alone the faith shaped by discussions in the ecumenical councils of the early church.

Those amongst the General Baptists who found it difficult to discover a fleshed-out doctrine of the trinity in the Bible were certainly not unique. Many Presbyterians, and some within the Established Church, especially encountered the same difficulties. It troubled the General Baptists more because it tended to divide the Kent and Sussex churches with their close association with Dutch Mennonites from the congregations in central England, which it has been argued had more of a Lollard inheritance.[7] Already by the 1690s, in the south

---

[6] Brown, *English Baptists*, p. 18.
[7] M. Watts, *The Dissenters* (2 vols; Oxford: Clarendon Press, 1978), I, pp. 283-84 citing A.H.J. Baines, 'The Signatories of the Orthodox Confession of 1679', *Baptist Quarterly* 17.1 (1957), p. 43. [sic] Watts actually refers to *Baptist Quarterly* 17.1-4 (1957), pp. 35-42, 74-86, 122-28, 170-78.

east Mathew Caffyn seemed to be championing a strangely aberrant christology which challenged both Christ's true humanity after the manner of the sixteenth-century Anabaptist, Melchior Hoffman, and, in an Arian fashion, Christ's divinity.[8]

Such teaching was strenuously opposed by the Buckinghamshire messenger, Thomas Monk, causing a split between those churches who, loyal to Caffyn, remained in the General Assembly and those who, committed to an orthodox view of the Trinity, organised themselves in a new body called the General Association. Whilst attempts to reunite the two bodies, seemed only to weaken the Association, a sizeable rump of its churches would eventually join the New Connexion. These were also the years of the Salter's Hall debate [1719] when dissenters generally debated the issue of subscription to specific [trinitarian] doctrinal articles. It is significant that all but two Particular Baptists present were happy to subscribe, but only one General Baptist. Of course, whilst we know exactly what beliefs the subscribers were committed to, we do not know what the non-subscribers actually believed other than that they took scripture to be their authority in all matters of faith and conduct, not any man-made reduction there from.[9] By 1703 the orthodox amongst the General Baptists had lost a number of their most able defenders by death [Thomas Grantham, Thomas Monk, John Griffith and Joseph Wright], whilst at the same time a number of more able younger leaders left to become Particular Baptists [Richard Adams, Richard Allen, John Piggott, and Mark Key] as Benjamin Keach had done rather earlier.[10]

The denomination's christological problems were, in part, the result of sincere believers reading scripture apart from the historic traditions of the church in which the doctrines of the trinity had been hammered out, especially since the General Baptists were estranged from other orthodox dissenters as not belonging to the larger Calvinist family, and therefore lacked appropriate confessional points of reference. Their doctrinal struggles were not the result of any post-Enlightenment reductionism but genuine problems with interpreting the Biblical text. What the General Baptists experienced at the beginning of the eighteenth century was mirrored among the Particular Baptists at the end of the century especially amongst those with Bristol connexions, some indeed amongst the extended family of Hugh and Caleb Evans, most notably John Evans [1767-1827], who became the minister of the Worship Street congregation in London, combining anti-trinitarian views – he denied the Spirit a separate identity from that of the first and second persons of the trinity - with a firm commitment to the idea of final judgment.

---

[8] Brown, *English Baptists*, pp. 16-17, 21-2.
[9] R. Tudur Jones, *Congregationalism in England, 1662-1962* (London: Independent Press, 1962), pp. 133-38.
[10] Brown, *English Baptists*, p. 25.

## The Baptist Denomination on the Eve of the Evangelical Revival

Both wings of the denomination were therefore facing severe difficulties on the eve of the Evangelical Revival. Not only were there weakening theological disputes which robbed them of both relevance and attractiveness, but small congregations had become increasingly inward-looking and defensive. Joseph Ivimey cites John Gill's qualitative judgment and mathematical calculations made by John Ryland of Warwick; Gill speaks of both a lack of zeal and a widespread diffusion of error, together, with rare exception, of an absence of able young leaders to take the place of older men. To this Ryland adds the calculation, admittedly of a highly speculative nature, that membership of Particular Baptist churches in England was around 5,500 with a community strength of around 16,500 in 1750. To this he adds a note that the General Baptists were at that time few in number with congregations 'small and languishing', but there is reason to believe that he was over pessimistic about the numerical strength of the General Baptists at this time.

This represented a severe decline on the situation obtaining in 1688; Ivimey concludes 'that prosperity has indeed slain more than the sword', a judgment well confirmed by the evidence of the Evans List derived from data collected between 1715 and 1718 where the figures for adherents are 40,500 Particular Baptists and 19,000 General Baptists. The second quarter of the eighteenth century had seen a worrying reduction in both membership and attendance. Were such a decline to be perpetuated, a once strong denominational tradition was in danger of extinction in many parts of the country and that within a generation. Ivimey alludes to 'the cold, dry, uninteresting doctrinal statements of the leading Baptists' asserting that 'had not God raised up the Methodists.... the rapid decline of the churches must have gone on with an accelerated motion.', identifying in particular the influx of Whitefield's converts into the churches of dissent and his renewing influence on the dissenting ministry.[11]

## The Impact of the Revival on Both Components within the Denomination

The rebirth of the denomination occurred as the general forces of revival began to impact upon Baptist life. In 1770, some of those who had been influenced by the Methodist Revival came to see the strength of the arguments for baptism by immersion and the restriction of the ordinance to believers only. However, after

---

[11] J. Ivimey, *A History of the English Baptists* (4 vols; London: n.p., 1811-30), III, pp. 277-82. I have subtracted the figures for Wales from the Ryland calculation to make comparison with Evans' figures easier. The 1718 figures are those provided by Michael Watts who has moderated Evans figures and submitted them to substantial testing for reliability. Watts, *The Dissenters,* I, pp. 268-70, 282-84 and Appendix, pp. 491-508 See also W. Morgan Patterson, 'The Evangelical Revival and the Baptists', in W.H. Brackney, P.F. Fiddes, and J.H.Y. Briggs (eds), *Pilgrim Pathways: Essays in Honour of B.R. White* (Macon, GA: Mercer University Press, 1999), pp. 243-62.

some initial overtures, finding no sympathy with the increasingly heterodox existing Arminian Baptists, they formed the New Connexion of General Baptists espousing an orthodox and evangelical Arminianism. As this new group became established, so it attracted to itself those churches of the old connexion that had remained orthodox, principally to be found in Lincolnshire, the south midlands, and the home counties to the north of the Thames. The churches in Kent and Sussex, by contrast, increasingly identified themselves with Arian and Socinian views. The New Connexion's heartlands were to become the East Midland counties east of the Pennines, stretching up into Yorkshire. In London, the new and old connexions existed side by side.

At the same time a number of those influenced by George Whitefield, and by transatlantic thinking associated with the name of Jonathan Edwards, entered the Baptist ministry. In the last third of the century a sequence of significant books began to articulate a new theological outlook. In 1768 Abraham Booth, a General turned Particular Baptist, published his much reprinted *Reign of Grace*, a year before he entered on his long pastorate of the Prescot Street Church in London. In 1781 the elder Robert Hall published a sermon he had preached two years earlier as the influential *Help to Zion's Travellers*. In 1785 Andrew Fuller finally set down in orderly form ideas that he had been pondering for four years in *The Gospel Worthy of all Acceptation*, spelling out a new Evangelical Calvinism, which came to underpin a new and vibrant vision of world mission.

At home the impact of the revival was to help the Particular Baptists to spread out from their heartlands, indicated by such centres as London, Bristol, Northampton, Cambridge, with strengths in the neighbouring counties of Essex, Bedfordshire, Northamptonshire, Hertfordshire, Buckinghamshire, Berkshire, Somerset, Wiltshire, and Devon, as well as considerable strength in south east Wales. Church planting now saw the denomination spread into Cornwall, along the south coast, into the West Midlands and up into Yorkshire as well as to the North West whilst the ancient Baptist churches of the area around Newcastle upon Tyne were reinforced. All in all the spread of the denomination at the end of the century was far more comprehensive than it had been at its beginning.

New theological emphases and a new vision of winning the world for Christ was also the fruit of a renewed spirituality which found its focus in John Sutcliff's Prayer Call of 1784. In that year he proposed to the Northamptonshire Association that churches hold a special prayer meeting on the first Monday of every month 'that sinners may be converted, the saints edified, the interest of religion revived, and the name of God glorified': 'let the whole interest of the Redeemer be affectionately remembered, and the spread of the gospel to the distant parts of the habitable globe be the object of your most fervent prayers.'[12]

---

[12] E.A. Payne, *The Prayer Call of 1784* (London: Baptist Laymen's Missionary Movement, 1941).

Of course, dissenters, devoted to the hymnody of Isaac Watts, once the congregational hymn singing controversy, [which for a number of years seemed set fair to divide the churches], was put behind them, had been singing about a world-wide faith for at least two generations. That is since at least the writing of Watts' hymn 'Jesus shall reign where're the sun/Doth his successive journeys run,' which was published in 1719 in his Psalms of David, where it appears as a paraphrase of Psalm 72 under the title 'Christ's Kingdom among the Gentiles'. Recognised as 'the earliest notable hymn on overseas missions', two verses omitted in modern hymn books make this even more clear:

Behold the islands with their kings
And Europe her best tribute brings;
From north to south the princes meet
To pay their homage at His feet.

There Persia, glorious to behold,
There India shines in eastern gold;
And barbarous nations at His word
Submit and bow, and own their Lord.[13]

It was one thing to affirm a missionary faith in hymnody, something else to set up an organisation able to sustain international mission and to enthuse the home constituency to support it as the major imperative in church life.

### Discovering a Wider Baptist Family

Fuller was the theologian turned administrator, who secured the vision in practical action as he took on the task of being the first secretary of the 'Particular Baptist Missionary Society for propagating the Gospel among the Heathen', which was founded in 1792 with William Carey and his colleagues setting up the first overseas mission station in Danish territory at Serampore. This involved not just a new commitment to share the gospel with unbelievers but a new discovery of the world, that is, the global perspectives of Christian faith in contrast to the 'parochialism' of a narrowly insular British faith. Not only was there a world to win but a world of fellow believers to link up with in the pursuit of that mission.

Such ideas had partially been advocated by the General Baptist, Thomas Grantham, at the end of the seventeenth century but now found a ready advocate in John Rippon, Gill's successor at Carter's Lane, who in 1790 began *The Baptist Annual Register* as a vehicle for sharing intelligence both about Baptist history and heritage as well as about Baptists around the world. Not only did it

---

[13] Hugh Martin (ed), *The Baptist Hymn Book Companion* (London: Psalms and Hymns Trust, 1962), p. 178.

share information about the different English associations now revived or founded as agencies of determined mission, but also laid down the record with regard to churches in Wales, Scotland and Ireland. Subsequent to a renewal of correspondence between individual British and American ministers following on the War of Independence, Rippon sought to institutionalise the publicizing of American religious news, responding in his words to 'a pretty general wish on both sides of the Atlantic, of obtaining a more comprehensive knowledge of each others religious circumstances'.[14] Indeed the *Register* was designed to meet the needs of a Transatlantic Baptist community. One particular aspect of this was recording the story of black Baptists in Georgia, South Carolina, Nova Scotia, Jamaica and Sierra Leone, and more than that securing practical help for them. At the same time he also engaged with the black diaspora in Britain, a large congregation of whom uniquely crowded Carter's Lane Chapel on 27 March, 1807 to celebrate the abolition of the slave trade in the British Empire.[15]

In the *Register* for 1793 there appears what purports to be a grand 'Catalogue of the Professors and Ministers among the Baptists within and out of the United Netherlands ... for 1791', to which he adds details of churches in Prussia, Poland, Lithuania, Saxony, the Rhineland, Switzerland France and Russia. The difficulty for the critical historian is that none of these several hundred churches were Baptist congregations, rather they were Mennonite congregations conceptualised by Rippon as part of a larger Baptist/Anabaptist cousinage.[16] The same *Baptist Annual Register* carried a dedication printed on an unnumbered page after the title page, 'to all the baptized ministers and people in America, England, Ireland, Scotland, Wales, the United Netherlands, France, Switzerland, Poland, Russia, Prussia and Elsewhere ...... in serious expectation that before many years elapse (in imitation of other wise men) a deputation from all these climes will meet probably in London to consult the ecclesiastical good to the whole.' So behind the lists lie not only geographical aspirations but interesting historical assumptions. As Ken Manley observes, 'Thus the historical and continuing distinctions between Mennonites and English Baptists were largely ignored in the desire to establish a world identity for all "Baptists".'[17] Already by the beginning of the nineteenth century British Baptists were developing a sense of being part of a worldwide family which was more developed than that of any other denomination, and which would be further increased both by patterns of migration and by the missionary endeavours of the new century

---

[14] J. Rippon (ed.), *Baptist Annual Register* ([London]: n.p., 1790-93), p. iv.
[15] K.R. Manley, *'Redeeming Love Proclaim': John Rippon and the Baptists* (Carlisle, UK: Paternoster, 2004), ch. 5, especially pp. 143, 243-45.
[16] Rippon (ed.), *Baptist Annual Register*, 1793, pp. 303-18.
[17] Manley, *'Redeeming Love'*, pp. 173-74.

## A Covenanted People of God

The revival necessarily changed the way Baptists conceived of the church. Historically, Baptist understandings of the teachings of scripture were essentially worked out within the deliberations of the covenant community, where, for all their disdain for man-made creeds, they respected the inherited understanding of the fathers as expressed in the classic confessions of the previous century, to which each church might add its own covenant, in which commitment to such confessions, and a practical order of living the Christian life in good order, was spelt out. Indeed the church covenant became the foundational document which underpinned the life of every newly constituted church. Thus, for example, the frequently-copied covenant drafted by Benjamin and Elias Keach in 1697 relates the church covenant to God's 'eternal covenant' of free grace, and in that context asks church members to undertake eight solemn pledges. Eighteenth-century covenants survive for the churches at Bourton on the Water, [1719-20], Caerleon [Wales], [1770], New Road, Oxford, [1780], and Stony Stratford, [1790].[18]

Within such covenant communities the life of the believers and of their children was carefully and patiently nurtured with the expectation that under proper instruction these children of Christian homes would grow into faith and thus come themselves to be baptised on confession of a lively faith. This sedate dissent was soon to be challenged by the revival fire of the Evangelical Revival in which a man might walk into church a deceiver, a drunkard and a blasphemer and walk out of it, having experienced the new birth, with the saint's assurance of faith. The religion of gradual nurture was giving way to the revival experience of sudden conversion, as now representing an alternative norm in Christian experience.

This change can be expressed by undertaking an architectural comparison. Consider first a seventeenth-century meeting house, and note the language, this is *not* a church, for such high language is for people, not for bricks and mortar. The building is domestic in scale, perhaps with thatched roof. It will be twice as wide as it is deep, with the pulpit set against the long wall opposite the entrance. In front of the pulpit will be the big pew encircling the communion table, where the deacons may well have had their seats. John Betjeman described it as having the quality of a well-scoured farmhouse kitchen, for this is a building, built for business, – it is where the saints, well-versed in scripture met around the open Bible and the Table for their nurture and growth in grace. All was good quality, the best that men and women of modest means could provide.[19]

---

[18] W.L. Lumpkin, *Baptist Confessions of Faith* (Chicago: Judson Press, 1959); C.W. Deweese, *Baptist Church Covenants* (Nashville, TN: Broadman Press, 1990); T & D.G. George (eds), *Baptist Confessions, Covenants and Catechisms* (Nashville, TN: Broadman & Holman Publishers, 1996).

[19] John Betjeman, *First and Last Loves* (London: Murray, 1952), pp. 97-105.

Contrast with this, a Tabernacle of the late eighteenth and early nineteenth century. The language has changed, and although this may be a Baptist *Tabernacle* it will be found to be far from temporary or portable, especially if equipped with classical portico to spell out a proper defiance of Catholic Gothic. The interior is changed as well. The scale and the orientation have both been altered. The pulpit is set against the short wall opposite the entrance. Behind it will be ranged, in commanding fashion, an array of impressive organ pipes, as if these trumpets, great and small, were of major theological significance. The model was now not so much the domesticity of a farm house, but the performance of a theatre, with the preacher lifted six feet high above contradiction. Everything was done to accommodate as many hearers as possible, in serried ranks of pitch pine pews, with galleries taking the seating up the rear and around the side walls. There was much less sense of sharing here: the preacher had a message from God and the people, many of whom might be present for the first time, were present to receive it, not to engage in theological debate. This was a building for mission, a building to accommodate the unbeliever as much as the committed disciple. What might appear like a communion rail was there for a different purpose, for this was the penitents' bench, where those seeking Christ could make public display of that intention. The invitation will surely both be given and pressed in a service, when the preacher will be anticipating the presence of sinners needing conversion, amongst those present. Indeed the whole service will be constructed to lead up to a climax which will be found as those present respond to the gospel appeal. In this new chapel layout, mission to the unchurched was as important as the nurture of the saints of the church. R.W. Dale, writing of a wider congregationalism expressed the change in this way. 'The Evangelical Revival insisted on the union of the individual saint with Christ; but the union of the Church – an organised society of saints – with Christ, was not familiar to it.'[20]

As the revival renewed Baptist life and spawned more adventurous mission so the need for churches to co-operate with one another was underlined, and so the idea of association, was revived. Certainly Baptists had learnt to associate with one another in the seventeenth century but another mark of early eighteenth-century weakness was that such efforts had become 'limited, faltering and invariably inward-looking'. By contrast, both the older associations now revived and the new associations which date from the second half of the eighteenth century had an urgent missionary purpose. Archetypal of the new purposefulness was the Northamptonshire Association founded in 1764. Impelled by Fullerism, it witnessed both the issuing of the Prayer Call of 1784 and the founding of the BMS. Lovegrove is therefore right to assert that 'despite contemporary emphasis upon the resilience and vitality of the congregational principle, it is impossible to ignore the real movement towards association, interde-

---

[20] R.W. Dale, *A History of English Congregationalism* (London: Hodder and Stoughton, 1907), p. 590.

pendence and the growth of external authority: a process not capable of reversal, arising as it did from the conflicting pressures of permanent social change and the practicalities of concerted evangelism.'[21]

## Itinerancy and the Renewal of the Church at Home

Thus the organisation of overseas missions also revolutionised the church at home with the founding of the Itinerant Society ushering in a remarkable period of church growth: particular Baptist churches grew from around 400 in 1789 to more than 1,000 by 1835. Baptists were concerned to avoid the criticism of showing concern for the heathen abroad but neglecting the mission field on their doorstep.[22] Whilst George Mitchell and David Cro[s]sley had been active in church planting in the North West at the beginning of the century,[23] for much of the century the energies for such activities were not forthcoming. The last decade of the century, however, saw a reversal of such lethargy and the resumption of aggressive itinerancy, with churches and revived associations moving outside the comfort zone of their own domestic activities in determined outreach.[24] Thus benefiting from the new energies of revival, Baptist growth was considerable as Baptists were able, like other evangelical dissenters, to respond to population growth, and the growth of new urban communities consequent upon the beginnings of the industrial revolution in contrast to the Established church which was hampered by the need for a separate act of parliament to establish each new parish.

At the same time the life of local churches became much more varied. Worship services now pretty universally embraced hymn-singing, which was made much more enjoyable by the spread of literacy and the emergence of the hymn book, though still climaxing in the preaching of the sermon. Churches, by the end of the century, were beginning to operate Sunday Schools which sometimes had an almost autonomous existence with separate buildings. And everywhere there was an engagement with philanthropic outreach into society.

In this period of growth the denomination developed new educational institutions; alongside a reformed Bristol, [1770], new colleges emerged at Horton/Rawdon [1804, as the Northern Education Society] and Stepney [1811]. A

---

[21] Lovegrove, *Established Church, Sectarian People*, pp. 29-31; G.F. Nuttall, 'Assemblies and Association in Dissent', *Studies in Church History* 7 (1971), pp. 304-305.

[22] Lovegrove, *Established Church, Sectarian People*, especially ch. 2 and p. 25.

[23] W.T. Whitley, *Baptists of North West England* (London: Kingsgate Press, 1913), pp. 71, 99; I. Sellers (ed), *Our Heritage: The Baptists of Yorkshire, Lancashire, and Cheshire, 1647-1987* (Leeds: Yorkshire Baptist Association and the Lancashire and Cheshire Baptist Association, 1987), pp. 11, 14.

[24] See the *Minute Book of the Baptist Society for the Encouragement and Support of Itinerant and Village Preaching*, deposited in the Angus Library, Regent's Park College, the University of Oxford.

better educated society argued the need for a better-trained ministry. Before this, educational funds and societies had sponsored suitable young men for training for the ministry and a number of senior ministers had such living in their manses for a programme of supervised initiation into the skills required of a minister. Whilst this semi-structured pattern of ministerial formation heralded the development of the collegiate system, it remains remarkable that a large number of men proved themselves successful autodidacts, self-taught scholars, whose achievements stand as a lively tribute to their scholarly application and discipline.

### The Eighteenth-Century Pulpit

The preaching of eighteenth-century evangelical dissent majored on well thought-out argument. Contrary to the belief that Evangelicalism and orthodox dissent were antipathetic to the forces of the Enlightenment, it has been shown that there is as much convergence as tension in their mutual concerns: at its best the Baptist pulpit was both rational and evangelical, able to relate to the changing cultural context whilst demonstrating that the exploration of revelation required hard intellectual analysis.

Sermons preached by Baptists against the slave trade amply illustrate this connection.[25] The securing of this reform was seen in Whiggish fashion as an aspect of the growth of that freedom to which they, with many of their fellow citizens, aspired. In arguing for this, the preachers indicated that, whilst the teaching they were commending to their churches derived from revelation as recorded in scripture, it was also congruent with basic rationality, thereby making an appeal to a wider than church constituency. For example, Abraham Booth argued that the law against 'man-stealing'[slavery], though received by revelation, was based on general moral principle, what he later called 'the broad basis of common rectitude, of justice and of humanity'. 'Manstealing ... must be considered a moral evil – universally evil, in every age and every nation.' He described the slave trade as 'this outrage on the sacred rights of liberty, of justice, and of humanity', against which 'reason and conscience, the common sentiments and feeling of mankind, will all unite if not debauched by avarice or blunted by habit.' A major reason for this was that the equality of men, as all made by God, was fundamental Christian doctrine. 'Did we not all spring from one common stock?..... we are all brothers and sisters, members of one great family'.[26] In so arguing the Baptist pulpit articulated what one might call a doctrine of Creation Humanism; thus James Dore of Maze Pond argued that liberty was the gift of God to every man: 'And can we trample on the sa-

---

[25] J.H.Y. Briggs, 'Baptists and the Campaign to Abolish the Slave Trade', *Baptist Quarterly*, 42.4 (2007), pp. 260-83.
[26] A. Booth, *Commerce in the Human Species....* (London: printed by L. Wayland, 1792), p. 6.

cred rights of the human kind without invading the prerogative of Heaven?' Freedom was a matter of natural right, 'belonging to men, *as men*'. Natural rights he particularised as 'their right to their lives, their limbs, their liberty, the fruit of their labour, and to the use, in common with others, of air, light, and water' for which declaration he referred his readers to Blackstone and Paley. As rights these things should be inalienable, and certainly ought not to be removed by a superior possession of power. Indeed it was essential to civilisation to protect 'the evident distinction between power and right'.[27]

A little later Robert Hall embraced in his preaching a similar form of rational evangelicalism that put a high premium on thought and learning. He believed that education was crucial in liberating the permanent 'moral and spiritual' worth of the individual from the 'incrustations of poverty and ignorance'. Whilst happy to argue his case in the context of a prevailing philosophy of 'utility', education was properly a religious task in so far as it equipped humankind to realise the stature of the personhood with which God created men and women as distinct from all other creatures. In the creation economy, the ability to acquire and respond to a wide range of knowledge was deemed to be unique to humankind. The negative correlative of this was that to deprive someone of education was to deprive them of something essential to their divine creation, an indispensable mark of their humanity. Conversely, ignorance parented disorder: Hall believed that revolution in France was a product of a want of education. Reflecting his doughty protestantism, he argued that, whilst the Church of Rome was 'a friend to ignorance', the churches of the Reformation had a vested interest in rationality and truth. Religious education was especially important because it both provided 'an authentic discovery of the way to salvation' and supplied 'an infallible rule of life'. Once individuals had overcome the distortion of truth brought about by human sin, the Scriptures, duly read, revealed the mind of God, often alluded to by Hall in the rather remote language of the 'Supreme Being'. This provides another clue to the consonance of his thinking, thoroughly evangelical though it was, with the rationality of the age. Abstract learning offering an insufficient goal; thus Hall stressed the importance of Sunday school scholars understanding 'the necessity of the agency of the Spirit, to render the knowledge they acquire practical and experimental.'

---

[27] J. Dore, *A Sermon on the African Slave Trade....* (London: printed by L. Wayland, 1788), pp. 19-21.

## United in Mission, Divided at the Table[28]

Since Baptist growth was in part the fruit of united evangelical witness, Robert Hall began to ponder how it could be right for Christians to be united under the Spirit in mission but separate at the Lord's Table, hence his advocacy of open communion, which was fiercely resisted by others, not least Andrew Fuller and Abraham Booth. Hall's most extended debate on the issue, was however, with Joseph Kinghorn of Norwich. Fuller, Booth and Kinghorn all believed that 'closed' or 'strict' communion was necessary for protecting the distinctiveness of Baptist beliefs and ecclesiology.

Revisionist Calvinism had no necessary association with the extension of table fellowship to those not baptised as believers. Thus whilst Fuller was perplexed by those who wished to open the table, John Ryland, Senior, in his Northampton pastorate, one of a number of churches to embrace in membership both Baptists and Paedo-Baptists, associated open communion, and indeed open membership, with a rather old-fashioned high Calvinism.[29] From the very earliest days there were churches which combined those committed to believers' baptism and those happy to baptise infants, representing in fact the way in which many Baptist churches came into being, emerging out of independent separatist congregations which did not immediately secure, and some never securing, agreement to practise only believers' baptism. Bunyan is rightly famous for his pamphlet, *Water Baptism No Bar to Communion,* and accordingly a number of churches in Bedfordshire and the surrounding counties were formed on open-membership principles. Where local circumstances made open membership difficult there sometimes existed separate church rolls for each category whilst sharing, for the most part a common diet of worship, thus the existence of the 'big' and the 'little' churches within the fellowship at Broadmead, Bristol. Perhaps the most principled arguments for open membership came from men like Daniel Turner and Abraham Atkins, discussed by Professor Fiddes in this volume.

Within the communion debate lay two contradictory principles – the commitment to specific Baptist views of the church and the testimony of its distinctive sacramental practice, on the one hand, and a commitment to the 'catholic-

---

[28] See J.H.Y. Briggs, 'The Baptist Contribution to the Sunday School Movement in the Nineteenth Century' in Stephen Orchard and John Briggs (eds), *The Sunday School Movement* (Milton Keynes: Paternoster, 2007), pp. 45-46 citing R. Hall, 'The Signs of the Times', a sermon preached in Bristol, 1820, and 'The Advantage of Knowledge to the Lower Classes', a sermon preached in Leicester, 1810 in Olinthus Gregory (ed.), *The Works of Robert Hall...* (6 vols; London: Bohn, 1866 edn) ii: pp. 149-64; vi: pp. 186-87.

[29] See J.H.Y. Briggs, *Baptists of the Nineteenth Century* (Didcot: Baptist Historical Society, 1994), pp. 44-45, 61-65. See also, Naylor, *Calvinism, Communion and the Baptists*, especially ch. 7, and M. Walker, *Baptists at the Table: The Theology of the Lord's Supper amongst English Baptists in the Nineteenth Century* (Didcot: Baptist Historical Society, 1992).

ity' of the one church of Jesus Christ and the danger of espousing the sectarian, unchurching all other Christians, on the other. The latter position was reinforced by an emerging partnership in mission which emerged in those years when English society seemed threatened by the contrary forces of violent revolution and chauvinistic imperialism across the channel in France. Accordingly there was much agonizing discussion around the rival claims of pan-Evangelical mission and distinctive Baptist ecclesiology and practice.

### Living under the Stigma of Second-class Citizenship

The Act of Toleration did not give dissenters equal rights under the law with churchmen. It stated that certain punishments were not to be imposed on loyal and orthodox protestant dissenters, but left the disqualifying Test and Corporation Acts on the statute book. Specifically it excused Baptists from affirming the validity of infant baptism. In 1753, Lord Hardwicke's Act made all weddings illegal except those celebrated by the clergy of the Established church, a situation that existed until 1836. Dissenting baptisms – infant as much as believers – were not recognised and so innumerable dissenters were denied burial in parish churchyards, a disability suffered by some dissenters in remote rural areas even into the twentieth century.

Notwithstanding increased numbers and wealth as the century progressed, Baptists remained second-class citizens suffering penal legislation until 1828 when the Test and Corporation Acts, limiting their ability to take civil offices, were repealed. This did not involve complete exclusion from civic and national responsibilities – David Bebbington identifies three eighteenth-century Baptist MPs, Thomas Guy of hospital fame, [representative for Tamworth, 1695-1708], Frederick Bull, Lord Mayor of the City of London 1773-4, [MP for London, 1773-1784] and Sir George Caswell, Sheriff of London 1720-21 [MP for Leominster, 1717-21, 22-41].[30]

Notwithstanding such exceptions, the limitation of toleration was keenly felt with local oppression fostering resentment in many places. The number of such cases calling for legal defence led to the founding of the Dissenting Deputies in 1734, a committee of twenty-one laymen elected by the Presbyterian, Independent and Baptist congregations of London to protect the civil rights of their members, and to work for the repeal of the obnoxious Test and Corporation Acts. Between 1740 and 1800 they handled some 143 cases of claimed abuse of dissenting rights. This lay representation paralleled the rather older clerical

---

[30] D.W. Bebbington, 'Baptist MPs in the Seventeenth and Eighteenth Centuries.' *Baptist Quarterly*, 28.6 (1980), pp. 261-62, and D.W. Bebbington, 'Baptist MPs: a Supplementary Note', *Baptist Quarterly* 42.2 [part 2] (2007), p. 153. For Bull and Baptist involvement in the governance of London, see Ivimey, *History*, IV, pp. 42-46, and for Baptist involvement in the government of Bristol, see R. Hayden, 'Caleb Evans and the Anti-Slavery Question', *Baptist Quarterly*, 39.1 (2001), pp. 7-9.

'General Body' [four Presbyterian, three Baptist and three Independent ministers] who had from the accession of Queen Anne in 1702 secured the right to address the throne. In such bodies Baptists were able to act in unison with other dissenters, especially in defence of the limited freedom that was theirs.

At the heart of the Deputies' work in the first thirty odd years of their existence was the infamous Sheriff's Cause in the City of London. The ploy here was to appoint dissenters to the office of Sheriff, and then to fine them for refusing office, on the profits of which, it is said, the City Corporation built the Mansion House. Such an abuse of justice was brought to an end by the judgment of Lord Mansfield in the House of Lords in 1767 when Mansfield at the conclusion of his judgment affirmed 'It is now no crime for a man to say he is a Dissenter.' The man at the centre of the case was Allen Evans, by then 82 year of age. The case had been before the courts for thirteen years since 1754 when Evans was fined £600 for declining office because of the sacramental test required. A Dissenting Deputy himself, 'he was a man of considerable opulence, and great respectability' though by his faithfulness to the dissenting cause, 'he exposed himself to the displeasure of the Great as to suffer considerably in his secular affairs.' Ivimey tells us that at the time of initial prosecution Evans was a member and deacon of Little Wild Street, but in late 1756 he transferred his membership to the General Baptist Church meeting at the Barbican. A merchant of good standing in the city, he was sometime a member of the Baptist Board.[31]

## Conscience and Politics

Baptist attitudes towards both state and society were initially conditioned by the desire of the founders of the denomination to distinguish themselves from continental Anabaptism and the excesses that occurred in Münster in 1532-5 in particular. Unlike such radical sectarians, the English Baptists, in their confessions, go out of their way to underline their willingness to obey a properly appointed magistracy, even if they did indicate clear limits to the extent to which the magistrate's writ might legitimately run, and those areas where conscience in the church took precedence over magisterial demands. But even then, recognising the authority of the state, they did not object to such punishment as might follow conscientious dissidence. There were, however, difficulties for the promotion of this peaceable law-abiding image nearer at home than sixteenth-

---

[31] B.L. Manning, *The Protestant Dissenting Deputies* (Cambridge: Cambridge University Press, 1952), pp. 119ff and especially p. 129; W. Brock, 'John Ward' *Transactions of the Baptist Historical Society* 4 (1914), p. 25; S. Wilson, 'The Baptist Board', *Transactions of the Baptist Historical Society* 5 (1917), p. 214. The General Baptist Minister celebrated Evans' achievement in a funeral sermon. See 'Daniel Noble' *Baptist Quarterly* 1 (1922), p. 214 where Evans is said incorrectly to have been the Chairman of the Dissenting Deputies, J. Ivimey, *History*, III, pp. 284-87.

century Germany. Amidst all the turmoil of what is now called the English Revolution some Baptists had been attracted to programmes that challenged even the Cromwellian state both politically and socially. In its early stages the Leveller movement derived some sympathetic support from Baptists, some of whose number also entertained millenarian, and in particular Fifth Monarchist, views, which they adopted alongside their membership of Baptist churches. As a consequence it is not surprising that Baptists were still sometimes portrayed as potentially dangerous sectarians.

Only slowly then did Baptists in the eighteenth century develop the confidence to engage with political issues, but that they most certainly did. The causes provoking such engagement were threefold: first the American Revolution, then the campaign first to end the slave trade and then the institution of slavery itself, and finally events across the channel in France, where an early welcoming of the revolution soon gave way to condemnation as events there turned to violence and attacks on the Christian religion. In so engaging they readily identified themselves with a Whig interpretation of history, which cast the record of the past in terms of a conflict between reactionary aristocratic forces [including, of course, the interests of the established church] and those liberal progressive forces which were working for the extension of true liberty to all free-born Englishmen. Their political engagements were accordingly seen as parts of that process, which they were confident was swiftly moving towards its goal.

Not surprisingly the reactionary forces that they attacked easily conceived of them as politically dangerous, particularly in the context of unrest at home and revolution abroad, and used both the forces of the law, and the pressure of popular excitement to seek to constrain them. Caleb Evans of Bristol and Rees David of Norwich both demonstrated how forthright Calvinist Baptists could be in their condemnation of government in their mistaken oppression of their brethren, the American colonists.[32] Many preachers were forthright in their condemnation of the slave trade. James Dore, minister of that highly engaged congregation at Maze Pond, Southwark, was eloquent on this topic which presumably gave the church's deacons confidence to petition their minister to deliver a series of lectures on the French Revolution or as they expressed it about that 'wonderful Revolution, that a neighbouring Nation hitherto groaning under ecclesiastical and civil Tyranny has so recently experienced.' Instead of a na-

---

[32] Representative sermons include the following: R. David, *The Hypocratical Faith* (Norwich, 1781); Rees David, *The Fear of God* (Norwich, 1782); C. Evans, *British Constitutional Liberty* (Bristol, 1775); C. Evans, *The Death of a Great and Good Man ... James Rouquet* (Bristol, 1776); C. Evans, *British Freedom Realized* (Bristol, 1788). See James Bradley, *Religion, Revolution and English Radicalism: Nonconformity in Eighteenth-century Politics and Society* (Cambridge: Cambridge University Press, 1990), pp. 130 n.28 [for Rees David], 127 n.18, 128 n. 19, 137 n. 47 [for Caleb Evans]. Tracing these sermons in Starr proves impossible.

tion 'groaning under ecclesiastical and civil Tyranny', the deacons rejoiced in 'The ardour for Liberty extending itself to other countries'. Domestic developments they found less encouraging: 'we have much to complain of in this;- that the Consciences of Britons are tampered with by the allurements of temporal advantage, and their minds shackled by the terror of persecution – nevertheless we encourage hopes, that by the divine blessing accompanying a steady, temperate and persevering discussion of the subject, such an alteration will be produced in the opinions of the Public, and in the resolves of the Legislature, as may raise us to an eminence on the scale of Freedom, which we have never yet obtained.'[33]

William Winterbotham, assistant to, co-pastor with, and eventually successor to, the Revd Philip Gibbs in Plymouth was not so fortunate. His two sermons on the Revolution led to his imprisonment for four years from November 1793 to November 1797, during which time alongside other literary endeavours he published in three volumes a new edition of John Gill's *Body of Divinity*.[34] Radical political views and allegiance to strict Calvinism happily inhabited the same intelligence.

In general terms J.B. Bradley concludes, 'The pulpit rhetoric of the Dissenting ministry had a profound impact on the politics of ordinary men, and the only documentable instances of the indifference of the laity at Liverpool [and Sudbury] can be traced to the failure, or at least the passivity, of the Dissenting pulpit.' He also suggests that Liverpool dissent's deep involvement in the slave trade 'may well have dampened interest in radical causes.' He accordingly speaks of 'the lack of progressive leadership' from the dissenting pulpit in Liverpool.[35] Clarkson certainly found Liverpool less welcoming than Bristol, describing the people as 'more hardened' and speaking about the trade with more coldness and less feeling. Certainly the hymn-writer, Samuel Medley, pastor of the principal Baptist chapel in Liverpool 1772-1799, adopted a no-politics rule. In an unfortunately undated series of verses, he thanks a North American friend for a present of 'Salt Fish and Cyder' dispatched from that country. It was suggested that Medley might find a gift from such a source difficult to receive, because in recent years the American colonies had troubled the mother nation, to which Medley replies,

> Why true, sir, I am ready to own,
> American conduct has oft made me groan,
> And if on this subject I wrote my whole mind,
> It is much but you'd think me severe or unkind.

---

[33] '"A Diaconal Epistle, 1790", dated October 1790', *Baptist Quarterly* 8.1 (1936), p. 21.
[34] W.H.W. [presumably W.H. Whitley], *The Rev William Winterbotham: A Sketch* (Ballantyne, Hanson and Co, London, [for private circulation], 1893), pp. 22-44.
[35] Bradley, *Religion, Revolution and English Radicalism*, p. 411, p. 392.

> On the whole, it is therefore, perhaps for the best
> To say little or nothing, and so let it rest.[36]

There seem to have been some comfort in some situations in resorting to such ambiguity on political issues.

### Everyday Lives: The Layman's World

One of the areas most demanding of further research, is a purposive exploration of what being a member of a Baptist church meant to the lay folk of the congregation in their workaday lives. The emphasis on seriousness seen in their church life and their domestic spirituality was clearly carried over into the world of employment whether as employers or employees. Far from being an arena surrendered to the powers of Mammon, the secular world, – the school, shop and market place, the farm, mill or factory, the office, banking hall, publishing house, or surgery – all were seen as subject to kingdom principles of energetic commitment and high morality. Church books testify to the fact that failure here as much as deviance in theology would be the subject of church discipline. But even with the prominent lay persons in the denomination more is said of their churchy activities than of their working lives, the exact nature of which in some cases remains difficult to identify.

Membership of a dissenting chapel did, however, place a person within a network of relationships which could afford useful introductions in a world of developing trade and industry, and of migration across the country. Search the membership lists of London churches, such as Prescot Street, Little Wild Street, Carter's Lane, and Maze Pond, and names from the leading families of provincial churches will soon be found. Similarly provincial causes were often strengthened when deacons of these central London Churches decided to set up in business on their own account in the provinces. Amongst the General Baptists this interplay between London and provincial church life became so common that it provoked an experiment in the exchange of employment intelligence. The General Baptist Assembly meeting on May 27 1795, records a letter from the Revd J. Kingsford of Portsmouth offering 'an advantageous situation in trade now to be disposed of'. This provoked the Assembly to decide to set up a register of such opportunities 'whether in trade or as Masters or Servants' with Thomas Brown of Gainsford Street, Southwark appointed to maintain this register.[37]

---

[36] Samuel Medley, *Works* (London, 1800), p. 297.

[37] 'Minutes of the Assembly of the General Baptists' transcribed by W.T. Whitley; May 27 1795, pp. 231-32. The minute was continued in subsequent years including 1796 when reference was made to the proposal of names for 'the binding of apprentices.' [p. 236] and 1797 when Thos Cook[e] of Newport in the Isle of Wight joined Brown in this work. Further reference is made in 1798, p. 247.

## Wealth, Taste, and Culture

Baptists played their part in developing the nation's industries both as manufacturers and traders, and as those who serviced these new international enterprises as bankers or those who insured such enterprises, which soon brought them its due rewards. They were not always people on the periphery of society but in many places enjoyed both influence and status, nor were they strangers to the development of refinement in taste. The most often cited case here is that of Thomas Sheraton, the furniture designer who gave his name to one of the century's most elegant styles. Indeed he entered the world of theological publishing, with works on Regeneration and the subject of Baptism, printed when he was just thirty, these before he thought of publishing on design. Sheraton was originally a Scotch Baptist in Stockton on Tees but after he had moved to London, he joined the Particulars holding his membership at Prescot Street. Douglas tells us that from 1799 to 1802 he shared the pastorate of the church in Darlington.[38]

Another cameo of both economic mobility and the forming of taste, not to mention women's history, can be seen in the life of Eleanor Coade, whose family came from the west country where Eleanor, born in Exeter, developed an association with the Baptist Chapel in Lyme Regis, which suggests she may have had interests with the supply of west country clays, though she first appears in London records as a linen draper in 1766. Around 1769 she established 'Coade's Lithodipyra, Terracotta, or Artificial Stone Manufactory', to exploit the patent of the artificial stone that bears her name, a remarkably effective ceramic imitation of natural stone. This impressive creation is to be found in use at Buckingham Palace, St George's Windsor, and the Royal Naval College. Exploiting classical statuary, vases and a variety of forms of architectural embellishment, produced for wealthy arbiters of decorative fashion, including royal patrons, Coade Stone remains a collector's item to the present day. In fact, Eleanor Coade, who is sometimes allocated to the wrong gender, and sometimes provided with an entrepreneurial sister, seems to have been a member of a group of dissenting or evangelical craftsmen that worked in association with John Bacon, sculptor and clay modeller, who oscillated between Dissent and Evangelical Anglicanism. In London, she was 'a most benevolent and useful member' of James Upton's congregation in Blackfriars.[39]

Amongst the many people associated with Eleanor Coade, were Robert and Thomas Parsons of Bath. Robert Parsons combined craftsman's skills with pas-

---

[38] D. Douglas, *History of Baptist Churches in the North of England* (London, 1846); Obituary, *Gentleman's Magazine* (1806), II, 1082.

[39] L. Jewitt, *Ceramic Art of Great Britain* (Chicheley, England: P.P.B. Minet), pp. 93-94; A. Kelly, *Mrs Coade's Stone* (Upton upon Severn, 1990); Baptist Magazine, 1822; D. Rosman, *Evangelicals and Culture* (London: Croom Helm, 1984), pp. 158-62, and entry on Bacon in D.M. Lewis (ed.), *Dictionary of Evangelical Biography* (2 vols; Oxford: Blackwells, 1995), I, pp. 44-45.

toral ministry, forming the Baptist congregation in Bath in 1759 and serving them gratuitously as pastor for forty years. Robert Parsons, the father, mason and sculptor, worked not only in bath stone but in marble. His work was to be found not only in many country houses across the country, both in fine rooms and in excellent garden ornaments, but also as an artist of England's eighteenth-century urban renaissance. Thus his work is to be found at that greatest of English gardens at Stourhead, as also in the Bristol Exchange, accepting commissions both from the aristocracy as well as the emerging princes of British commerce. The son was also an effective mason and sculptor, but not being chosen to succeed his father in the pastorate, became estranged from Bath Baptists. Nevertheless, he took a leading role in Bath society as a founder member of both the Bath and West Agricultural Society and the Bath Philosophical Society. It was almost inevitable at this time that masons, encountering fossils in their cutting of their raw materials, should become interested in the emerging science of geology. This interest is reflected in a collection of fossils other geological material given by Parsons to the museum of Bristol College.

Once more the Baptist network comes into play for an engraving of the son survives, derived from a painting by Samuel Medley, son of the hymn-writer pastor of Liverpool of the same name, a member, along with Robert Bowyer, water-colourist to the King and miniature painter to the Queen, of Rippon's congregation at Carter's Lane but later a member of F.A. Cox's congregation at Hackney and with him involved in the foundation of London University and the work of the Baptist Missionary Society.[40] A large donation from William Ashlin [a substantial manufacturer of gilded and carved mirrors, who had premises in the Strand[41]], one of John Martin's deacons at Grafton Street enabled the church to move to new purpose-built premises in Keppel Street, near Bedford Square, in 1795. Here Martin collected and ministered to a very prestigious congregation. Thomas Chevalier was surgeon to the Prince of Wales but also wrote a preface to distinguished religious publisher and fellow member, Samuel Bagster's Polyglot Bible. Also in the congregation were the Tatham and Varley families, the Palmers and the Linnells who together made an important contribution to the art and architecture of the turn of the century. The evidence also indicates that they interconnected with one another largely though their association with Keppel Street, a congregation producing a quite remarkable number [9] of entries in the Dictionary of National Biography.

A further example of royal appointments is to be found in the Barbican congregation which in the eighteenth century enjoyed the learned ministries of Dr James Foster, Dr John Gale, and the Revd Joseph Burroughs, all of whom were or became General Baptists. Both of the latter two studied, as did the most able

---

[40] Information from the Revd Kerry Birch of Worcester. See Birch, 'The Contribution of the Baptists'.
[41] *Universal British Directory, 1790* (5 vols; London, 1790-98), I, Part II, p. 57; *Holden's Triennial Directory* (London, 1805), unpaginated.

of dissenters, at the University of Leyden. Indeed the PhD degree which had not been awarded in living memory was specially revived for Gale whose family was well-connected and whose portrait was painted by the court painter, Joseph Highmore, 'one of his hearers', who painted both the English and the Danish royal family. But the court connexion is stronger than that: Emmanuel Bowen [1693/4-1767], cartographer, was geographer to George II, and is described as both a 'Welsh Baptist of gentle birth' and very involved in the affairs of the Barbican Baptist Church. One of Bowen's apprentices was Thomas Kitchin [1719-1784] also a renowned cartographer, who became hydrographer to the King, notwithstanding the fact that dissenters could not officially hold offices of profit under the crown. Kitchen also used his skills to engrave portraits of leading Baptists – producing, without theological partisanship, images of James Foster, John Gill and Isaac Kimber. Large parts of the minutes of the Barbican church are in Kitchin's hand whose religious commitment is clearly revealed in his annotations of the churches and chapels of the city in his map of London and even more clearly in his allegorical. *THE JOURNEY OF LIFE, or An Accurate MAP of the ROADS, COUNTIES, TOWNS &c in the WAYS to HAPPINESS & MISERY*, which has the pilgrim travelling from impenitence and 'the Borders of Hell' to Glory. Kitchen's son, Thomas Bowen Kitchen, also active in the Barbican church followed his father as Hydographer to the King. Further engravers/cartographers in membership with the Barbican church and part of the Kitchin network were Thomas Jefferies, geographer to the Prince of Wales, later George III, and the Joseph Collyers, father and son, the latter being engraver to Queen Charlotte.[42] Such a congregation, as the individuals it attracted, was exceptional but it does point to a number of congregations with considerable influence on both local and national cultural developments

Representatives of Baptist achievement in the literary field include Anne Steele whose poetry, including hymnody, was written under the name of Theodosia, one of a group of Baptist women acknowledged for their poetic gifts, which sustained the reflective side of the evangelical revival. Joseph Cottle was a successful Bristol bookseller who became the intimate and publisher of Coleridge, Southey and later Wordsworth. A benefactor of Bristol College and a member of Hannah More's circle, he took a particular interest in Coleridge's movement from Unitarianism to orthodox belief. Associated with him were those Bristol tutors who maintained the highest standard of intellectual apologetic at the end of the eighteenth century: James Newton, John Foster, Joseph Hughes and Robert Hall.

---

[42] Lawrence Worms, 'Thomas Kitchin's "Journey of Life", Hydrographer to George III, mapmaker and engraver', Parts I & II, *The Map Collector*, 62/3 (1993) and individual entries in the *Oxford Dictionary of National Biography*.

## The Shape of the Discussion in this Volume

Such is the overall pattern of development in which the essays in this volume are set. Benjamin Keach, who died in 1704, here presented to us by Austin Walker, only just gets in to the eighteenth century but he provides a useful departing point for the Particular Baptist tradition, there being so much more to his ministry than his work as hymn-writer and protagonist in the congregational singing controversy. Given the importance of the local church in Baptist theology it is right that two further essays celebrate the pastoral ministry exercised there; Karen Smith's exploration of the spiritual counsel offered by James Fanch of Romsey, and Michael Haykin's portrayal of the life and work of Benjamin Beddome of Bourton on the Water, another hymn-writing pastor, though both through their published writings reached a larger audience.

The story that Stephen Copson tells is of three enquiring spirits attracted to the non-subscribing life of the General Baptists, receiving amongst them believers, or immersion, baptism, but by the leadership they assumed, reinforcing those developing unorthodox christologies. Gilbert Boyce fought valiantly to defend the orthodox position amongst the Old Connexion General Baptists of Lincolnshire; indeed it was he who ordained Dan Taylor, but his attempt to bridge the division caused by the founding of the New Connexion was doomed to failure. Of course, the Methodist Revival was critical to the life of the General Baptists as offering a new and lively series of congregations of Evangelical Arminian outlook. Here Clive Jarvis discusses Boyce's controversy with John Wesley over baptism.

Daniel Turner of Abingdon, the subject of Paul Fiddes' essay, alerts the reader to the open-membership and open-communion tradition within Particular Baptist churches, which lived alongside the majority that were of a more exclusive outlook from the beginnings of Baptist life. His concern was no easy matter of pragmatic convenience, but was rooted in his Covenant Theology, and his commitment to the Universal Church of Christ, and the eschewing of anything that smattered of the sectarian. Andrew Fuller was both a product of the Evangelical Revival and a major force within it in providing the Particular Baptists with a new missionary Calvinist theology, 'a theology which', as Peter Morden shows, 'set human responsibility alongside divine sovereignty.'

The last two essays look at the impact of theology on the life of Baptist people particularly as they struggled with the ugly consequences of the part played by the United Kingdom in the Atlantic Slave Trade and attempts to secure its abolition, preliminary to securing the abolition of the institution itself. Roger Hayden looks at the way that this split the Broadmead congregation in Bristol, whilst Timothy Whelan looks at the crusading endeavours of the London bookseller, publisher and author, William Fox, and his associate Martha Gurney of the influential family of that name at that time associated with the Maze Pond Church in Walworth, an important chapter in the history of conscience.

CHAPTER 2

# Benjamin Keach (1640-1704): Tailor Turned Preacher[1]

Austin Walker

Harrowden in Bedfordshire, Paulerspury in Northamptonshire, and Stoke Hammond in Buckinghamshire do not appear to have a great deal in common. In fact, few people are likely to have heard of these three small English villages. They are all within an hour's drive of each other, and they are the birthplaces of three notable Christian men, all of whom left their mark on their own and subsequent generations. One started life as a tinker, another a cobbler, and the third a tailor; yet all of them became famous preachers of the gospel of the Lord Jesus Christ. The tinker was John Bunyan, born in Harrowden in 1628. Well over a century later, in 1761, William Carey was born in the village of Paulerspury. He too learned an ordinary trade, that of a cobbler, before God called him to be a preacher and missionary to the Indian sub-continent. The third was the tailor, Benjamin Keach, born on 29 February 1640 in the Buckinghamshire village of Stoke Hammond to John and Joyce Keach.[2] He was baptized in the local parish church, where his father had served as a churchwarden.[3]

It appears that Benjamin Keach, like Bunyan and Carey, had little formal education and was largely self-taught. But, like Bunyan before him and Carey after him, he became a powerful preacher of the gospel of the Lord Jesus Christ. In 1668, Keach moved from rural Buckinghamshire to London where, by the end of the seventeenth century, he had become one of the leading Dissenters, and the foremost Particular Baptist pastor, theologian, and writer. He

---

[1] This is a slightly edited version of the annual lecture of the Strict Baptist Historical Society given in March 2004 in London and entitled *Benjamin Keach (1640-1704) Tailor and Preacher*.
[2] *A perfect and Complete Regester of Marrages, Nativities and Burials belonging to the Congregation that Meeteth on Horsely:down, over whom Benjamen Keach is Overseer*, Public Record Office, The National Archives, Kew, London, RG4/4188.
[3] *Parish Registers 1537-1758, Stoke Hammond*, Bucks. Record Office, Aylesbury, PR195.

was for thirty-six years the pastor of the largest Baptist congregation south of the Thames, in Horselydown, Southwark, serving faithfully there until his death at the age of sixty-four in 1704. This congregation was subsequently served by one of Keach's sons-in-law, Benjamin Stinton (from 1704 until 1718); Dr John Gill followed him (1720 until 1771), and he was succeeded by Dr John Rippon (who served from 1773 until 1836). Thomas Crosby (1685-1756) was another of Keach's sons-in law, and he not only provided a home for Susanna, Keach's widow, but was also the first Baptist historian, and an important source of information about Keach.[4] By 1854, the Southwark congregation had moved its meetinghouse to New Park Street, and they called a young man from the Fens by the name of Charles Haddon Spurgeon to be their minister. Spurgeon, writing a short account of the history of the Metropolitan Tabernacle, referred to his predecessor as 'one of the most notable pastors of our church' and 'one of the most useful preachers of his time', whose teaching was 'sweetly spiritual, intensely scriptural and full of Christ'.[5] Today, if the name of Keach is known at all, it is usually associated with his promotion of congregational hymn singing and the ensuing controversy both in his own congregation and among the London Particular Baptists in the 1690s. However, Keach deserves to be remembered for far more than his introduction of hymn singing into the normal services of worship. For example, it is a little known fact that during his lifetime (and for some time after his death) Keach was as well known as John Bunyan as a writer of allegory: Keach's *War with the Devil* was a best seller along with Bunyan's *Pilgrim's Progress*.[6] In our own day, Benjamin Keach is not as well-known as William Carey and John Bunyan. It is fitting that in the three hundredth year since his death on 18 July 1704 we draw our attention to this faithful servant of Jesus Christ, who regarded preaching the gospel as his life's work.

## A Thumbnail Sketch of the Life of Benjamin Keach

Keach was christened and brought up in the local Anglican Church in Stoke Hammond. At about the age of fifteen, he was converted to Christ through the ministry of Matthew Mead in the neighbouring parish of Great Brickhill.[7] Mead was only there for a short time before leaving for London, eventually to

---

[4] Thomas Crosby, *The History of the English Baptists* (4 vols; London, 1738-1740). Facsimile copy recently published by The Baptist Standard Bearer, Inc., Arkansas, n.d.

[5] C. H. Spurgeon, *The Metropolitan Tabernacle: Its History and Work* (Pasadena, TX: Pilgrim Publications, 1990), pp. 18, 25, 26.

[6] Ian Green, *Print and Protestantism in Early Modern England* (Oxford: Oxford University Press, 2000), pp. 590-672.

[7] The details of the proof that Matthew Mead was the instrument of Keach's conversion are complex. Readers are referred to chapter 1 of Austin Walker, *The Excellent Benjamin Keach* (Dundas, Ontario: Joshua Press, 2004).

become an Independent pastor in Stepney. Mead probably held to Calvinistic theology at this time, but after the young Keach became convinced of believer's baptism, he joined the General Baptists, whose theological sympathies were Arminian, and became associated with the small market town of Winslow that was only seven or eight miles from his birthplace. In 1660, when he was twenty, he married Jane Grove of Winslow. They had five children, three of whom survived infancy: Mary, Elias and Hannah. Hannah eventually became a Quaker, much to the grief of her father. Elias went to Philadelphia and – following his conversion to Christ while in Pennsylvania – founded several Baptist churches in the Philadelphia area, before returning to pastor a church in London. He died a few years before his father in 1699.

The young Keach's preaching and teaching abilities were soon recognized among the General Baptists in Buckinghamshire. However, he was often in trouble with the civil authorities for his activities. These were dramatic days in England. The first decade of Keach's life was dominated by the civil wars; in 1649, when he was nine, Charles I was executed. His teenage years saw the days of the Commonwealth and the Protectorate of Oliver Cromwell. However, in 1660, when he was only twenty years old and still a very young and inexperienced Christian, a dark shadow was cast over the cause of Dissent. The death of Oliver Cromwell and, the failure of his son Richard to secure power, led to the return of Charles II. Varying degrees of persecution rapidly became the common experience of many dissenting congregations and preachers.

Keach did not escape; he fell foul of the Act of Uniformity. On 8 and 9 October 1664 he found himself on trial before the Lord Chief Justice, Sir Robert Hyde, at the Quarterly Assizes held in Aylesbury. He was charged with the crime of being a 'seditious, heretical and schismatical person'. He had published his first book, *The Child's Instructor*, in which he had (in the eyes of the court) adopted doctrine contrary to the Book of Common Prayer and the Liturgy of the Church of England. Among those deemed damnable doctrines by the authorities was the question of who should be baptised. Keach's answer was simple and clear: 'Believers, or godly men and women only, who can make confession of their faith and repentance.'[8]

For his convictions, he was fined and placed in the pillory first at Aylesbury, and then at Winslow. This event was one of several persecutions he suffered, one of which certainly threatened his life. Keach became a marked man in Buckinghamshire, and in 1668 he decided to move to London. He came to Southwark, a large parish south of the River Thames, which was a hotbed of Dissent, with a reputation for many illegal 'conventicles'. He deemed it wisest to live north of the river (at least until 1689, when it appears he moved to Freemans Lane in Southwark, subsequently obliterated by the building of Tower Bridge in the 1890s). Keach joined himself to a General Baptist congregation in Tooley Street, Southwark, and very shortly succeeded William Rider

---

[8] *Calendar of State Papers, Domestic Series*, 1603-1714, 1663-64, p. 595.

as the pastor. Two years after their arrival in London, his wife Jane died, leaving him with the responsibility of caring for a young family alone.

During these early years in London, his theological convictions developed and advanced, primarily through his understanding of God's salvation and the covenant of grace. Whether this was due to his contact with Hanserd Knollys (1599?-1691), a prominent London Particular Baptist, or with Susannah Partridge, the lady who was to become his second wife, or a combination of both, is not clear. Whatever the actual influences, Keach became a Particular Baptist. He became so convinced that the eternal covenant of grace was the basis of salvation, with Christ the only Mediator and Surety, that he could not remain a General Baptist: his views of salvation were now decidedly Calvinistic. This is his account of the change:

> Brethren, next unto the grace of God in my conversion, I have often said, I do look upon myself bound to admire the riches of God's love and goodness to me, in opening my eyes to see those Arminian errors, which when I was young, I had from some men of corrupt principles sucked in; nay, and when I was about 23 years old (1663), I wrote a little book for children, in which some of those errors were vindicated; which after my eyes were inlightened, and the book with alterations being again reprinted, I left out, and now do declare my dislike of the first impressions, and do disown what I there asserted: When I was a child, I thought as a child, I understood as a child, as the apostle speaks. And let me intreat you to study the nature of the covenant of grace; for until I had that opened to me, I was ignorant of the mysteries of the Gospel.[9]

It is not clear if the Tooley Street congregation split as a result of this advance in Keach's thinking, or how many were persuaded of his new convictions. However, from the remaining group the church began to grow, and – at the time of the Indulgence granted by Charles II in 1672 – obtained a license to build a meeting house in nearby Horselydown. For Keach, the die was cast: his new understanding of the covenant of grace was decisive, and for the remainder of his life he remained a firmly persuaded Calvinist, one of the many who signed the 1689 *Confession of Faith* at the Particular Baptist Assembly of that year. In April 1672, Hanserd Knollys married Keach and Mrs Susanna Partridge (a widow from Rickmansworth). They had five daughters: Elizabeth, Susanna (who in 1699 married Keach's successor Benjamin Stinton), Rachel, a second Rachel, and finally Rebekah (born in 1682, who married Thomas Crosby).

Even as a young Christian, Keach displayed some evidence of ability to preach. Within three years or so of his conversion, he was preaching among the General Baptists. In his early twenties, he also began publishing his writings and never stopped. During his life, he produced over fifty works: a number of

---

[9] Benjamin Keach, 'The Blessedness of Christ's Sheep', in *A Golden Mine Opened* (London, 1694), pp. 314-15.

allegorical and poetical works (including an epic of over 60,000 words, called *The Divine Lover,* together with some 300 hymns), as well as polemical works dealing, for example, with baptism, the laying on of hands, the teachings of the Quakers, and the Neonomian controversy where he drew swords with Richard Baxter, together with sermons on a wide range of subjects. It is these sermons in particular that we shall consider.

It should also be remembered that for his first twenty or so years in London he carried out his ministry illegally along with many other dissenting preachers. Harassment by the civil authorities was commonplace. He referred to these sufferings as the 'ten hot persecutions', the hottest of which was the last in the early 1680s.[10] However, it is very difficult to detail the extent to which Keach himself suffered.

### Keach's View of the Preacher

Keach wrote the following about preaching:

> What a great blessing faithful gospel-ministers are to a people, and to the church of God. Can a house be built without builders, or such who are skilled in that art and mystery? So how can souls believe without a preacher sent of God, or churches be built, unless God raise up some men, endowed with wisdom and skill in gospel mysteries, who well know both the matter and the form of a true church, and how to build it by the rule Christ hath left? And how should builders be encouraged and honoured for their work sake, they being labourers together with God, and stewards of the mysteries of Christ?[11]

The conviction that 'faithful gospel-ministers' are one of God's great blessings to the church informed both the method and the manner in which Keach undertook all his work as a minister of Jesus Christ. He saw himself as a steward in the house of Christ. Faithfulness to the Lord Jesus Christ was Keach's controlling principle as he engaged in the task of being a preacher and a pastor. He understood this to mean that he was called to a builder of the church of Christ, preaching the Word of God so that people would be converted and also to oversee the life of the church and build it by the rule that Christ had left in his Word. During the 1670s, he kept sermon notes from the figures of speech used in the Bible that eventually were published as *Tropologia* and that work was to contain a significant section entitled 'Ministers and Churches'.[12] Explaining

---

[10] Benjamin Keach, 'The sower', in *Parables One,* p. 140. *Gospel Mysteries Unveil'd, or exposition of all the parables, and many express similitudes* (London, 1701) has been reprinted as *Expositions of the Parables, Series One and Two* (Grand Rapids, MI: Kregel, 1991). It is the modern edition that is referred to, here, as *Parables One,* or *Two.*
[11] Keach, 'The vineyard', in *Parables Two,* p. 33.
[12] Benjamin Keach, *Types and Metaphors,* Section 12, pp. 828-58. *Tropologia, A Key to Open Scripture Metaphors* (London, 1681) has been reprinted as *Preaching from the*

this faithfulness, he said that

> every Minister of Christ ought to be faithful in all things, wholly studying the profit, honour and interest of the Lord Jesus. They ought to be continually about his affairs, not leave the management of the Church, and concerns of the ministry, like some self-seeking priests of our days, to those, who are inexperienced, negligent, and worse; to follow their own concerns, and living in ease and pleasure, pursuing after the riches and vanities of this world, mattering not whether Christ be honoured or no, of whether his interest sink or swim, so that things go well with them, and they thrive in the world. There are too many such in this day, so that we may well say with the apostle, 'All seek their own, and none the things that are Christ's.'[13]

The dawning of persecution during the 1660s did nothing to dampen Keach's conviction about the importance of preaching, and he continued to preach during the years of persecution even if it meant suffering as a consequence, persuaded as he was that preaching was God's 'own ordinance'. Furthermore, since he was persuaded that God had called him to be a preacher, his disposition was to obey God rather than man, in the same spirit as the New Testament church.[14]

In Keach's eyes, preaching had the place of primary importance in the work of a pastor. In 1697, he published *The Glory of a True Church, and its Discipline Displayed,* written for Baptist churches but 'particularly to that under my care'. It contained a summary of what he believed should be the work of a pastor.[15] Keach describes a fivefold function: to feed the flock by preaching the Word of Christ; to administer all the Gospel ordinances and to be faithful and hard-working in carrying out these tasks, 'studying to shew himself approved unto God'; to visit the flock; to pray for them at all times; to be a good example in conduct, love, faith and purity of life; and, to carry out the work with impartiality and humility.[16] Here again, ministering the Word of Christ occupies the prime position.

Keach believed that the work of a true gospel minister was a great and a weighty work. His view was shared by many other Dissenters, not least his

---

*Types and Metaphors of the Bible* (Grand Rapids, MI: Kregel, 1972). It is the modern edition that is referred to in this lecture as *Types and Metaphors.*

[13] Keach, 'Ministers compared to stewards', in *Types and Metaphors,* p. 843.

[14] Peter and the apostles when on trial before the high priest and the Jewish Sanhedrin had been commanded not to preach anymore and had answered, 'We ought to obey God rather than men', (Acts 5:29).

[15] Benjamin Keach, *The Glory of a True Church, and its Discipline Displayed* (London: 1697), p. iii. A reformatted edition, with new pagination, was produced by M.T. Renihan (Spokane, WA & Oxford: 1995). Page numbers refer to the original 1697 edition. Keach used the words 'pastor', 'bishop' and 'overseer' and 'elder' interchangeably, reflecting scriptural usage.

[16] Keach, *The Glory of a True Church,* p. 9.

fellow preachers among the London Particular Baptists. Writing on behalf of the 1689 Particular Baptist Assembly, and addressing the congregations of baptized believers, Keach, speaking of pastors, said:

> 'tis a Holy and sublime Office; he is placed in a very high Sphere and Station, hence called the Ambassador of Christ; What higher Dignity can be conferred on Man? The greatness of the Prince whose Messengers they are, sets forth their Dignity; they are in Christ's stead Imployed in the great Affairs of His Spiritual Kingdom; and have received Authority from Him, and are also prepared and qualified for this Sacred Work by Him, and indeed therefore ought to be blameless, *as the Stewards of God*: And hence it is that those who are said to receive them, receive Him; and those who despise them, despise Him. O! with what Holy Fear, Dread, and Reverence ought they to enter upon this Work and Office, least they should dishonour their great and glorious Prince and Heavenly Sovereign, whom they represent! Is it not a weighty thing to be made the Mouth of Christ?[17]

The churches of this day, so many of which seem geared to entertainment, would do well to consider Keach's view of preaching, and to search the Scriptures to see if what he said is faithful to the Word of God. In particular, pastors who seek to be faithful to Christ should seek to teach their people what the Word of God says about the preaching of the Gospel. If Keach is right, then maintaining the primacy of preaching is a matter of life and death for the churches of Christ.

## Keach's Sermons

The sermons of Benjamin Keach constitute the greater part of his writings; the majority of them were published in the last fifteen years of his life. Nothing has survived of his sermons from his days in Buckinghamshire. The sermon he preached at John Norcott's funeral in 1676 is the earliest sample we have of his preaching.[18] *Tropologia*, published in 1681, was developed from some of his sermon notes and was a massive undertaking, and too expensive for the pockets of the ordinary folk of Keach's day. The contents do not read like sermons, however, and it may be that the publication was intended as more of a reference work. Nevertheless, these sermon notes on the types and metaphors of the Bible

---

[17] Benjamin Keach, *The Gospel Ministers' Maintenance Vindicated. Wherein, A regular Ministry in the Churches is first asserted, and the objections against a Gospel maintenance for ministers answered* (London, 1689). I am indebted to Dr James M. Renihan of the Institute of Reformed Baptist Studies, Westminster Theological Seminary, Escondido, CA. for a reprinted version of this treatise. The quotation is taken from the section in Keach entitled, 'The Great and Weighty Work of a True Gospel Minister opened', p. 36 in Renihan's repaginated version.
[18] Benjamin Keach, *A summons to the grave, or the necessity of a timely preparation for death* (London, 1676).

are the closest Keach came to producing a systematic theology. They form an important source of information for understanding Keach and the theology he preached. They show how his biblical and Calvinistic theology was not only well-established during the 1670s, but also how that theology undergirded the remainder of his ministry until his death some thirty years later in 1704.

It was not until after 1689, when freedom of the press became a reality, that Keach published his sermons more widely. The books of sermons he published in the decade or so before his death varied in length. A second tome (comparable to *Tropologia* for length) appeared in 1701, called *Gospel Mysteries unveil'd or Exposition of all the Parables*. These had begun life as lectures preached at seven o'clock in the morning, delivered soon after the Act of Toleration had been passed in 1689 – Keach was eager to seize the new opportunities provided by the new freedom to meet and preach.

On a much smaller scale, in 1696 he published a single sermon on Proverbs 3:6 called *God acknowledged: or the true interest of the nation,* preached originally on 11 December 1695, a day appointed by William III for public prayer and humiliation. A larger work, consisting of fourteen sermons based on Isaiah 54:10, and called *The Display of Glorious Grace or the Covenant of Peace opened,* followed in 1698.

The latter sermons were among many he preached that addressed the issue of justification by faith in the light of the neonomian controversy that raged in London in the 1690s. Keach was not slow to preach or take up his pen against the teaching that was being promoted by Richard Baxter, Daniel Williams and Samuel Clark. Keach vigorously defended the Reformation doctrine of justification by faith in his published sermons, which included not only *The Display of Glorious Grace* but also *The Marrow of True Justification,* published in 1692, *The everlasting Covenant, a sweet cordial for a drooping soul* (1693), and *A medium betwixt two extremes* (1698). He also made frequent references to the controversy in other published sermons such as *A Golden Mine Opened,* and in his extended series of sermons on the parables.

These volumes by no means exhaust the writings of Keach. A full bibliography should be consulted to appreciate the full range of his writings.[19] Here we are concerning ourselves primarily with his preaching and his sermons.

## Keach's Characteristics as a Preacher

It is not possible for us to consider every aspect of Keach's ministry and the detailed subject matter of his sermons. Rather, I have attempted to provide an overall picture of the content, the style, and the manner of his preaching.

---

[19] Such a bibliography can be found in Walker, *The Excellent Benjamin Keach,* pp. 395-407.

Firstly, **Keach was a preacher of the Word of God**. He firmly believed that the Bible is the Word of God, and preached it as such. No estimate of Keach will ever be accurate unless his conviction regarding the Bible is fully appreciated, for this conviction forms the bedrock of all his preaching. He was supremely a man of integrity, who not only made it his aim to live by biblical principles and convictions, but who also sought to preach biblical truth. The Bible, as the Word of God, was his supreme authority and guide; his religion was one of sincere obedience to that Word. He asserted this of the Bible:

> Yea, it is a book by the inspiration of God, as all holy scriptures were. All other books, save the Bible are human, but this is sacred and divine.... It is a book of all truth and no error, can that be said of any other book?[20]

And again:

> Of all the writings in the world, the sacred Scriptures assume most unto themselves, telling us, they are the Word of God, the words of eternal life, and given out by the inspiration of the Holy Ghost, the testimony of Jesus, the faithful witness, Rev 2.19; and that they shall judge the world John 12; that they are able to make men wise unto salvation 2 Tim 3.16; they are the immortal seed, 1 Pet 1.23; their tenor is, 'Thus saith the Lord'...and no conclusion but 'the Lord hath spoken', 'hear the word of the Lord', and 'He that hath an ear let him hear'.[21]

Furthermore, Keach believed that the greatness and glory of a nation was bound up with that nation having the privilege of the light of the Word of God, together with the faithful preaching of that Word. Today, sadly, many in our nation scorn such an opinion, but his was no uncommon conviction among our dissenting forefathers of the seventeenth century. He earnestly desired God's blessing upon his nation:

What a mercy and blessing it is to have the holy Scriptures, or the sacred oracles, and what a loss and dismal judgment it would be should God take the ministration of the Gospel from us, or bring upon us a famine of the Word. The glory of England lies in this, it enjoys the light of God's word, it is a land of vision; but if God should take from it the Gospel, it would soon become a land of darkness: no judgment...is like to such a judgment, as many in our neighbouring nation find by woeful experience.[22]

Such convictions provided Keach with one of his principal motivations for his preaching ministry in Southwark week by week for over thirty years. He was firmly persuaded that the reading and the preaching of the Scriptures was the ordinary and effectual means for the conversion of sinners and that when those Scriptures were read and preached that they were made effective by the

---

[20] Keach, 'The word of God compared to light', in *Types and Metaphors*, p. 533.
[21] Keach, 'The rich man and Lazarus', in *Parables Two*, p. 405.
[22] Keach, 'The rich man and Lazarus', in *Parables Two*, p. 413.

power of the Holy Spirit. Such effectiveness was not true of any other means. Preaching was God's own chosen ordinance for the salvation of sinners and was not to be abandoned for other methods of human invention.

Furthermore, these same convictions governed the content of his preaching. He made it his aim to preach 'nothing for doctrine, but what is the direct and undeniable truth and mind of God; they [preachers] must not corrupt the Word, not intermix it with the traditions of men.'[23] He sought to be balanced in the content of his preaching, declaring everything that was in the Word of God, and all in its biblical balance. Preachers, he counselled, should take care and

> must not harp too much on one string, or have only one distinct note. So a preacher that would make right gospel-music, must not always preach on one particular gospel truth, but he must touch melodiously upon every string.[24]

This breadth of sermon content is demonstrated most clearly in *Tropologia* and in the sermons on the parables, showing that throughout his ministry Keach maintained this necessary variety. Some of his other published sermons were more thematic, but those tended to be relatively short series. Among the most important were *The Blessedness of Christ's Sheep*, examining the biblical doctrine of perseverance, and *The Display of Glorious Grace*, focusing on the biblical doctrines of the covenant of grace and salvation.

That brings us to consider, secondly, that **Keach was a preacher of Christ and God's sovereign covenant grace**. Attention has already been drawn to Keach's adoption of Calvinistic views, and his understanding of the covenant of grace which he regarded as the most significant change in his life after his conversion to Christ. Keach believed that the covenant of grace was a source of great consolation to every Christian, in whatever condition they found themselves. Preaching at the funeral service of a friend and fellow preacher Henry Forty in 1693, Keach said:

> This Covenant stands firm, this Foundation of God is sure, it was established from all eternity by an Eternal act of God, that cannot be repeated, altered or changed: God is thine, Christ is thine, if thou hast Union with him, all is thine; and the Oath of God, the Truth and Faithfulness of God is engaged for the making good all the Blessings that are contained in this Covenant; God is thine and Christ is thine for ever.[25]

This brings us to the very heart of Keach's understanding of the covenant of grace. In his sermons it is not only a repeated theme, but it is the underlying theme and basis for his understanding of the way in which the triune God

---

[23] Keach, 'Ministers compared to watchmen', in *Types and Metaphors*, p. 834.
[24] Keach, 'Children in the market place', in *Parables One*, p. 280.
[25] Benjamin Keach, *The everlasting covenant a sweet cordial for a drooping soul* (London, 1693), p. 43.

works out his salvation. Keach laid great emphasis on this unbreakable and unchangeable covenant made in eternity between the Father and the Son and – through the Lord Jesus Christ, the Son – with the elect. The work of the Spirit was to bring that salvation into effect in the lives of the elect.

In detail, this meant that each person of the Trinity undertook to fulfil a distinct role in the covenant of grace. Keach believed that the Father took the initiative in establishing the covenant of grace. It was his eternal decree and electing love that underlay the sending of the Son and the Holy Spirit in order to bring salvation to this fallen sinful world: 'The decree of God on his part is irrevocable...it is the high, unalterable and supreme law of heaven.'[26]

Keach acknowledged that the Son, Jesus Christ, displays his glory in his deity and also in his love by undertaking to save sinners. It is the righteousness of the Son that provides the basis for the sinner's justification, and it is the Son who continues to intercede for them in heaven, thus providing grace to persevere for all who believe in him. And, finally, he taught that it is the Holy Spirit who carries out and applies the covenant to sinners so that salvation becomes their experience. The Spirit's role is to ensure that all the legacies left in Christ's last will and testament are given to all believers. It is, therefore, the Spirit's work to regenerate, sanctify and preserve, and to make the saints ready for their eternal inheritance by working Christ's image in them. All this, Keach concluded, was the result of the infinite wisdom and the inconceivable love and goodness of God. Any assurance of salvation could not, then, be founded on man, but rather on God who had made an unbreakable and unchangeable covenant; the same God who took the initiative in salvation and undertook to ensure the salvation of all the elect.

In his preaching, Keach was full of Christ. He said that the covenant of grace was made primarily with him as the second person of the Trinity. He believed that, as the Mediator, Christ was appointed as the root, or the common head, or the representative, or the surety in this covenant, for and on behalf of all that the Father has given to him, namely his elect.[27] The covenant between God in the person of the Father, and man in the person of Christ, was the foundation of the covenant of grace.[28] As Mediator, in order to heal the breach caused by sin, Christ undertook to merit eternal life for his elect by his perfect obedience, to die in their place, to bear the wrath and curse due to their sin and bring them to glory, body and soul. Christ, as testator, confirmed and ratified this covenant by the blood of the cross. The death of Christ was, then, the price Christ paid to redeem his people:

---

[26] Keach, 'The Blessedness of Christ's sheep', in *A Golden Mine Opened*, p. 177.

[27] 'Surety' is a favourite term used by Keach. It means a guarantor.

[28] Keach is here expressing what the 1689 London Baptist Confession of Faith teaches, 'This covenant...is founded in that eternal covenant transaction that was between the Father and the Son about the redemption of the elect,' Chapter 7, *Of God's Covenant*.

> The Death of Christ was that Price by which all Grace is purchased for us...was the Pacifying, or Atoning Sacrifice, his Precious Blood quenched the fire of God's Wrath, and so it is the only way by which we come to be delivered from Hell: Our Jonah was cast overboard to make a Calm and caused the Storm of Divine Vengeance to cease.[29]

Keach had his own vivid way, using biblical metaphors, of expressing the way in which the three persons of the Godhead fulfill their respective redemptive roles in the covenant of grace:

> Salvation is called a garment...the Father may be said to prepare the matter which this robe is made of; the Son wrought it, he made the garment, and the Holy Spirit puts it on the soul; the garment of salvation is Christ's righteousness. Again, the Father sought out, or chose the bride, the Son espouses and marries her, but it is the Holy Ghost that inclines her heart and stirs up, nay that causes the soul to like and love this Blessed Lover, and brings it to yield and consent to accept heartily and willingly of Jesus Christ. We were sick of a fearful and incurable disease, and the Father found out the medicine; the blood of Christ is that medicine, and the Holy Spirit applies it to the soul. We were in debt, in prison, and bound in fetters and cruel chains, and the Father procured a Friend to pay all our debts; the Son was this our Friend, who laid down the infinite sum; and the Holy Spirit knocks off our irons, our fetters and chains, and brings us out of the prison-house. The Father loved us, and sent His Son to merit grace for us; the Son loved us and died, and thereby purchased that grace to be imparted to us; and the Holy Spirit works that grace in us. O what is the nature of this salvation; how great, how glorious! That the whole Trinity, both the Father, and the Son, and the Holy Ghost, are thus employed in and about it, that we might have it made sure to us for ever.[30]

Firm Calvinist as he was, Keach did not lean towards hyper-Calvinism, nor did he by his doctrine contribute towards the development of hyper-Calvinism in the succeeding generation, as has been sometimes suggested.[31] Keach believed in what is called the 'free offer of the gospel': that preachers had a biblical warrant freely to offer salvation to all and to urge unbelievers to come to Christ, pointing out their responsibility to repent of their sins and believe on

---

[29] Benjamin Keach, *The Display of Glorious Grace, or the Covenant of Peace Opened* (London, 1698), pp. 115-16.

[30] Keach, 'The Great Salvation', in *A Golden Mine Opened*, pp. 382-83.

[31] J. Barry Vaughn in 'Benjamin Keach', in Timothy George and David Dockery (eds), *Baptist Theologians* (Nashville, TN: Broadman Press, 1990), p. 60. Vaughn suggests that Keach was close to Hyper-Calvinism because of his attitude towards foreign missions. Tom J. Nettles firmly refutes this suggestion made by Vaughn in 'Benjamin Keach, 1640-1704', in Michael A. G. Haykin, (ed), *British Particular Baptists 1638-1910* (3 Vols; Springfield, MO: Particular Baptist Press, 1998), I, pp. 120-26. Nettles also quotes Joseph Ivimey's persuasion that if some of Keach's Baptist successors had preached in the same manner as Keach and others, then the churches would not have experienced decline as a result of their Hyper-Calvinism.

Christ. This is something foreign to hyper-Calvinism. Picking up the imagery of a preacher as an ambassador of Christ, he affirmed that this picture informs us not only of the high value that we should place on the gospel, but also of the 'great and absolute necessity of Preaching the Gospel'.[32] Such preaching included this 'free offer of the gospel', which is very evident in his earnest exhortation to the unconverted at the conclusion of one of his sermons:

> Sinners be ye exhorted, and fully persuaded to hearken to Christ's Ambassadors, and carefully to receive their Message.... To accept of Terms of Peace by closing with Christ, by believing in him.... What do you say Sinners? Will you strive to take hold of Jesus Christ? Believe in him, cry to him for Faith, resolve to lay down your Arms: What answer shall I return to my Great Master? Do not make a Pause, but speedily come to a Resolution, your lives are uncertain.[33]

In expounding the parable of the pearl of great price he asserts that it is 'an indispensable duty' that sinners actively seek Jesus Christ:

> Will any say it is in vain to seek Jesus Christ, they may as well say it is in vain for ministers to preach to sinners, and in vain for them to read, hear and pray; hearing and living are joined together; for as 'faith comes by hearing,' so life comes by hearing also: 'Hear and your soul shall live,' Is 55.3. This finding, this hearing, and this believing is all one and the same thing: when seeking of Christ is of no use, preaching will be of no use also. But know, O ye sinners, that seeking of Christ, and finding him are joined together. Therefore it is an indispensable duty for sinners to seek Jesus Christ.[34]

This urging of sinners to turn to Christ in this way was one of the joys of preaching for Keach, and it is frequently found in his printed sermons. He regarded it as nothing less than his calling 'to proclaim that Peace which is already made, and endeavour to persuade Sinners to accept of it on those Terms offered to them, that they may be reconciled to God.'[35]

Thirdly, **Keach was a pastoral preacher.** He maintained a special affection for his congregation that met in Horselydown, Southwark. When in Buckinghamshire, it seems he was not a pastor of any one congregation, but, once he came to London, he was settled and preached to them regularly until his death. He regarded them as 'the ornament of my poor ministry', many of them having been converted to Christ as a result of his preaching.[36] On one occasion near the end of his life, aware of his increasing age, he expressed the close bond that he felt between pastor and people, telling them that if they continued living in

---

[32] Keach, *The Display of Glorious Grace*, p. 146.
[33] Keach, *The Display of Glorious Grace*, pp. 149-50.
[34] Keach, 'The pearl of great price', in *Parables One*, p. 200.
[35] Keach, *The Display of Glorious Grace*, p. 145.
[36] Keach, 'Epistle,' *The Articles of the Faith of the congregation of Horseley-down [Back Street]* (London, 1697), p. 1.

love

> you will cause my latter days to be most sweet and comfortable to me, after all those Troubles, Sorrows, and Reproaches I have met with, both from within and without.[37]

Some of those troubles were recent in his memory, as a result of the hymn singing controversy. This controversy led to the departure of a number of members from the church, some of them longstanding families. Such troubles were a considerable cause of grief to this under-shepherd of the flock of Christ.

Crosby has recorded the manner in which Keach preached, indicating that there was a natural manliness about him and that – while he may not have been endowed with the greatest gifts of language – his sermons were marked by sound biblical teaching. His flock would have gone home satisfied, acknowledging that their preacher had not tried to entertain them with clever words and wit but rather had fed them with meat.

Of his pulpit ministry, Crosby testified:

> He affected no unusual tones, nor indecent gestures in his preaching, his stile was strong and masculine. He generally used notes, especially in the latter part of his life; and if his sermons had not all the embellishments of language, which some boast of, they had this peculiar advantage, to be full of solid divinity; which is a much better character for pulpit discourses, than to say, they are full of pompous eloquence and flights of wit.[38]

We have noted that one of Keach's greatest pastoral concerns was the conversion to Christ of his hearers and readers, but this does not mean that he was concerned solely with conversion and with believers as individuals. He was concerned also for the corporate life of the church, that his members might understand not only the nature and calling of a minister of the Gospel, but also that they would understand the nature of the church itself, and how it was to be governed and ordered, and how each of the members were to fulfill their responsibilities.

Fourthly, **Keach was a discerning preacher**. Keach lived towards the end of the age that was marked by the effective ministry of many distinguished preachers of the gospel. The majority of those men were renowned for their adherence to biblical orthodoxy as expressed in the three seventeenth-century confessions of faith put forth by the three main branches of Calvinistic Dissent: the Presbyterians, who drew up the *Westminster Confession of Faith,* the Independents, who adopted the *Savoy Declaration*, and the Particular Baptists, who compiled what became known as the *Second London Baptist Confession of Faith*. There was a great deal of common theological ground among these three

---

[37] Keach, 'Epistle,' *The Articles,* p. 2.
[38] Crosby, *History*, IV, p. 305.

groups of Dissenters.

However, not all preachers or churches adhered to biblical orthodoxy and Keach, while no lover of controversy, was invariably alert to error. He was the kind of man who would confront false teaching of any kind, in order to warn his people against it. For example, he was aware of the dangers and tendencies of Arminianism to his flock:

> Arminians by their doctrine intimate men are endowed with power to repent, without any special or supernatural grace; which notion may put people upon undoing temptations, even to delay, or defer the great work of regeneration until sickness, or death comes, or until they are grown old; for if they have such ability or power as they say, men are subject to conclude, that they may have the same power tomorrow, which they have this day.[39]

Keach also warned against others errors, principally Roman Catholicism, Socinianism, Quakerism, and – in particular – the Neonomian teaching of Richard Baxter. Although Baxter died in 1691, the controversy did not die with him. Keach played a major role in this dispute, which focused on justification by faith and, most specifically, on the nature of a believer's righteousness. It became known as the Neonomian (or 'new law') controversy, arising out of Baxter's teaching that obedience to a new law brought in by Christ (an obedience that took the form of saving faith and holy living) was the basis of one's personal saving righteousness.

Keach consistently opposed this Neonomian teaching as a fundamental error. Towards the end of a sermon based on Matthew 3.12, preached at some time in the 1690s to his regular London congregation in Horselydown, Southwark, he affectionately but plainly warned them:

> And to you, sinners, if you would be found wheat in the day of Christ, then receive Christ's true doctrine, labour to distinguish between truth and error; beware of that strange and new scheme that darkens the free-grace of God, and tends to destroy the covenant of grace; remember to exalt Christ alone in your salvation. How do some turn the gospel of God's free grace into a law, by the performance of which, as the conditions of life and justification, tell thee, thy salvation doth depend. See what subtle opposers (of the clearest gospel) are risen up amongst us, and labour to avoid them; though their tongues should seem to be tipped with silver, yet their doctrine is copper.[40]

Finally, **Benjamin Keach was an earnest and discriminating preacher.** Keach's preaching was marked by earnestness. Crosby portrayed his life as 'one continued scene of labour and toil', and preaching the gospel of the Lord Jesus Christ as his greatest pleasure.[41] Keach did not have a strong constitution and his diligence in the study and in preaching exhausted him. He was not

---

[39] Keach, 'The two sons', in *Parables Two*, p. 353.
[40] Keach, 'The fan in his hand', in *Parables One*, p. 52.
[41] Crosby, *History*, IV, p. 304.

ashamed of his Christian faith, or of his Calvinism, or his Baptist convictions. He was not the kind of man who would hold back any truth that he believed, and he was always anxious to press the truth home to the conscience of all kinds of hearers.

Earnestness was one of those characteristics that made Keach a useful and winsome preacher in his lifetime. He preached the Lord Jesus Christ, and the grace of God not only as one who had discovered and understood the truth of the grace of God in the teachings of the Bible, but also as one who had experienced the power of that grace in his own life. He asked the question, 'who can admire sovereign and undeserved mercy more than they that have been in the depths of sorrow and misery, and are forever delivered and raised to glory and eternal happiness?'[42]

Indeed, he regarded this experience of God's grace through Jesus Christ as one of the essential elements in faithful and effective preaching:

> He that ministers the Word, ought principally to experience the grace of God in his own heart, and the power of it, in that grand and evangelical work of regeneration; as also to understand those blessed mysteries of the sacred Scriptures, that he may unfold them to others, and have a lawful call, which altogether constitutes, though he never saw a university.[43]

He was determined that as much as it depended on him, his hearers would also experience the power of that same grace in their own lives. This explains why his preaching was marked by such evident fervency and zeal. For Keach this was an essential element in preaching – preachers should deliver their sermons hot: 'cold meat is not so refreshing and sweet as that which is hot; a minister must preach with life, and holy fervency of spirit; cold and lifeless preaching, makes cold hearing.'[44]

He preached to the mind and heart and conscience of his hearers. He was earnest with them, not only urging them to repent of their sins and flee from the wrath of God, but also pleading with them to turn to the Lord Jesus Christ. As we have shown, Keach was a Calvinist: he believed that God saves sinners, and his understanding of the Bible's teaching on regeneration and conversion clearly showed his clear grasp of those doctrines. These doctrines never prevented him from earnestly urging his hearers to

> receive this Saviour, believe in him, and you shall be saved whosoever you are: It is not the greatness of your Sins that can hinder or obstruct him from saving your

---

[42] Keach, 'The Pharisee and the publican', in *Parables Two*, p. 430.

[43] Keach, *Types and Metaphors*, p. xi.

[44] Keach, 'The Scribe', in *Parables One*, p. 271.

Souls; though your Sins be as red as scarlet, or as red as Crimson, he will wash them all away, and shall make you as white as Wool, as white as Snow.[45]

Linked to this earnestness was the element of discrimination in his preaching. He wanted to make sure that his hearers had not been deceived into thinking that they were Christians when they were not. He regarded hypocrisy as alive and well, and needing to be exposed. He was very aware of the dangers of hypocrisy to a person's soul, and was quick to recognize the hand of the devil in such deception. When Keach preached on the parable of the sower from Matthew 13:3-23, he drew attention to the fact that Christ deals with different kinds of hearers and observed that one weakness on the part of contemporary preachers was the failure to discriminate between different kinds of hearers. Keach did not fall into the trap of simply assuming that everyone to whom he preached was a true Christian. He inferred from his exposition of this parable

> that it is no certain sign a man is a child of God, and shall be saved, because he hears the Word of God preached, or loves to hear sermons, or makes a visible profession of religion, and becomes a church member, and does many things that are commendable, or praiseworthy, for all these things are common to reprobate or unsound professors as with elect ones; nay, though a man holds out in religious practices for many years unsuspected, yet afterwards he may decay and wither.[46]

Such sermons did not make for easy preaching, or for comfortable hearing, and may give the impression that Keach was a somewhat harsh preacher. This would not be an accurate impression however. Recalling Spurgeon's overall estimate of his preaching as 'sweetly spiritual, intensely scriptural and full of Christ', sets this feature of his preaching in its fuller context. Keach had a passionate concern for the souls of his hearers, and believed that deception was a very real danger. Had Keach omitted this searching aspect in his sermons he would have regarded himself as being unfaithful to Christ and guilty of misleading his hearers. Keach believed that such an emphasis was not only necessary but also biblical. He saw this discrimination as a vital part of his work as a faithful watchman:

> Ministers, or Christ's spiritual Watchmen, must give warning when they see danger approaching, and therefore had need be men of knowledge. They are called seers; if they have no eyes, they cannot be called seers.[47]

## Some Concluding Observations

We have seen that Keach began life in an obscure village in Buckinghamshire.

---

[45] Keach, 'The Great Salvation', in *A Golden Mine Opened*, p. 385.
[46] Keach, 'The sower', in *Parables One*, p. 149.
[47] Keach, 'Ministers compared to watchmen', in *Types and Metaphors*, p. 834.

He was an ordinary man, with little or no formal education, a tailor by trade, who left the Church of England because of his biblical convictions. Bunyan and Carey were likewise ordinary men. Yet each one of them became famous and preachers of the Christian gospel. Surely this is a marked example of God's sovereignty, who takes the obscure, the unknown, and the uneducated, saves them, and then gives them a thirst for true knowledge and sends them out as his ambassadors. It reminds us of 1 Corinthians 1:26: 'For you see your calling, brethren, that not many wise according to the flesh, not many mighty, not many noble are called.'

Furthermore, Keach's life and ministry is a reminder of the power of God and the importance of maintaining historic biblical Christianity, namely evangelical Calvinism. The Christianity current today tends to be more of a hybrid, a mongrel version of the distinctive faith and life set out in the Scriptures. The church is apparently suffering from a bad attack of amnesia. It was a wise and discerning contemporary of Keach's who wrote:

> The principles of Arminianism are the natural dictates of a carnal mind, which is enmity both to the law of God, and to the gospel of Christ; and next to the dead sea of Popery, (into which this stream also runs), have since Pelagius, to this day, been the greatest plague of the church of Christ, and it is like will be till his second coming.[48]

Keach maintained his commitment to biblical truth, and he consistently defended that truth. Today, in our generation, where to be dogmatic is often regarded as an example of intolerance and bigotry, we do well to ask ourselves what is the biblical truth that we must continue to believe and preach. The future of the church and the glory of God are at stake.

Finally, Keach's congregation was a truly blessed congregation, because they enjoyed the ministry of a man who preached the Word of God to them. So were many other congregations of the day, whether their preachers were Presbyterians, Independents or Particular Baptists. These men preached because they believed in the primacy of preaching. Is the church today suffering from a crisis of confidence? Keach believed that preaching was God's chosen way of saving sinners and building the church. Has the Word of God changed? If not, then neither should our own methods, nor our confidence in God, to honour the means he has appointed.

---

[48] Robert Traill, 'The Doctrine of Justification vindicated from the Charge of Antinomianism', *The Works of Robert Traill* (4 vols; Edinburgh: Banner of Truth Trust, 1975), I, p. 279.

CHAPTER 3

# Stogdon, Foster, and Bulkeley: Variations on an Eighteenth-Century Theme

Stephen Copson

In this article I would like to introduce you to three Dissenting ministers who were baptized by immersion in the early eighteenth century, two probably at the London Barbican baptistry although they were not residents of the capital. I want to follow the trajectories of their movement to conviction of believers baptism, what they held in common and the way that their stories intersect, in order to shed some light and perhaps raise some questions. You may recognise these individuals as they are found in the pages of the *New Dictionary of National Biography*, and often appear with references or footnotes in Baptist histories of the eighteenth century. By looking at these men, I hope we shall appreciate again the mistake of expecting people to conform to categories of denominational labels of a later creation. Indeed, it may not seem that we are talking about Baptists at all, but please be patient as the story unfolds!

## Hubert Stogdon (1692-1717/18)

The first person to present is Hubert Stogdon.[1] Stogdon was born in 1692 at Bodicote near Banbury. He was the son of Robert Stogdon, a Presbyterian minister who died in 1697. Robert's mother, Elizabeth Hubert or Hubbard, was the daughter of an ejected minister. Dissent flowed in the blood. When his father died, Hubert went to live with relatives in Devon, where he was educated first by the Presbyterian minister of Withycombe Raleigh and then at the Free School in Exeter, and thence at Hallett's Academy in Exeter. In 1714 he wrote *A Defence of the Caveat against the New Sect of Anabaptists* which, whilst appearing to be anti-Baptist, was actually a polemic against some Exeter Anglican clergymen who were zealous in insisting that those from a dissenting upbringing, particularly Independent and Presbyterian, must undergo the Anglican rites. In 1715, he became for a while Chaplain to Sir John Davy at Creedy Park, Crediton before returning to be preacher to the congregation at Thorverton,

---

[1] For Hubert Stogdon, see *New Dictionary of National Biography* (hereafter, *NDNB*).

where he was apparently very content. In 1714 he had been examined by the Exeter ministers for public preaching and found acceptable, and he was requested to defend a thesis before coming for confirmation of ordination in Devon or Cornwall where the ministers writ ran. The Assembly of the United Meeting of Presbyterian and Independent ministers in Exeter controlled the process of ordination. Before Stogdon's interview, however, rumours had begun to circulate about his orthodoxy.

'It seems Mr.Stogdon said that himself was an Arian and hoped Arianism would be as extensive as the Gospel' wrote one bemused Devon Dissenting minister.[2] Whilst once decidedly orthodox, Stogdon had been impressed in 1717 by reading Samuel Clarke's *Scripture-Doctrine* and in that year wrote to the author to explain how he had been greatly influenced by it. Nicholas Billingsley noted that 'he came to it by slow degrees, laborious and humble enquiries, with many prayers and tears, with much fear and trembling'.[3] Stogdon himself was less than discreet, declaring to some fellow students 'I am an Arian, and glory in the name'.[4] The rumours fed into a wider feeling of unease that orthodox ministers in Exeter had about the Academy and its tutors Joseph Hallett III and James Peirce. In 1710, Hallett had corresponded with William Whiston, an Anglican clergyman and Lucasian Professor of Mathematics at Cambridge (1703-11), whose *Primitive Christianity Revived* (1712) challenged traditional trinitarian doctrines (although now perhaps he is better remembered as the translator of Josephus). Peirce had also been friendly with Whiston when he was in Cambridge. Peirce had come to Exeter in 1714. If he or other members of the staff and students at the Academy held reservations about the nature of Christ or doctrine of the Trinity, they were careful not to disclose them. The concern over Stogdon and his ordination threatened to provide the opportunity for this concern to be made public. In fact, the simmering dispute erupted as the orthodox ministers took advice from the ministers in London, paving the way for the Salters Hall Debate in 1719 where, famously 'The Bible carried it by four' and London and provincial Dissent was divided into two camps, subscribers and non-subscribers marked by an angry pamphlet battle.

In the event, Hubert Stogdon did not appear before the Exeter ministers. He was given a letter of commendation signed by Joseph Hallett II, Peirce, and John Withers, another Exeter minister who Stogdon had defended in his 1714 pamphlet, and in 1718 he moved to Somerset, beyond the jurisdiction of the Exeter ministers. This was achieved largely due to the intervention of Nicholas

---

[2] 'The Diary (1705-1726) of Rev Samuel Short, Dissenting Minister of Uffculme', *Devon & Cornwall Notes & Queries* 23.7 (July 1948), p. 157 (see the letter of 20 December 1719).

[3] N. Billingsley, *A sermon occasioned by the death if the late Revd Mr Hubert Stogdon preached at Trowbridge in the county of Wilts on January 7 1727-8*, p. 20.

[4] A. Brockett, *Nonconformity in Exeter 1650-1875* (Manchester: Manchester University Press, 1962), p. 82.

Billingsley, who proposed him to the congregation at Wookey, holding out to the people there the prospect of 'constant worship'.[5] Indeed, he lived with Billingsley at nearby Ashwick. Billinsgley was also embroiled in the controversy in Exeter, and was accused of promoting Arian views amongst the ministers in Devon, a claim he vigorously denied. He was not quite perhaps as innocent as he suggests. In 1716, he had preached at the ordination of Thomas Morgan, who less than five years later was a deist writer. In vindicating his views later, Billingsley acknowledged that he found some good sense in Thomas Emlyn's writings but asserted that 'I take the Bible only for my Rule'.[6] As others in the dispute were aware, this appeal to scripture was not necessarily a guarantee of orthodoxy. 'I believe that every private Man has a right to and is bound to search the Scripture and judge for himself. I am of the mind of Locke and Howe in this'.[7] The Evans Manuscripts confirm that Stogdon moved to Wookey and its associated church at Wells, then under the pastoral charge of John Moore, Jr. In August 1718, he was ordained at Shepton Mallett, the church pastored by Matthew Towgood. Orthodox opinion in Exeter was outraged at this manoeuvre. John Ball raged: 'Must I hold my peace and see the church overrun with Arianism to dethrone Christ and bring in worship of a creature?'[8] Hubert Stogdon remained at Wookey from 1717-21 and lived in the home of Nicholas Billingsley, where he was joined by James Foster, the second of our guests. The household broke up when Foster moved on in 1720 and Stogdon left when he married in 1721. From 1721, he preached both at Wookey and Colesford, alternating with another minister, following James Foster, who had also ministered at Colesford.

According to Billingsley in a funeral sermon, during his time at Wookey, Stogdon read John Gale's *Reply on Mr. Wall's history of infant Baptism*, which had been reprinted in 1720. Gale was a preacher at the Paul's Alley Barbican General Baptist church, where Joseph Burroughs was the pastor. Gale was a subscriber at Salters Hall, although he was also involved in Whiston's Society for Promoting Primitive Christianity.[9] Gale's arguments convinced Stogdon of the need for believers baptism but seemingly not of the form of congregational government. He did not act on this conviction until 1722 or perhaps 1723, when he was apparently baptised at the Barbican baptistery in London. Did he not know of more local Baptist congregations? What connections did he have

---

[5] Billingsley, *A sermon occasioned* p. 21.
[6] N. Billingsley, *Rational and Christian Principles the best rule of Conduct with an Appendix containing a Vindication of the Author from some unjust Censures and groundless Aspersions cast upon him* (1721), p. 69.
[7] Billingsley, *Rational & Christian Principles,* p. 69.
[8] John Ball of Honiton quoted in Brockett, *Nonconformity in Exeter* 1650-1875 (1963). Ball was father-in-law to John Lavington, a fellow student of Stogdon, who became one of the leaders of the orthodox party in the Exeter dispute.
[9] For John Gale and William Whiston, see *NDNB*.

with London? Gale himself had died in 1721. Nicholas Billingsley who might have known contacts in London was not sympathetic to Baptist views. In January 1723, Stogdon's name was considered by the Paul's Alley Barbican church as a possible co-pastor to Joseph Burroughs, but he apparently refused the invitation. Two others had been considered, one being Joseph Morris, a London General Baptist and the other James Foster, and it was James Foster who eventually moved to Paul's Alley.

Stogdon's treatise in 1719 *Seasonable Advice Relating to the Present Dispute about the Holy Trinity* came amidst the noise of an increasingly agitated stream of accusation and counter-accusation. In his pamphlet, Stogdon cast himself as the moderate between extremes, but there was little doubt about his sympathies. The pamphlet was printed for John Clark, whose publications included authors from both camps, although tellingly he published works by Peirce, Billingsley and Foster. In the pamphlet, Stogdon described the two sides as Trinitarians and Unitarians. He appealed for a measured discussion in Christian charity but reserved the stronger rebuke for the orthodox party. He gave himself away in his appeal to biblical criticism, and 'free and impartial Enquiry', looking for the 'reasonable way'.[10] Nicholas Billingsley had noted 'One thing I observed of him from his first coming to me viz He would not entertain opinions from the judgements of others. He always called for proof. He had no notion of taking up his sentiments from human authority. Nothing would move him but reason and argument'.[11] Stogdon showed in his pamphlet his mistrust of revealed religion in the light of rational religion and its social expression, 'The Morality in religion is above the Mystery of it'.[12] With reasoning akin to Foster's, he asked whether the doctrine of the Trinity was fundamental to salvation i.e that without a belief in it a man or woman cannot be saved? He argued that the doctrine was far from clear and thus not clearly revealed in scripture and appealed for a measured consideration from both sides until such time as 'we come into the World of Intellectual light'.[13] It was reported that he had applauded the outcome of the Salters Hall debate. In 1722, Stogdon wrote to Isaac Watts about his book, *The Doctrine of the Christian Trinity*. Watts had voted with the minority at Salters Hall that did not require ministers to subscribe. This underlined the complexity of the Salters Hall votes, that there was not a simple division of orthodox and heterodox views on the Trinity but for some a genuine quandary over authority. Watts warmed to Stogdon's 'charity' but not his views, commenting, 'I do not think it is a matter of small impor-

---

[10] H. Stogdon, *Seasonable Advice relating to the present disputes about the Holy Trinity address'd to both contending parties* (1719), p.15.
[11] Billingsley, *A sermon occasioned*, p. 19.
[12] Stogdon, *Seasonable Advice*, p. 20 quoting unknown author.
[13] Stogdon, *Seasonable Advice*, p. 33.

tance whether we believe his godhead or no'.[14]

Here was one of the key points of dispute in the Arian or Trinitarian dispute: the use of Scripture. In *Seasonable Advice*, Stogdon was content to argue that some Scripture passages were not original, showing a subtle analysis of the texts. Scripture alone, and in particular dominical commands, was the key that unlocked the metaphysics and inexplicable revelations as it pointed the way to reason. This clarified why Stogdon and Foster had qualms about the Trinity but held a conviction about immersion baptism. In his response at his ordination in 1718, Stogdon highlighted the dilemma 'Some of my Brethren tell me that they also have a right to insist upon certain conditions which our Lord and master has no where specified... therefore I am obliged to seek my ordination from those who profess to do it upon gospel terms'. He went on to say:

> Having declared my faith as a Catholic Christian.... I acknowledge no other revelation of the mind and will of God as necessary to be believed in order to eternal salvation but the writings of the Old and New testaments the primitive and Protestant bible only. I renounce that doctrine which denies to any man the liberty of reading the scriptures or any part of them under the pretence of the danger of broaching heresy or his insufficiency to judge or the necessary infallibility or safety of the public faith. I protest against that tyrannical antichristian tenet which denies to any man a liberty of judging for himself in matters of religion or that obliges him to surrender his judgement to any mortal man or men whether Pope or council synod or assembly.[15]

Fine words and a bold assertion of the sufficiency of scripture, freedom of enquiry, and liberty of conscience—all values which would have rung bells in many reformed orthodox circles except that they were now used to dispute orthodoxy. Stogdon summed up his own attitude as he described the 'Unitarian' party in *Seasonable Advice*, 'The character you industriously aim at, and upon all Occasions recommend, is that of Reasonable Creatures, impartial Examiners, unbigotted Protestants, Catholick and charitable Christians, willing to hear and soberly to consider any thing that shall be offer'd to you in the Spirit of Meekness, Simplicity and Good Will, let it come from which Quarter it will etc...'.[16]

After his baptism, Stogdon apparently turned down an offer of a congregation because of his views on baptism, his unorthodox views scared off another, and, after refusing the Barbican church in midsummer 1724, Stogdon became minister of a congregation of paedobaptists in Trowbridge that did not cavil at his convictions on believer baptism. Here he remained until his death on 20th January 1727/8. Billingsley preached the funeral sermon, firstly in Stogdon's

---

[14] T. Milner, *The Life, Times and Correspondence of the Rev Isaac Watts DD* (London: Simpkin and Marshall, 1834), pp. 405-10, letter dated 4 August 1722.

[15] Quoted in Billingsley, *A sermon occasioned*, p.32.

[16] Stogdon, *Seasonable Advice*, p. 39.

meeting house and, later the same day, in the Baptist meeting house of Thomas Lucas' congregation.

### James Foster (1697-1753)

We have already met James Foster in the parlour at Nicholas Billingsley's house in Ashwick.[17] Foster was born in Exeter in 1697 into a nonconformist family, although his paternal grandfather had been a clergyman in the established church. Foster was educated at the Free School in Exeter from 1702 and then at Hallett's Academy. He was a favourite of James Peirce. He left the Academy at the time that the Arian controversy was stirring. This might be said to have been expedient. He went to Milborne Port, Somerset for a short time. Whilst it was a paedobaptist congregation, Milborne Port was later served by John Elms of Wincanton who received a grant from the Particular Baptist Fund in 1722, then Samuel Fry and John Bosher, both Sabbatarian Baptists. Fry later moved to Horsleydown in London in 1737, whilst Bosher had a strong influence in the South West, becoming first Arian then Unitarian over the years. After a short stay at Milborne Port, Foster went to live at Nicholas Billingsley's home with Stogdon. Here in 1719 or 1720, it was reported that he composed his influential *Essay on Fundamentals*. A stone set in the gardens later commemorated this.[18] He was preaching at Wookey and Coleford although his payments were very small. In 1720, he moved to Trowbridge where he had a small congregation of 20 or 30 and very slim means, although Murch's *History of the Presbyterian and General Baptist Churches in the West of England* (1835) does not appear to record this congregation. In 1720 the *Essay on Fundamentals* was published along with a sermon on the resurrection preached at Trowbridge. The main thrust of the Essay was that the doctrine of the Trinity was not essential to salvation, a view he shared with Hubert Stogdon.

Foster had, most likely, known Stogdon in Exeter, and he probably owed his arrival in Milborne Port in some measure to Billingsley. Foster quoted Stogdon's *Seasonable Advice* approvingly in his *Essay on Fundamentals*. The two

---

[17] For Foster, see *NDNB*.

[18] J. Collinson, *A History of Somerset*, (3 vols; London: T. Payne, Mews-Gate, 1791), II, p. 449. 'In the garden is an old summer house almost covered with ivy – where Dr James Foster having embraced the obnoxious tenets of the dissented dissenters and retired hither out of the way of clamour and confusion, studied and penned many of his works. A small stone placed therein is inscribed to his memory in the following words 'Sacred to the memory of the celebrated James Foster DD who in this humble and retired mansion, secluded from the fury of bigots, and the cares of a busy world, spent several years: and composed many of the excellent discourses on natural religion and social virtue (and the annexed offices of devotion) which have been read with universal admiration during the last and present ages; and which while they exhibit to posterity the most beautiful display of the divine attributes and important duties of human life, will immortalize the name and memory of their learned and pious author'.

of them were good friends with Robert White, Presbyterian minister at Coleford, who Billingsley was later accused of having insinuated into the church. It seems probable that the three exchanged views on the Arian controversy and that Billingsley participated. White also left Coleford in 1720, around the same time that James Foster moved to a small congregation of Presbyterians in Trowbridge. During his time in Trowbridge, Foster read Gale on baptism and was convinced. Perhaps he discussed it with Stogdon. As a result, Foster was baptised at the Barbican and possibly by Gale himself. As Gale died in December 1721, this meant Foster was baptized before Stogdon. Again, this poses fundamental questions. There were Baptists in Trowbridge. Why not there? In 1712, the Baptist John Davisson had started a small academy in the town, and in 1721, Thomas Lucas came to be a tutor. Lucas had previously been minister of the Baptist church in Exeter and had on occasions been present at the meetings of the orthodox students at the Exeter Academy, as Peirce later noted. Around the time that the *Essay on Fundamentals* was published in 1720, Foster became chaplain to Robert Houlton of Farleigh Castle. An Arian and a Baptist cannot have had hopes of much income. In July 1723, Foster's name came to the attention of the Barbican congregation when they were looking for a copastor. He was invited by the church in March 1723 and ordained in July 1724. In 1737, some of the books owned by the Barbican church were sent to the Trowbridge academy.[19]

During his time in London, Foster's reputation flourished. From 1728, he gave the Sunday evening lecture in Old Jewry to a 'conference of persons of every rank and station and quality. Wits, free-thinkers, members of the clergy who whilst they gratified their curiosity had their pre-possessions shaken and their prejudices loosened...', according to Caleb Fleming.[20] His pulpit oratory was thought particularly attractive to women. He was lauded by Alexander Pope in rhyme.[21] A phrase cited in a 1733 sermon and quoted by Bolingbroke among others, 'Where mystery begins, religion ends', has resonances of the Stogdon quoted above, that 'The Morality in religion is above the Mystery of it'.[22] In 1741, Foster preached the funeral sermon for Thomas Emlyn, who had long been accused of Socinian views; indeed he, unlike Doddridge, was willing to allow Emlyn the use of his pulpit. In 1719, the second edition of Emlyn's *A Full Enquiry into the Originality of that text 1 John v.7* had used biblical criticism to explore orthodox doctrine as had Stogdon in his pamphlet, 'that there is

---

[19] Paul's Alley, Barbican Church Book entry for 25 Sept 1737, quoted in Vidler (ed.), *Universal Theological Magazine* (London, 1803) vol. 8.
[20] C. Fleming, *A sermon preached at Pinners Hall on the occasion of the death of the late reverend James Foster DD who departed this life Nov 5 1753* (1753), p. 9.
[21] A. Pope, prologue to the *Satires*, I.132-3: 'Let modest Foster, if he will, excel/Ten Metropolitans in preaching well'.
[22] From 'On Mystery', in J. Foster, *Sermons on the following subjects* (London: Printed for J. Noon, 1733).

a Truth in those Texts which contain the Scripture doctrine of the Trinity all believe, but what that truth is the dispute'.[23] Whiston and Samuel Clarke, too, had brought a fresh rigour to study of the scriptures, and when Whiston very publicly left the Church of England in 1747, he joined Foster's General Baptist church. Foster preached the funeral sermon for John Ashworth, Baptist minister of White's Alley in October 1742. Ashworth was the brother of Caleb Ashworth, Doddridge's assistant and successor at the Northampton Academy, and he was also a friend of Charles Bulkeley, Doddridge's pupil who we shall meet shortly. Bulkeley overlapped with Caleb who came to Doddridge in 1739 and may owe his friendship with John to Caleb. A controversialist, Foster engaged in debate on the nature of heresy and deism.[24] In 1744, the Paul's Alley congregation discussed the issue of open membership and decided against it. Later in 1744, Foster accepted an invitation from the Pinners Hall Independent church to be their pastor. The two decisions were linked. Pinners Hall gave him equally greater latitude on church membership and a welcome to his Christology. When he died in 1753, one funeral sermon was given by Caleb Fleming who succeeded him at Pinners Hall and another by Charles Bulkeley, the pastor of White's Alley General Baptist congregation.

We return to the *Essay on Fundamentals*. A major thrust of the argument was for the clarity and simplicity of Christian faith: 'No doctrine is a fundamental and necessary article of a Christian's faith but what is so plainly and distinctly revealed as that an ordinary Christian in his enquiries can't miss the knowledge of'.[25] How reasonable was it of God to offer salvation to the world but make the apprehension of that salvation dependent on doctrine that most ordinary believers could not understand? Foster continued,

> since it is plain that no christian who uses his bible can avoid knowing what doctrines are essential and indispensably part of Christian faith, I think it fairly and naturally follows that no doctrines can be as the word has been explained fundamental about which Christians using their bibles are disagreed and divided into parties and consequently that none of those points which are at present debated by great numbers on all sides in the protestant world are as such vast and infinite

---

[23] Stogdon, *Seasonable Advice*, p. 28.

[24] Foster exchanged a flurry of pamphlets (1735-37) with Henry Stebbing, Archdeacon of Wiltshire on the issue of heresy and also responded to the deist Matthew Tindal in *A Short View of some of the most notorious inconsistencies, absurdities and contradictions contain'd in a late book falsly entitled The Usefulness, Truth and Excellency of the Christian Revelation defended* (1731).

[25] J. Foster, *An Essay on Fundamentals with a particular regard to the Doctrine of the Ever-Blessed trinity.... to which is annexed The Resurrection of Christ prov'd .... in a sermon preached at Trowbridge* (London: printed for J. Clarke, 1720), p. 4.

consequence: to mention particulars not the doctrines of the Trinity, original sin, Absolute election, perseverance etc.[26]

Foster was clearly moving away from the earlier Calvinist background toward an Arminian view of salvation. His sympathies in the Exeter dispute were underlined as he spoke out against the treatment meted out to Peirce and Hallett, who had been turned out of their churches, and he also quoted Emlyn and Whiston with approval.[27]

Foster was a disciple of the rational in religion. 'In all matters of religious speculation, he justly asserted the honour and vindicated the use of human reason ... He looked upon reason as the ornament and glory of human nature and upon religion as its proper province',[28] commented Charles Bulkeley. 'He despised the systematic jargon of the schools; the absurdity and mystery of human systems he severed and cut away from the pure and rational instruction of the gospel', noted Caleb Fleming.[29] His ideas drew a sharp attack from the high Calvinist, John Brine, in his *A Vindication of some truths of natural and revealed religion* (1746).

As for Stogdon, so for Foster it was scripture that held the key, and around this all Christians should unite, in affection if not in opinion. However, Scripture had to be properly interpreted by reason. Nothing should be required from reasonable people that the gospels did not command, which, of course, left vast tracts of speculative and systematic theology fair game for discussion. Foster saw the primacy of ethics over doctrine as the touchstone of faith, the practical expression of Christianity that informed the everyday relationships of people in their moral and civil duties to one another. 'What I mean is that the main scope and tenor of his preaching was practical and moral. He considered mankind not as being merely rational but as formed for social connections and for cultivating and cherishing social dispositions'.[30] This can be traced in the volumes of his sermons that were published, highly prized at the time but quickly forgotten after his death. 'Moreover all his labours shew that he understood the great design of Christ's mediation to be the reconciling men to God by promoting virtue and advancing the interests of truth and goodness in the world'.[31]

---

[26] Foster, *Fundamentals*, p. 14.

[27] Foster, *Fundamentals*, p. 26.

[28] C. Bulkeley, *A sermon preached at the Evening Lecture in the Old Jewry on Sunday November 18 1753 on occasion of the death of the late Revd James Foster DD who departed this life November 5 1753 in the 56$^{th}$ year of his life* (London: printed for J. Noon, 1753), pp.11-12.

[29] Fleming, *A sermon preached at Pinners Hall*, p. 18.

[30] Bulkeley, *A sermon preached at the Evening Lecture*, p. 17.

[31] Fleming, *A sermon preached at Pinners Hall*, p. 24.

### Charles Bulkeley [or Bulkley] (1719-1797)

In 1753, Charles Bulkeley (or Bulkley) preached one of the funeral sermons for James Foster. A decade earlier, Foster had preached the funeral sermon for John Ashworth, Bulkeley's predecessor at White's Alley General Baptist church. Bulkeley was born on 18 October 1719.[32] His mother was a daughter of Matthew Henry, the Bible commentator. His father was a silk merchant of London with dissenting connections in Hampshire and Wiltshire, one sister belonged to Nicholas Pearson's dissenting church in Lymington, and another was married to Moses Always, minister of a dissenting congregation in Frome. Orphaned at the age of 9, Bulkeley was brought up by three aunts, firstly in Whitchurch and then in Chester where he received his early education under an Anglican clergyman. In 1736, he entered Doddridge's academy in Northampton. His aunt Susannah was a correspondent of Doddridge, who visited Lymington where she lived. A very capable, if erratic, student, Bulkeley irritated Doddridge with his failings: 'ungoverned love... indolence, neglect of study... chat, disputation, indevotion, pride and error' as he confided to Isaac Watts in April 1740, but Doddridge seemed to have a particular affection for Bulkeley. Though fearing Bulkeley might turn out 'Arian, Socinian or Pelagian', he was still hopeful.[33] Bulkeley preached his first sermon in Northampton in May 1740, and in August, Doddridge wrote to his wife that the church at Welford was considering Bulkeley only to reject him a fortnight later because of unorthodox views. He went to Colchester but had moved on by 1741 when another minister was recorded. Thomas Coleman, writing in 1853, said that Bulkeley changed his views on doctrine and baptism early in 1741 and was asked by the Colchester church to resign from his office.[34] In November 1741, Bulkeley was invited to preach fortnightly at White's Alley and allowed 15 shillings. When the church came to discuss a successor to John Ashworth in 1742, the options were Bulkeley or Richard Barron, a London General Baptist. A decision was held back pending an affirmation that only those baptised on immersion were acceptable.[35] In November 1742, Bulkeley was accepted into membership (presuming therefore that he was baptised) following a letter of recommendation on his character from Dr Daniel Scott of Colchester. Scott was the half-brother of Thomas Scott, minister of the Independent church at Hitchin and then Norwich, whose son (also Thomas), a fellow student of Doddridge, became an evangelical Arian in ministry at Ipswich. Another brother, Joseph Nicoll Scott, trained as a doctor after ejection from his post as co-pastor with his father at Norwich

---

[32] For Charles Bulkeley, see *NDNB*.
[33] G. F. Nuttall (ed.), *Calendar of the Correspondence of Philip Doddridge DD (1702-1751)* (London: H.M. Stationery Office, 1979), letter no. 605.
[34] T. Coleman, *Memorials of the Independent Churches in Northamptonshire* (London: 1853), p. 166.
[35] The mss records of the White's Alley General Baptist church are held at The Guildhall, London.

because of his unorthodox views on the Trinity.[36] Doddridge kept in close touch with the family, visiting them in Norwich and Ipswich, and also with Daniel Scott, for whom he had the highest regard. Daniel Scott had trained at Utrecht where he had been baptised by the Mennonites. Returning to England, he kept aloof from committing himself to one tradition or other. He settled in Colchester, where two, or possibly three, Baptist causes met but his name was not linked with any of them. It seems possible that Bulkeley's views on baptism were changed by acquaintance with Scott, whose *New Version of St. Matthew's Gospel* had been published in 1741 with its strong advocacy of immersion baptism. Scott's trinitarian views may also have been attractive to Bulkeley—his *Essay towards a Demonstration of the Scripture Trinity* [1725] had been first thought to have James Peirce as its author. Why does the letter to White's Alley come from Scott and not from one of the Baptist churches in Colchester? Had Bulkeley been convinced of the necessity of immersion baptism by Scott without becoming a member of a church? In April 1743, Bulkeley was chosen pastor at White's Alley after affirming his Arminian convictions, a shift from the Calvinism of the academy. On 15 June, he was ordained to the church. His entries in the church book for much of the following half century were minimal.

When Foster gave up the Old Jewry lecture, Bulkeley succeeded him. He was a popular and capable orator with a list of published works, mainly sermons. In 1751 and 1752, he published two defences of Shaftesbury's ethics, an unusual cause to champion for a dissenting minister.[37] In 1754, he published *Two Discourses on Catholick Communion,* an appeal for mixed communion that two years later drew a response in print from Grantham Killingworth of Norwich, as Killingworth had earlier written against James Foster's sermon printed in 1749 on the same issue.[38] In 1758, came *On the nature and foundation of religious, Christian and social worship,* and in 1764, came his 576 page magnum opus, *The Oeconomy of the Gospel.* It was this work, especially the chapter on baptism, that had an impact on Joshua Toulmin, another academy-trained Presbyterian minister who became a convinced believer in immersion baptism, minister of a General Baptist church, and holder of less than orthodox trinitarian views.

As Doddridge had admitted to Watts, Bulkeley was a product of, and advo-

---

[36] For Thomas Scott, Daniel Scott, Thomas Scott, Jr, and Joseph Nicoll Scott, see *NDNB.*
[37] Philosophical works: *A Vindication of my Lord Shaftesbury's on the subject of Ridicule* (London: printed for J. Noon, 1751) and *A Vindication of my Lord Shaftesbury on Morality and Religion* (London: printed for J. Noon and R. Baldwin, 1752) and *Notes on the Philosophical Writings of Lord Bolingbroke* (London: printed for J. Noon, J Waugh, and W. Fenner, 1755). For more on this aspect of Charles Bulkeley, see I. Rivers, 'Charles Bulkley, the Baptist Shaftesburian', in *Il Gentleman Filosofo: Nuovi Saggi su Shaftesbury,* ed. Giancarlo Carabelli and Paola Zanardi (Padova: Il Poligrafo, 2003).
[38] G. Killingworth, *An Answer to Rev Mr C. Bulkley's Plea for mixt Communion as published in two discourses* (London: printed for R. Baldwin, 1756).

cate for, the system of 'free enquiry' in religion. As his memorialist, John Evans, noted 'In religious matters no one better understood the right of private judgement and what redounds still more to his praise no one more readily allowed the exercise of it to others'.[39] After a long single pastorate, Bulkeley died in 1797. He was succeeded by John Evans, a decidedly Unitarian Baptist. Most accounts add knowingly that the membership of the church was reduced to five men and three women at the time of Bulkeley's death. Heterodoxy entailed decline, we are meant to understand. The General Baptists of the eighteenth century were often categorised in this way; their doctrinal tendency to Arian or Unitarian views augured their downfall.

## The Authority of Scripture, Reason in Religion, and the Search for Simplicity

These three men reflected the desire to search for the basis of a simple Christianity. In the seventeenth century, reason had been part of the armoury used by Puritans and nonconformists when challenged about the raw appeal of their message, as they managed to hold together the experiential and doctrinal. Reason was allowed a limited function and had been wedded to an evangelical doctrine. Important works signalling this stream of thought were Baxter's *The Unreasonableness of Infidelity* and *The Reasons of the Christian Religion*. This approach was bolstered by Locke's *Essay Concerning Human Understanding*, and its latitudinarian arguments were an influential source where reason rather than doctrine was the higher priority. Baxter's wish was for churches to unite 'upon the terms of Primitive Simplicity'. Said Baxter, as quoted by Hubert Stogdon, 'The Lord Jesus in Wisdom and Tender Mercy establish'd a Law of Grace and Rule of Life, pure and perfect, but simple and plain. ... so that the Christian Faith is a Matter of great Plainness and Simplicity'. Billingsley quoted at length from Baxter's *Cure of Church Divisions* in his *Rational and Christian Principles* and also cited Locke and Howe.[40] John Brine appended to his attack on Foster '*a dialogue between a Calvinist, a Socinian, an Arminian, a Baxterian and a Deist*'. As the eighteenth century progressed, the rational tendency increasingly came to be set over against the experiential and the evangelical, creating a growing division between the Unitarian and Evangelical Revival mentalities. Professor Isabel Rivers catches this movement of thought well:

> In the eighteenth century especially among some of the Presbyterians the rational tendency further came to imply hostility to appeals to feeling and the influence of

---

[39] J. Evans, *A Sermon [on Job v.26] preached ... April 30 1797 on the decease of the ... Revd C.Bulkley ... with a sketch of his life etc* (London: printed by C. Whittingham, 1797), p. 44.

[40] Billingsley, *Rational and Christian Principles*, p. 69.

the Spirit in religion and a growing sympathy not only with the moralist latitudinarian strain in the established Church (to which Baxter had himself partly contributed) and its Arminian theology but with the covert Arianism of some of its members.[41]

Symptomatic of this concern for simplicity was an early interest in textual analysis – Stogdon, Emlyn and Bulkeley all wrote *Notes on the Bible*. With the three men of our essay, the search for fundamental Christianity was grounded in a scripture conviction about immersion baptism.

Some years ago, Geoffrey Nuttall argued that the Arminianism of Old Dissent was of the head whereas that of the Wesleys was of the heart.[42] The conclusion that all men will be saved could be derived logically from the nature of God. Such a scheme of general redemption could easily fall into a doctrine of general revelation, reducing the importance of the Incarnation in the plan of salvation. An Arminian theology could easily be drawn into an Arian Christology. So enthusiasm for mission could be blunted, as at the other end of the spectrum high Calvinism could vitiate the missionary imperative. Wesley's universalism, however, was rooted firmly in the power of Christ to save which fired his missionary passion.

It is noteworthy that these three ministers were the product of an academy education that exposed students to opposing points of view in theological debate. This certainly was the Doddridge method and was also followed by Caleb Ashworth. Did this openness encourage heterodoxy? In the change from Calvinist to Arminian theology, why did the General Baptists become the logical home? Was it because the General Baptists were ready to put more confidence in scripture as a rule of faith and less tied to systematic doctrine, hence their stance as non-subscribers at Salters Hall? Some commentators argue that there was an inevitable process leading from Arminian through Arian to Socinian or Unitarian views. This process was more complex than the suggestion that it simply reflects a shift in orthodoxy. Key for many General Baptist ministers was the relationship between the authority of scripture and the exercise of reason in religion.

These three cases illustrate a definite fluidity in 'denominational' loyalty. Labels do not work well. Stogdon was baptised but did not minister to a Baptist congregation and was still acceptable to a congregation of paedobaptists. Foster also ministered to a congregation of Presbyterians. He moved to an Arminian Baptist cause and when he did not agree with Paul's Alley on communion, he moved to an Independent congregation. Bulkeley emerged from Doddridge's Academy to pastor a General Baptist church. Characteristics that defined de-

---

[41] I. Rivers, *Reason, Grace, and Sentiment: a Study of the Language of Religion and Ethics, 1660-1780* (Cambridge: Cambridge University Press, 1991), p.165.

[42] G. F. Nuttall, *The Puritan Spirit: Essays and Addresses* (London: Epworth Press, 1967), p. 78.

nominations subsequently should not be imposed on earlier generations.

There is great regional diversity in eighteenth-century England. Can historians be guilty of projecting back a national and consistent character for General Baptists at this period? Two of the three ministers encountered ultimately gravitated to the capital. Stogdon, who did not leave the West Country, nonetheless had London connections. The other two were educated men drawn to the comparative freedom of London, where their auditors extended far beyond the reaches of the Baptist congregations. They were not the only General Baptist leaders active in London at this period but it is significant that their heterodox views were more accommodated in the capital and equally that some of the elite London churches were willing to search beyond the obvious Baptist candidates to find suitable candidates for ministry.

The minutes of the General Baptist Assembly revealed only a couple of dozen churches attending or reporting to the annual meeting in London in the 1720s.[43] The greater part of these was located in London, Kent, and Sussex, although Foster's church was not represented. It is easy to understand why association links between churches in a geographical area might be stronger than the relationship with a distant group, although the Lincolnshire Association did send letters to be read at the London meetings. This raises the question of distinctive regional character. It is sometimes suggested that the General Baptists died out as a consequence of adopting Arian or Unitarian views,[44] but there is room for further investigation to see whether reasons for the demise of General Baptist churches varied from area to area. If some did maintain traditional orthodox doctrines, perhaps their gradual decline could be down to other reasons, such as the preponderance of rural churches in a volatile period of employment, rigid rules about 'marrying out', the failure to produce capable leaders or to attract new members in sufficient numbers to make the communities viable. All may be elements in the story. When the New Connexion started in 1770, Dan Taylor and the other evangelical leaders continued to maintain links (admittedly not always uncritically) with the Old Generals for over 30 years, only finally severing the connection when the General Assembly embraced the universalist Elkanah Winchester. This surely indicated a basic level of acceptance. Perhaps we must turn to the missiologist and the sociologist as well as the historian if we are to understand what caused the obvious decline of these communities.

These are my three exhibits in a short essay. In this brief piece, it is not possible to do more than raise some questions about the links and similarities and ask whether they point to more general themes. The three men that we have

---

[43] W.T. Whitley (ed.), *Minutes of the General Assembly of the General Baptists 1654-1728* (London: printed for the Society, 1909).

[44] For example, A. C. Underwood, *A History of the English Baptists* (London: Baptist Union, 1948), p.127: 'In spite of their connexional organization, ruin came when they gradually adopted Arian and Socinian views of the Person of Christ'.

encountered in this essay are atypical of General Baptist life in the first half of the eighteenth century. Indeed, Stogdon is more baptist than Baptist. The two who ministered to Baptist congregations in London were well educated, paid by their churches, and enjoyed an audience beyond their church congregations drawn from many levels of society. They contrast with their humbler country cousins in small churches who often held manual occupations. Yet, if they are to be counted as General Baptists, and if their contemporaries also counted them as General Baptists, then we must beware of too easily categorising them in an unhelpful and anachronistic way.

CHAPTER 4

# James Fanch (1704-1767): The Spiritual Counsel of an Eighteenth-Century Baptist Pastor

Karen E. Smith

In 1951, Ernest Payne noted the need for more regional studies and recalled 'how more than once the late Dr W.T. Whitley emphasised that the next stage in the study of Baptist history in this country must be the completion of county and regional studies'.[1] For those who are interested in the study of Baptist devotion, one might add that further biographical studies, especially of women and men living outside London are needed as well. Over the years, our tendency in Baptist life has sometimes been to tell the story of Baptists by giving attention, to pastors and leaders who made notable contributions to denominational life. Yet, by focussing on 'great men' like Thomas Helwys, John Rippon, John Gill, Andrew Fuller, William Carey, John Ryland or C.H. Spurgeon, not only have we failed to hear the voices of women, who, though active, were often working behind the scenes, but we have sometimes failed to note the contributions of ministers of smaller churches in the provinces.

The purpose of this paper is to focus on the life of James Fanch (1704-1767) who was pastor of the church at Romsey in Hampshire from 1745 and also preached at the neighbouring village of Lockerley from 1751 until his death in 1767. He was a friend of the well-known hymn-writer, Anne Steele[2] (1717-1778) of Broughton in Hampshire.[3] He also wrote hymns and published several

---

[1] E.A. Payne, *The Baptists of Berkshire Through Three Centuries* (London: Kingsgate, 1951), p.7.
[2] Anne Steele (1717-1778) was a Baptist hymn-writer from Broughton in Hampshire. Her first volume of poetry was *Poems on Subjects Chiefly Devotional under the title Theodosia* (London, 1760). In 1780 it was reprinted by Caleb Evans with a volume of miscellaneous pieces. Her hymns were included in many different Baptist hymn collections. See J. R. Watson, 'Steele, Anne (1717–1778)', *Oxford Dictionary of National Biography* (Oxford: Oxford University Press, 2004); online edn, May 2005. [http://www.oxforddnb.com/view/article/26343, accessed 3 Nov 2006].
[3] Writing to his brother-in-law, Daniel Turner, several years before her poems were published, Fanch claimed of Anne Steele: 'Her poetical compositions, both of the seri-

books: *Free Thoughts On Practical Religion* (1761), *A Paraphrase of the Psalms of David from Latin* (1761), *A Compendium of the Principles of Religion (1752)*. A fourth volume, *Ten Sermons On Practical Subjects* (1768) was published posthumously.[4] In addition, there is also a memoir of his life and a treatise related to the ministry at Lockerley entitled, *A Brief and Faithful Narrative of the Extraordinary Rise and Present State of a Protestant Dissenting Congregation of the Baptist Denomination; at Lockerley, a small village near Romsey in Hampshire* (1758). Both the memoir and the treatise were written by Fanch's brother-in-law, Daniel Turner,[5] who served as pastor of the congregation at Abingdon for nearly 50 years. In addition, there is a collection of letters which were sent to Turner from Fanch which offer insight into his ministry and his understanding of Christian devotion. While it is not assumed that Fanch's views were held by all Baptists, even in Hampshire and Wiltshire, it appears that he was highly regarded in the area where he served, and his sermons con-

---

ous and amusing kind are almost inimitable, much beyond anything I have yet seen since those of Dr Watts. She aims not at the sublime or any high flights of imagination but her productions are admirably correct and delicate. I have several of them in my hands which she desired me to review, all which are truly delightful'. He also claimed that Anne Steele encouraged him to publish his verse. Daniel Turner, *A Brief and Faithful Narrative of the Extraordinary Rise and Present Sate of A Protestant Dissenting Congregation of the Baptist Denomination; at Lockerley, a small village near Romsey in Hampshire* (London, 1758), pp. 29-30.

[4] Fanch was preparing his sermons for publication, but had not finished when he died and Turner says that John Gill was 'kind to superintend the remainder and conduct the whole through the press'. Turner, *A Brief and Faithful Narrative*, p. 10. The extent of Gill's assistance is unknown. James Fanch, *Free Thoughts on Practical Religion Digested into Short Essays on Various Subjects Moral and Divine: Collected Chiefly with a view to assist young persons just setting out in Life. To Which is added an Appendix, A Short View of the Law and Gospel, With some Brief Observations on both* (London: George Keith at the Bible and Crown, 1761), *Ten Sermons on Practical Subjects* (London: G. Keith in Grace-Church-Street, 1768), *A Paraphrase on a select Number of the Psalms of David; to which are added, some occasional pieces*, (London: G. Keith at the Bible and Crown in Gracechurch-Street, 1764). *A Compendium of the Principles of Religion, Doctrinal and Practical; In a Short View of the Law and Gospel; With Some Observations on Both.* (Reading: S. Blackman at the Kings Arms in Fisher-pond, 1748, [2nd ed. 1752]).

[5] Daniel Turner (1710-1798) was pastor at Reading from 1743 to 1748 and after that at Abingdon from 1748 to 1798. He was born at Black Farm near St. Albans on 1 March 1710. Before going to Reading, he kept a boarding school at Hemel Hempstead and was an occasional preacher in Baptist chapels. His wife Ann (née Fanch) died in September 1744 and he later married a Mrs Lucas, of Reading. He wrote a number of treatises and hymns. See W.T. Whitley, *A Baptist Bibliography* (2 vols; London: Kingsgate Press, 1916–22), I, p. 230; S. L. Copson, 'Turner, Daniel (1710–1798)', *Oxford Dictionary of National Biography*, Oxford University Press, 2004 [http://www.oxforddnb.com/view/article/27845, accessed 31 Jan 2006].

tinued to be read by ministers in the locality.[6] His work provides an example of a warm evangelical devotion of a lesser known minister in the provinces in the eighteenth century.

Serving as a Baptist minister at time when 'enthusiasm' was stressed, Fanch's work stands as a reminder that for many within the old dissenting tradition, heart felt piety did not exclude attention to doctrine. Rather there was an insistence that for any sincere Christian believer there will always be a balance between heart and mind or the emotion and the intellect. As Daniel Turner put it in his memoir of Fanch: 'The religion of Jesus is to be felt as well as understood'.[7]

### The Early Years and the Call to Ministry

James Fanch was born at Hemel Hempstead in Hertfordshire in 1704. Although it seems that he first followed his father in 'the mechanic side of life', Daniel Turner claims that Fanch exhibited 'a very good natural understanding' and applied himself to the study of books and literature. 'By his unwearied application and the assistance of some learned friends', Turner says, Fanch learned 'Greek, Hebrew, and Latin and read the best classics with taste and judgment. The poets more especially'.[8]

Eventually, Fanch went to assist Turner at his boarding school at Hempstead.[9] When Turner and his wife, Ann, moved to Reading in 1741 so that Turner could serve as pastor of the Baptist congregation, Fanch went with them. While he was in Reading, Turner says that the congregation recognised that Fanch 'possessed very promising abilities for the ministry of the Gospel', and, after a 'proper trial' of his gifts, the congregation called Fanch to the work and 'recommending him by their prayers to the grace of God, sent him to supply the destitute churches as providence open'd the way'.[10]

---

[6] In May 1784, Jane Attwater, a member of the church in Bratton, recorded in her diary that she had gone to a service at Broughton where 'Mr Lewis read part of one of Mr Fanch's sermons'. 20 May 1784, *Jane Attwater Diary*, Angus Library, Regent's Park College. For Jane Attwater, see Marjorie Reeves, *Sheepbell and Ploughshare* (Bradford-on-Avon: Moonraker Press, 1978) and Marjorie Reeves, 'Jane Attwater's Diaries', in William Brackney, Paul Fiddes and John H. Y. Briggs (eds), *Pilgrim Pathways, Essays in Baptists History in Honour of B.R. White* (Macon: Mercer University Press, 1999), pp. 207-22.
[7] Daniel Turner, *Brief Memoirs of the Revd Mr James Fanch late pastor of the Baptist Church at Romsey, Hants.* by Daniel Turner, M.A., (MS IIC4, Dr Williams's Library), p. 28.
[8] Turner, *Brief Memoirs*, p.2.
[9] Turner, *Brief Memoirs*, p.3.
[10] Turner, *Brief Memoirs*, p.3.

Fanch was not an imposing figure. In fact, Turner claimed that Fanch's 'bodily presence ...was by no means favourable to his ministerial character'.[11] He had a speech defect that Turner felt 'stood rather in the way of his popular acceptance'.[12] However, Turner claimed that Fanch had a deep understanding of Scripture. He wrote of Fanch:

> his penetration into divine subjects was so deep, his knowledge so clear, his judgement so sound and his exertions accompanied with such primitive simplicity and earnest desire of doing good that those of his hearers who regarded the matter rather than the manner were highly delighted, and even those of a contrary cast often found their attention so arrested that they were compel'd to admire what at first they were disposed to despise.[13]

Among the congregations to whom Turner claims that Fanch first preached with great acceptance, were the Baptist congregation in Whitchurch and a 'paedobaptist congregation at Alton' in Hampshire. In 1744, when he went to Whitchurch, the congregation had been without a pastor for three years and had about 45 members.[14] He stayed there for a year, and it is not known if that church considered calling him to be their pastor. Judging from a letter he sent to Turner in 1746 after the death of one of the church members at Whitchurch, Mr John Benham, it would appear that his time there was not entirely happy. Apart from Benham, he had few kind words for other members of the congregation, but wrote, 'they are in the main a peevish, disconcerted, unhappy people and have not now one man either to call on or to steer them who is fit for it that I know of'.[15]

## Ministry at Romsey

In November 1745, Fanch accepted an invitation to serve the congregation at Romsey with the view to becoming their pastor, though not without 'much

---

[11] Turner, *Brief Memoirs*, p. 4.

[12] Turner, *Brief Memoirs*, p. 4.

[13] Turner, *Brief Memoirs*, p. 4.

[14] The church may have waited to call a pastor because of financial difficulties. Their previous pastor, John Grant complained about the lack of financial support. The congregation was receiving assistance from the Particular Baptist Fund. See a Letter from the Particular Baptist fund to the church, 3 November 1730, *Whitchurch Papers*, [FPC E8 MSS 3, C8], Angus Library.

[15] Letter from James Fanch to Daniel Turner, 11 December 1746. Dr Williams's Library [MS 126611]. The congregation at Whitchurch was able to support a minister thanks to a legacy of John Benham, a maltster, who was married to the aunt of Anne Steele, Mary. See 'Settlement in trust and counterpart (of £200) for the maintenance of the ministers of the Baptist Churches at Whitchurch, Broughton, Romsey and Newbury, 1747', Hampshire Record Office, [MS 46M71 T16-17].

doubting and fearing what kind of reception he should meet with and what might be the success of his ministry amongst them'.[16] Apparently, the congregation in Romsey had been 'exceedingly unhappy by means of unchristian contentions and discretions and the most lamentable confusion in the affairs of the church'.[17] However, there were those who appeared to desire peace and they pressed Fanch to accept the invitation to come to Romsey. In addition, he was encouraged by neighbouring ministers, such as William Steele, of Broughton, who believed that Fanch could help 'heal the breaches of the people at Romsey' and restore peace and order within the congregation.[18]

Although he was aware of differences among the people before going to Romsey, Fanch was overwhelmed by the problems he faced on his arrival. His main concern was the 'narrowness of the subscriptions' which he hoped would be 'in some way mended' if he stayed.[19] Apparently some of the members had left or had withdrawn their financial support. This meant that the subscriptions combined with twenty shillings a year from the Particular Baptist Board in London brought a total of six pounds a year for the ministry of the church.

In December 1746, Fanch was worried that he would have to leave Romsey. He wrote to Turner that he had sought the advice of Mr Stennett of London[20] who was a representative of the Baptist Board.[21] Describing the decline in the number of church members and the state of the church he wrote:

> the few that remain of the church are so spiritless and disconcerted that I have not been able to get them joyntly to take one regular step towards settling their affairs....in a word we are here the perfect wreck of a church. We have but three men members at present that belong to the church, besides those who have been set aside for disorders or have removed themselves thro disgust or if they still call themselves members, they are dead while they are alive.[22]

---

[16] Turner, *Brief Memoirs*, p. 4.

[17] Turner, *Brief Memoirs*, p. 4.

[18] Turner, *Brief Memoirs*, p. 4. William Steele was the father of Anne Steele and pastor of the Broughton Church from 1739 to 1769 and had from as early as 1718 assisted his uncle, Henry Steele, who served as pastor from 1699 until his death in 1739. They were both successful timber merchants.

[19] Letter from Fanch to Turner, 23 July 1747. Dr Williams's Library [MS 126611].

[20] Joseph Stennett (1692-1758) was the son of Joseph Stennett (1663-1713) the hymnwriter. In 1714 he served the congregation at Abergavenny and then went to Leominster. In 1719, he moved to Exeter, and in 1737, he went to the church in Little Wild Street in London, Joseph Ivimey, *A History of the English Baptists* (4 vols; London: n.p., 1811-1830), III, pp. 580-89. S. L. Copson, 'Stennett, Joseph (1663–1713)', *Oxford Dictionary of National Biography*, (Oxford: Oxford University Press, Sept 2004); online edn, May 2006 [http://www.oxforddnb.com/view/article/26360, accessed 3 Nov 2006].

[21] Letter from James Fanch to Daniel Turner, 11 December 1746. Dr Williams's Library [MS 126611].

[22] Letter from Fanch to Turner, 11 December 1746.

As time went on, Fanch became more discouraged. Some of the members of the congregation, who were now meeting at Southampton, were trying to acquire the financial rights to property at Southampton as well as to money left in trust. To establish their claim, they suggested that the church had been known as the Romsey-Southampton Baptist Church and had drawn its members from the surrounding area including the New Forest, Hursley, and Winchester, as well as Southampton and Romsey.[23] In effect, they argued that since previously members had been drawn from Romsey and Southampton, because they, who had been members of what was then the Romsey Church and had chosen to go to Southampton and 'raise up the cause there', they were entitled to the rights of the property and trust.[24]

In January of 1746/7 Fanch wrote to Turner saying that he had asked Mr Stennett to assist in the recovery of the papers concerning the Southampton property and if he succeeded the church would have about fifteen pounds a year besides money from the Particular Baptist Fund and subscriptions.[25] Moreover, he was hoping to draw up a covenant of peace for the church members to sign. He said he still sometimes felt he was preaching a 'funeral sermon for the church and cause at Romsey'.[26] While he desired to leave the church, he knew it would be difficult for them to find someone else if he went. He wrote to Turner:

> I have told them plainly that if things are not put upon a better foot by Lady Day or some proper measures taken in order to it they may take it for granted that I shall leave them. This positive resolution has much alarm'd them and well it may, for they know their affairs to be a manner desperate if I remove, their condition being so low and their character so bad that they will find it hard to procure or maintain a minister of any credit.[27]

Although he lacked the support of all the church members, Fanch was encouraged by other ministers in the area to remain at Romsey. John Lacy,[28] pas-

---

[23] Letter from James Sherwood to the Gentlemen Trustees of a hundred pounds left to the Baptist people at Southampton now in the possession of Mr Anstie of Devizes, 3 February 1770. Wiltshire Record Office [MS 1215 33].

[24] Letter from Sherwood, 3 February 1770.

[25] The congregation at Romsey received assistance from the Particular Baptist Fund in 1745 when they were listed as 2nd class and thereby granted £0-4-0. Fanch was given an additional £2-10-0 in order to purchase a copy of 'Poole's Annotations'. *Particular Baptist Fund* (1744-47).

[26] Letter from Fanch to Turner, 27 January 1746/7. Dr Williams's Library, [MS 126611].

[27] Letter from Fanch to Turner, 27 January 1746/7.

[28] John Lacy (1700-1781) was born at Clatford near Andover, on 22 May 1700 and moved with his family to Portsea in 1704. He married in 1728, and after that, joined the Meeting-house Alley church. He was called out by the congregation to preach in March 1732, and in July 1733, he was given pastoral charge of the congregation. Samuel

tor of the church at Portsmouth, supported the young minister, as did William Steele of Broughton.[29] In fact, after eight years of probation, when Fanch accepted an invitation to become pastor of the church, Steele preached the sermon at the ordination service.[30]

The legal dispute seems to have gone on for some time. In July 1747, Fanch reported to Turner that the congregation at Romsey had 'obtained the legal powers to demand the rents at Southampton arising from a cellar under the meeting place'.[31] Efforts to arrive at a peaceful settlement among the members at Romsey, however, proved more difficult. At a church meeting, Fanch was accused of trying to take control of the church's money, and a Mr Bye,[32] who had since moved to London and was therefore unable to defend himself in the meeting, was accused of tearing pages from the church book.[33] Moreover, a Mr Henning threatened to withhold the £9 per year of which he was a trustee.[34] Henning's position was upheld by Mr and Mrs Sherwood, members of the church, who, according to Fanch, resorted to using 'abusive language' against the church officers at the church meeting.[35]

In spite of the difficulties which Fanch faced at Romsey, there were some hopeful signs. He was encouraged by the number of people attending the weekly lectures at Romsey which, according to him, included some from the established Church, as well as a number of Independents.[36] The next month, he wrote to Turner saying that though at times he felt like leaving Romsey, he planned to stay:

> I have to stay a while longer. I can't help saying tis ten thousand pities a church should sink utterly in a populous town ... I having near double the number of people I had when I first came and I hope good has been done to some souls by my ministry.[37]

---

Rowles, *The Christian Soldier Waiting For His Crown, A Sermon, Occasioned by the Death of the Rev Mr John Lacy*, (London: J. Brown, 1781); Ivimey, *A History of the English Baptists*, IV, pp. 486-89.

[29] Letter from Fanch to Turner, 23 July 1747. Dr Williams's Library, [MS 126611].

[30] The ordination sermon was from the third verse of Jude. Later in the afternoon, he preached another sermon from Daniel 12:3. *William Steele Sermons*, Angus Library.

[31] Letter from Fanch to Turner, 23 July 1747. Dr Williams's Library, [MS 126611].

[32] William Bye of Rumsey, 'saro-merchant' was listed as a trustee for the Salisbury congregation. *Trust Deed*, 2 June 1748. Angus Library.

[33] Letter from Fanch to Turner, 12 August 1751. Dr Williams's Library [MS IIc4/6].

[34] Letter from Fanch to Turner, 12 August 1751.

[35] Letter from Fanch to Turner, 12 August 1751.

[36] Letter from Fanch to Turner, 11 December 1746. Dr Williams's Library [MS IIc4/2] 126611].

[37] Letter from Fanch to Turner, 27 January 1746. Dr Williams's Library [MS IIc4/3].

Fanch's letters to Turner provide an interesting picture of the financial difficulties faced by a young eighteenth-century pastor and illustrate dependence of Baptists in the provinces on the Particular Baptist Fund. There is no account of the way the dispute was finally resolved, though it appears that the managers of the Particular Baptist Fund did not acknowledge Sherwood's claim because in 1763 payment of £5 was made to 'Mr Fanch of Southampton and Romsey'.[38] However, as late as February 1770, two years after Fanch's death, Sherwood and his friends were still trying to establish their rights to the property.[39] In 1801, a notice appeared in the *Baptist Annual Register* that Baptists at Southampton had erected a new meeting-house. Though the article does not shed further light on the resolution of the previous dispute, it includes a reminder of the earlier difficulties with this comment: 'various circumstances of an unpleasant nature, relative to their former place of worship, has occasioned the erection of this; which is neat and convenient; and it is to be hoped, will be of much use to the cause of God in this populous town'.[40]

## At Lockerley

As the outlook for the congregation at Romsey slowly improved, Fanch was encouraged further when, in 1751, a group of believers at Lockerley who had some time before left the established Church asked him to go there each week to preach and conduct worship services.[41] A house was licensed for preaching. By February 1752, a baptismal service was held at Broughton when Fanch, assisted by William Steele of Broughton, baptised sixteen people, and the church was formed.[42] It was not, however, without opposition. According to Turner's account, many 'bigotted and prophane neighbours' did all they could to 'revile and scoff' at the members.[43] Nevertheless, by March 1753, five more believers were baptised.[44] Later in the year, Fanch reported that several new

---

[38] He was listed under the category '1st class' and was given £5-0-0. *Minutes of the Particular Baptist Fund* (1761-1764).

[39] Letter from James Sherwood to the Gentlemen Trustees of a hundred pounds left to the Baptist people at Southampton now in the possession of Mr Anstie of Devizes, 3 February 1770, Wiltshire Record Office [MS 1215 33].

[40] John Rippon (ed.), *The Baptist Annual Register for 1798, 1799, 1800 and part of 1801*, (London: Button and Condor, 1801), p. 342.

[41] Turner, *A Brief and Faithful Narrative*, p. 9.

[42] Turner, *A Brief and Faithful Narrative*, p. 1; 17 February 1752, *Diary of Anne Cater (Cator) Steele*, Angus Library, Regent's Park College, Oxford. Mrs Steele was the stepmother of Anne Steele, the hymn-writer.

[43] Turner, *Brief Memoirs*, p. 10.

[44] Turner, *Brief Memoirs*, p. 10; For Fanch's sermon on that occasion, see 'An Exhortation Given at the Settlement of the Church of Christ at Lockerley in Hampshire, 1753' in *Ten Sermons On Practical Subjects* (1768), pp. 83ff. He notes in his sermon that Wil-

members had been added, and there were a few 'occasional communicants' which brought the church membership to about thirty with 'nearly twice as many hearers and few of either originally Dissenters'.[45] With the increase in membership, a larger meeting place was needed; in 1757, an old house was purchased and converted into a meeting-house.[46]

Finance, of course, was a problem for the folk in Lockerley, and the congregation at Romsey offered no assistance to the fledgling cause. In fact, it is noted in the Romsey church book that the church had considered reducing the amount they gave to Fanch after he began to go to Lockerley regularly and was receiving a small financial remuneration from them. Fanch protested that the money he received from the congregation at Lockerley was for expenses, so the church decided not to take the Lockerley money into account.[47]

As a way of trying to gain financial support for the congregation at Lockerley, in 1758, Daniel Turner, wrote a pamphlet entitled: *A Brief and Faithful Narrative of the Extraordinary Rise and Present State of a Protestant Dissenting Congregation of the Baptist Denomination; at Lockerley a small village near Romsey in Hampshire.* In making his appeal for financial support for the work at Lockerley, Turner clearly wanted to avoid alienating other Christians or appearing to write 'out of a spirit of intemperate party zeal'. In fact, he stated that:

> I can with greatest sincerity add, that if these worthy people after their being turned from darkness unto Light and from the power of Satan unto God hands thought it their duty to have adhered to the established church, or to have embraced any other denomination of Protestants, we should have heartily rejoiced in the happy change, owe'd them as our brethren in Christ....[48]

In describing the beginnings of the work at Lockerley, Turner was careful to make a clear distinction between the practice of village preaching, in which many Baptists were engaged, and itinerant evangelism so often identified with the Evangelical Revival. Stressing that, for Baptists, it was important that congregations have 'a constant and settled ministry amongst them',[49] Turner emphasised that the congregation at Lockerley had first 'invited Fanch' there to preach and pointed out that the initial 'rise' of the congregation at Lockerley

---

liam Steele had preached 'a sensible and judicious sermon' earlier that day on Acts 8:36 (p. 90).

[45] Turner, *Brief Memoirs*, p. 12.

[46] It was opened on 13 October, 1757 with William Steele preaching in the morning and Fanch in the evening. *Diary of Anne Cator (Cater) Steele*, 12 October, 1757, Angus Library.

[47] According to the church records, he had to 'haire a horse' when he went to Lockerley. *Romsey Church Records 1751-1799*, Angus Library [II/449-450 Acc.28].

[48] Turner, *A Brief and Faithful Narrative*, p. 6.

[49] Turner, *A Brief and Faithful Narrative*, p. 15.

occurred without the 'use of external means', but, as the title suggests, was an 'extraordinary' event.[50] He described the people at Lockerley and the growth of the congregation by saying that, in the main, they were 'a sober, honest, industrious sort of people; yet too much addicted to country sports and revellings and to the horrid and scandalous sin of prophane swearing'.[51] However, he claimed:

> It pleased God (for the most part without any evident use of external means and nearly at the same time) to awaken several of these people and give them such a deep and lively sense of their sinful pollution and guilt and the danger they were in as to another world...until that time all were under a general profession of Christianity and most of them of the established church but nevertheless ignorant of their miserable condition.[52]

While clearly wanting to distance himself and the congregation at Lockerley from any accusation of 'enthusiasm', Turner seems to have wanted to draw a distinction between emotionalism and a healthy enthusiasm for religion. He commented that enthusiasm may be viewed in a bad sense if it is seen as 'a false and delirious feeling'.[53] Yet, he wrote:

> Some perhaps may be ready to call all this Enthusiasm, and therefore conclude we ought rather to discourage than countenance such a cause. To which may be replied—That if to be convinced of the exceeding sinfulness of sin, and to repent of it with hearty sorrow; if to dread the Divine Displeasure due to it as the greatest Evil and earnestly to endeavour to fly from it, if to hunger and thirst after Righteousness and the favour of God, as supreme Good and diligently to seek it in his House and Ordinances; if to believe in Christ, and embrace the promises of salvation by him, with affectionate Gratitude, Comfort and Hope; if to renounce in Deed as well as Profession the pomps and vanities of this wicked world, and all the sinful Lusts of the flesh, and to devote themselves to the Service and Will of God; in a word if to live as those who are fully persuaded they are living for Eternity, and to work out their salvation with a fear and trembling becoming an affair of such infinite importance; if all, or any of this be Enthusiasm it must be acknowledged these people are chargeable with it; for this appears to be intirely

---

[50] The pamphlet was written to appeal for a 'constant and settled ministry amongst them' and pay for 'fitting up the new place of public worship'. It was inscribed to the Gentlemen trustees and directors of the Baptist Fund in the cities of Bristol and London and signed by William Steele and John Kent, both of Broughton, John Lacy, of Portsmouth and James Fanch. Their signatures are also found on a general appeal for financial assistance printed at the end of the narrative. Subscriptions or other contributions for the Lockerley cause were to be sent to William Tomkins, of Abingdon, in Berkshire, William Steele, Jr, of Broughton in Hampshire, and Benjamin Forsitt in Leaden-hall Street or Mr John Ward in Cornhill, in London. Turner, *A Brief and Faithful Narrative*, p. 16.
[51] Turner, *A Brief and Faithful Narrative*, p. 8.
[52] Turner, *A Brief and Faithful Narrative*, p. 7.
[53] Turner, *Brief Memoirs*, p. 13.

(sic) their case; but who thinks seriously, and reverences his Bible, will venture to call it so?[54]

Turner's account of the congregation at Lockerley along with Fanch's letters to Turner and the story of the troubles faced by the congregation at Romsey provide a glimpse into some of the struggles and difficulties for this eighteenth-century pastor in the provinces. His evangelical fervour and enthusiasm for the Gospel may be noted in his desire to continue preaching to the congregations at Lockerley and Romsey in spite of the difficulties he faced. However, Fanch was not merely an 'enthusiast' but was seeking, as he counseled others, to find a balance between emotion and reason in Christian devotion.

### The Excellency of the Word: A Guide to Walking With God

The focal point for all devotion and the place where mind and heart were joined, according to Fanch, was in the study of the Bible. For Fanch, a clear understanding of God's word was at the heart of devotional practice. Like other Calvinistic Baptists, Fanch believed that the Bible was to be used as the only guide to faith and practice. The mind and will of God was revealed to the believer in the proclamation of the Word. 'In all points, essential to the salvation of mankind,' Fanch claimed, 'the divine oracles never deliver themselves ambiguously; but are plain, full and expressive, both as to their meaning and importance.'[55]

The primary principle used when interpreting Scripture was one which was based on the teaching embodied in the 1689 *Confession* that 'the infallible rule of interpretation of Scripture is the Scripture itself'.[56] Fanch emphasised that this approach to Scripture was true not only in public worship but in private devotion as well. Insisting that there must be constant meditation on the word, Fanch offered this advice for a better understanding of Scripture in private devotional reading: 1) begin with prayer 2) use the New Testament to comment on the Old Testament 3) study the New Testament as a fulfillment of Old Testament passages and compare one Scripture with another with the help of a Bible with a good marginal reference and a concordance.[57] Fanch also recommended that Christians should read the Psalms and the book of Job devotionally and always read all Scripture with a 'humble, unprejudiced and unbiased mind'. Finally, he concluded, 'do not teach your Bible, but let your Bible teach

---

[54] Turner, *Brief Memoirs*, p. 13.

[55] Fanch, *Free Thoughts*, pp. 28-29.

[56] *Confession of Faith Put forth by the Elders and Brethren Of many Congregations of Christians (baptized upon Profession of their Faith) in London and the Country* (1677), in William L. Lumpkin (ed.), *Baptist Confessions of Faith* (Valley Forge, PA: Judson Press, rev. edn, 1969), pp. 251-52.

[57] Fanch, *Free Thought*, pp. 32-35.

you'.[58]

Significantly, while not overlooking the importance of study and a reasoned approach to a clear understanding of the Word, Fanch seems to have emphasised the need for the heart to grasp the Word as well. In fact, in private devotion, Fanch stressed that what was needed first was for 'the view of the Law and Gospel be got by Heart first', and study could later follow.[59] Far from being something to which a Christian should give mere intellectual assent, Fanch stressed that in Christian faith there was an 'inseperable connection between the doctrinal, the experimental, and the practical part of Christianity: so that there is no doctrine of the gospel whatever, but what is capable of a close and home application'.[60] Moreover, once the word was taken to heart, it was to be reflected on throughout the week and could be used as a stimulus for self-examination.

## Self-examination

Like other Calvinistic Baptists in the eighteenth century, Fanch believed that self-examination was part of the ongoing life of the believer and essential to personal discipleship. It was not simply to be an exercise in self-awareness. Rather, the practice of self-examination was linked to the whole idea of preparation as a necessary discipline within the life of devotion. Self-examination was required before one could give a testimony of an 'experimental work of faith' and be baptised. It was also vital to the ongoing task of discipleship and considered essential before believers came to the Lord's table. Finally, of course, self-examination was an essential part of preparation for death.[61]

Since preparation was a focus of the ongoing Christian life for Calvinistic Baptists, it is not surprising to find that Fanch devoted a section of *Free Thoughts on Practical Religion* to the practice of self-examination. Likening the Christian way to a pilgrimage, he suggested that while we 'shall never go this journey twice over' self-examination provided a means for noting errors and amending one's ways.[62] Fanch argued that it was important to 'observe narrowly the workings of your own heart; for misconduct in life most commonly proceeds from some faulty inclination within'.[63]

Fanch seems to suggest that self-examination is one means by which heart

---

[58] Fanch, *Free Thoughts*, p. 33.
[59] Fanch, *A Compendium,* remarks in the preface, n.p.
[60] Fanch, *Ten Sermons on Practical Subjects*, remarks in the preface. n.p.
[61] I have discussed some of these ideas in 'Preparation as a Discipline of Devotion in Eighteenth Century England: a Lost Facet of Baptist Identity?', in Ian M. Randall, Toivo Pilli and Anthony Cross (eds.) *Baptist Identities* (Studies in Baptist History and Thought, 19, Milton Keynes: Paternoster, 2006), pp. 22-44.
[62] Fanch, *Free Thoughts*, p. 84.
[63] Fanch, *Free Thoughts*, p. 86.

and mind are both used together in the Christian life. He claimed, for instance, that self-examination 'will cost much labour and application of mind', but urged his readers to see the benefits of it which included: growth in modesty and humility, gratitude to God, and the ability to learn from past mistakes.[64] Significantly, he argued that by 'comparing the conduct of past years with the present, one is able the better to judge whether he makes any improvement in the practical part of things, since practice ought to be the main end of all knowledge and experience whatever'.[65]

## Prayer: Communion with God

Another important part of Christian devotion which brought together heart and mind, according to Fanch, was prayer. He believed, as the 1689 *Confession* described it, that prayer as other forms of worship was to be 'performed in obedience...with understanding, faith, reverence, and godly fear'.[66] Prayer was both a duty and a privilege. Answer to prayer, however, was not dependent on the believer. The fact that God does not immediately answer our requests was, according to Fanch, a way in which God may endeavour to 'keep up our diligence and fervency in prayer'.[67] Speaking of Paul's struggles against hardship in a sermon on 2 Corinthians 12:7-10, he wrote,

> My grace is sufficient for thee, will justify the dealings of God with his people; though he should not give an immediate and direct answer to their prayers in the way and manner that they expected. Although a wise and gracious God does not meet with his people, so as to answer them just in the line and track of their petitions; yet he answers them in the main, as to the principal scope and drift of their desires; which are the glory of God, and the spiritual good, and welfare of their souls.[68]

In addition to seeing prayer as an act of obedience to God, it was also viewed as a responsibility which members of the community of faith had toward each other. Prayer was not merely a matter of petition for oneself but also of intercession for others. Even those who believed they were unable to contribute a great deal else to the cause of Christ could make a contribution through prayer. Evidence of a faithful prayer life was seen as a measure of personal piety. James Fanch exhorted his listeners:

---

[64] Fanch, *Free Thoughts*, p. 84.
[65] Fanch, *Free Thoughts*, p. 86.
[66] Lumpkin (ed.), *Confessions*, p. 281.
[67] Fanch, 'Sermon V, St. Paul's Temptation; and his Behaviour in it', in *Ten Sermons on Practical Subjects* (1768), p. 188.
[68] Fanch, 'Sermon VI, St. Paul's Temptation, and his support under it; with the divine reasons for it', in *Ten Sermons on Practical Subjects*, p. 209.

> Would you then, O christians! do much for God, and his cause, much for Christ and the Gospel in your day and generation; live much with God and be frequent in breathing out your desires to him for the public good. Let it be no discouragement to thee, because thou art situated in low life, and seemest to be buried in obscurity; since thy prayers are not to him that hath eyes of flesh, or seeth as man seeth; but to that God who regardeth the prayer of the humble... If you cannot assist the church of Christ by your contribution, you may do much another way, by your prayers and supplication at the throne of grace...[69]

While noting the need for prayer and urging his readers to 'walk with God' and have fellowship and communion with him' in prayer, Fanch was eager to point out that prayer was not to be judged by the 'multitude of words' spoken but the way in which the believer offered 'the multitude of desires' to God.[70] The emphasis on contemplative wordless prayer is a good example of the way Fanch saw 'heart and mind' joining together in practical devotion. Like the Puritans before him, he stressed the importance of meditation and contemplation, or what some have called 'mental' prayer.[71] Fanch did not believe that this type of prayer was achieved in an instant. Rather, he stressed that approach to prayer took time and effort:

> The soule of man, labouring under the effects of weakness and depravity, like some heavy body, rises upward slowly, though it descends to the earth swiftly, and therefore the human affections must have some time allowed them to rise, and to grow warm; and besides, the things that are to be offered to God in prayer, as the matter of it will certainly need some time for deliberation; and it ought not be supposed that confession of sins, thanksgiving for mercies spiritual and temporal, petitions for blessings for ourselves, our friends, the Church of God, the nation, and the world, which things take in various concerns and interests of ourselves and of mankind, that all these can be run over in a hurry...But allowing that the duties of the closet are attended with some expence (sic) of time; can any one lay out time to better advantage? Is it reasonable that men should serve God only with that which costs them nothing?[72]

While he urged his listeners to take time to focus on God, Fanch admitted that believers may often be troubled by distractions. One of the greatest distractions, according to Fanch, was what he described as worldly cares. While he

---

[69] Fanch, 'Sermon IV, On the Same Subject, Philippians 1:27' in *Ten Sermons On Practical Subjects*, p. 133.
[70] Fanch, 'Sermon I, Walking With God, the Great Concern of the Christian Life', a sermon on Genesis 5:24, Hebrews 11:5', in *Ten Sermon On Practical Subjects*, p. 4, 18.
[71] See Gordon Wakefield, *Puritan Devotion, Its Place in the Development of English Piety* (London: Epworth Press, 1957), p. 85. He says that Thomas Hooker defined meditation as a serious intention of the mind whereby we come to search out the truth and settle it effectually on the heart.
[72] Fanch, *Free Thoughts*, pp. 51-52.

admitted that it was easier for some to be 'masters of their time', nevertheless, he wrote, 'upon the whole, to be in necessity, or to be unavoidably incumbered with much worldly business, is one thing, and to be needlessly fond of it is quite another'.[73]

Even though he urged his readers to avoid a great deal of worldly cares, at the same time, he stressed that one could still 'walk with God' in worldly business. Claiming that solitude is needed so that 'both mind and body may be more capable of renewed labour', he also emphasised the need to be involved in the public business of the world. While acknowledging that everyone needs rest, he seems to stress that if a person is called to a task by God, one must be completely focussed on that task. He wrote that:

> He that in his mind is determined to serve God, and do good in his generation, will never want employment. He that has gained the prudence to gather up the little particles of his time, which the most throw away, has attained in some good measure to the most useful and pious end of living. Whatever divine Providence has made to any one his main business of life, this ought to be his main study, be the calling whatever it will, and on this most time ought to be spent: there are those who instead of employing the main part of their time to one thing, continually divide and subdivide their time and their employment into a multitude of parts; these have commonly a smattering of almost everything, at last are perfect in nothing. It will be found upon observation, that the strongest brain, and the firmest constitution, will at times stand in need of relaxation; the mind being weary, will need rest as well as the body: and if it be much overstrained, like a bow that is kept continually bent, it will in time lose its force; so that whoever imagines he shall gain by these excessive measures, will, in the end, find that he loses time instead of redeeming it.[74]

Fanch urged believers not to think that shutting themselves up from work will necessarily mean that they have shut out all temptation. What was essential was a determined effort to redeem the time; that, too, was a matter of the mind and the heart.

## Spiritual Guidance

While Fanch embraced religious enthusiasm and readily engaged in evangelistic outreach, he also took seriously the need to challenge people to think about the faith. Two helps for the devotional life which Fanch believed might aid a believer trying to find the right balance between heart and mind in the Christian life were: 1) a spiritual friend 2) good reading. Fanch suggests that in order for a person to grow spiritually, it is important to be guided by a faithful friend.[75]

---

[73] Fanch, *Free Thoughts*, p. 51.
[74] Fanch, *Free Thoughts*, p. 90.
[75] Fanch, *Free Thoughts*, p. 80.

This spiritual advisor should be chosen carefully. Fanch argued that one should only choose a friend who was 'judiciously severe upon his own conduct' and had the ability both to discuss and advise on personal reading.[76] Fanch argued that books should be chosen with care and read with a purpose.

> For the choice of the best authors, make use of some able and well-studied friends; and with them converse frequently and closely on the main subjects of every book you read, as time and opportunity will permit: and having so done, put down your main thoughts, in some well-methodized common-place-book, in as succinct and concise a manner as can be conveniently done.[77]

Fanch was in favour of study, yet, he warned against reading too much. He suggested that too much reading could render an individual incapable of independent thought. He wrote:

> Read no more books than you can well digest: over-reading hinders thinking, and tends to fill the mind with other mens sentiments instead of one's own. Very few men, comparatively, are able to be at once both very great readers and close thinkers; it is but little imagined how much sound knowledge may be gained by a few good books well-studied. Some, by the multitude of their quotations, would seem as though they had read everything, and understood everything; but, at a nearer view, they do not appear such extraordinary proficients; for sometimes a great reader and a considerable linguist, proves but a dull reasoner.[78]

Fanch concluded with these final points of advice about reading: 1) 'make your collection of standard-books deliberately' 2) 'read books of controversy slowly and studiously, and no more than you have just cause to consult' 3) 'read books of meditation, practical piety and devotion frequently and most seriously' 4) 'read the Bible daily'.[79]

Fanch's emphasis on reading as part of the devotional life is another important reminder of the way he believed that Christian faith must find expression through thought and action. While there was a willingness to proclaim the Gospel in spite of hardship, expense, or opposition, at the same time, devotion was never to be reduced to mere enthusiasm. The emphasis on a heart-felt piety and enthusiasm being joined with a critical and reflective faith was one of the important features of Calvinistic Baptist devotion in the eighteenth century. Certainly, it seems that for James Fanch, the sobriety of Calvinistic faith could join hands with a warm evangelical experience and the outcome would be practical religion, the kind which realised, as he put it, 'that there is no doctrine what-

---

[76] Fanch, *Free Thoughts*, p. 86.
[77] Fanch, Free *Thoughts*, p. 79.
[78] Fanch, *Free Thoughts*, p. 80.
[79] Fanch, *Free Thoughts*, p. 81.

ever, but what is capable of close and home application'.[80]

---

[80] Fanch, *Ten Sermons on Practical Subjects*, remarks in the preface. n. p.

CHAPTER 5

# Gilbert Boyce: General Baptist Messenger and Opponent of John Wesley[1]

Clive Jarvis

## Introduction

Gilbert Boyce, who was minister at Coningsby, Lincolnshire, as well as Association Messenger, for sixty-two years, 1738-1800,[2] played a significant part in the story of Dan Taylor (1738-1816), who was one of the most significant Baptists of the eighteenth century as founder of the New Connexion of General Baptist Churches in 1770. In the autumn of 1763, Boyce as Messenger ordained Taylor. Taylor had been a convert of the Methodist Revival and then minister of a small group of believers in Wadsworth, Yorkshire, who soon abandoned their Methodist inclinations, becoming convinced of the validity of believers' baptism. Local Particular Baptists would not baptize Taylor because of his Arminian views, but they directed him to the General Baptists in Lincolnshire. Taylor left Wadsworth in February 1763 and eventually came to the General Baptist Church at Gamston in Nottinghamshire. After persuading one of the ministers, John Dossey, that he was a genuine and suitable candidate for baptism, he was baptized in the River Idle by Gamston's senior minister, Mr Joseph Jeffries [also written as Jeffery], on Wednesday, 16 February 1763.[3] Taylor threw himself into General Baptist church life, joining the Lincolnshire Association and forming a lifelong friendship with the minister at Boston, William Thompson, who went with him to Wadsworth in May 1763 to baptize fourteen believers and help form them into a church under Taylor's leadership.[4]

---

[1] A version of this paper first appeared in *Baptist Quarterly* 39.5 (2002), 244-59.
[2] Nehemiah Curnock (ed.), *The Journal of John Wesley*, (7 vols; London, 1909-16), III, p. 360 n. 2.
[3] Adam Taylor, *The History of the English General Baptists of the Seventeenth Century* (Two Parts) (London, 1818), pp. 73-4, 256-57, for Jeffries/Jeffery. Dossey is referred to on pp. 73, 75, 257, 264, as preaching at Gamston, assistant preacher at Gamston, co-pastor there from 1763-78, when he died in his 63$^{rd}$ year. He also took monthly services at Ashford. With Jeffery he was co-founder of building the new meeting-house at Gamston.
[4] Taylor, *History of the English General Baptists*, p. 76.

Boyce was quick to see the potential in Taylor, and in 1765 and 1767, he took Taylor with him to the General Baptist Assembly in London. This exposure to the wider life of General Baptists, however, also exposed Taylor to weaknesses that his insularity in South Yorkshire and in Lincolnshire amongst new-found friends had hitherto kept from him, especially the widespread lack of evangelistic zeal and the equally prevalent drift amongst General Baptist churches towards Unitarianism. In a letter to Gilbert Boyce, Taylor blamed the decline of the General Baptists on the acceptance of Arianism and Socinianism and consequent laying aside of the gospel.[5] There was evident disarray among General Baptists, for when Taylor accompanied Boyce to London in 1765, it was the first time in forty years that the Lincolnshire Association had sent representatives.

The New Connexion historian, J.H. Wood, wrote, 'In 1769, the disputes were so violent, both at the Lincolnshire association and the General Assembly, and some circumstances occurred of so unpleasant a nature, that the friends of the great truths of the gospel were led to conclude that a separation was necessary for the support of the faith; they therefore determined to withdraw from their present associations.'[6]

## Wesley and Paedo-Baptism

Those mid-century General Baptists epitomized by Gilbert Boyce had reason to be suspicious of the Methodist Revival. Although attracted to the revival's Arminianism, Boyce and many of his fellow Baptists found John Wesley's adherence to the practice of infant baptism unacceptable.

Wesley's attitude to baptism as conducted by dissenters, reflecting his high-church background, is also revealing. In a discussion with the Bishop of London, Edmund Gibson, Wesley stated that he would consider it his duty to re-baptize any who were dissatisfied with 'lay-baptism', should they desire episcopal baptism.[7] By 'lay-baptism' Wesley meant all baptisms carried out by dissenters, since he only viewed those ordained by the Church of England as true priests. The Bishop did not favour Wesley's view and urged him to recon-

---

[5] J. H. Wood, *A Condensed History of the General Baptists of the New Connexion* (Leicester, 1847). John Stanger, minister of the General Baptist church at Bessell's Green, Kent, gave a similar verdict on the decline: 'Their declension in principles and preaching proved the annihilation of the denomination', cited in a review of J. Taylor's, *Statistics of the New Connexion of General Baptists from its Formation in 1770 to 1843* (ed. J. Goadby), *Baptist Magazine*, May 1844, p. 244. Quotation attributed to Stanger as written 50 years earlier, i.e. c. 1794, referring to the condition of the Old Connexion at the time of the founding of the New.

[6] Wood, *A Condensed History of the General Baptists*, p. 175.

[7] Edith C. Kenyon, *John Wesley: The Founder of Methodism* (1891), p. 181. For Gibson, E. G. Rupp, *Religion in England 1688-1791* (Oxford: Clarendon Press, 1986), pp. 379-80.

sider, but shortly afterwards, against the Bishop's advice, Wesley re-baptized one such person. Baptists had cause to be wary of him.

Boyce was not unknown to Wesley. Fairly early in his ministry, on Tuesday, 5 July 1748, John Wesley had visited Boyce at his home in Coningsby, staying overnight. To his *Journal* Wesley confided, 'I was scarce sat down in his house before he fell upon the point of baptism. I waived the dispute for some time; but finding there was no remedy, I came close to the question, and we kept to it for about an hour and a half. From that time we let the matter rest, and confirmed our love toward each other.'[8]

Boyce, however, was not content to let the matter rest and, according to John Telford, editor of one of the more comprehensive collections of Wesley's letters,[9] a correspondence between Boyce and Wesley ensued. In 1770, Boyce went so far as to place his objections to Wesley in print with his *A Serious Reply to the Rev. Mr John Wesley,*[10] a substantial 198-page work which challenged Wesley vociferously from beginning to end. The *Serious Reply* was not the result of a twenty-year correspondence but rather of a decision by Boyce, at the urging of his fellow ministers, to publish the objections he had presented to Wesley many years earlier.[11] Interestingly, it is not clear from either Wesley's *Journal* or from his *Letters* that he was aware of Boyce's publication. This is surprising given their correspondence and also because the *Journals* otherwise indicate that Wesley was very widely read. However, *A Serious Reply* appeared twenty years after Wesley's visit to Boyce and their subsequent correspondence, so this might explain either his ignorance or lack of interest.

Wesley found dissenters generally irritating and tiresome, and their predisposition toward disputation especially irksome. He tended to lump Baptists, Congregationalists, Presbyterians and others together as 'dissenters', although his *Journal* and *Letters* have some references to 'Anabaptists'. He said of Baptists that from their first appearance in England, 'They immediately commenced a warm dispute, not concerning the vitals of Christianity, but concerning the manner and time of administering one of the external ordinances of it. And as their opinion hereof totally differed from that of all other members of the Church of England, so they soon openly declared their separation from it, not without sharp censures of those that remain therein.'[12] To Boyce, Wesley wrote, 'I wish your zeal was better employed than in persuading men to be either dipped or sprinkled. I will employ mine by the grace of God in persuading

---

[8] Curnock (ed.), *Journal*, III, p. 360.
[9] John Telford (ed.), *The Letters of John Wesley*, (8 vols; London, 1931).
[10] Gilbert Boyce, *A Serious Reply to the Rev. Mr John Wesley in particular, and to the people called Methodists in general; In much love and Christian friendship recommended to his and their very serious consideration* (Boston, 1770). A copy can be found in the British Library.
[11] See Boyce's opening remarks to the first letter in *A Serious Reply*.
[12] Gerald R. Cragg (ed.) *The Works of John Wesley* (2 vols; Oxford, 1975), II, p. 319.

them to love God with all their hearts and their neighbour as themselves.'[13] In a letter to James Clark, he repeated some welcome advice received from his father, 'You may have peace with the Dissenters, if you do not so humour them as to dispute with them; if you do, they will outface and outlung you, and at the end you will be just where you were in the beginning.'[14]

Boyce's letters to Wesley do not survive, but from Wesley's initial replies something of the substance of their disputations is clear. The opening paragraph of the letter of 22 May 1750 revealed that Boyce was raising questions about what he presumed to be 'Methodist Claims' for the Church of England to be the one true church, a claim that Wesley strenuously denied, concluding, 'But I conceive every society of true believers to be a branch of the one true Church of Jesus Christ'.[15] As on the occasion of their meeting, baptism remained a point of disputation for Boyce, who appeared to be upholding a very high view of baptism as necessary to salvation. Wesley contended, 'You think the mode of baptism is necessary to salvation: I deny that even baptism itself is so; if it were, every Quaker must be damned, which I can in no wise believe.'[16]

The third matter Wesley dealt with was the accusation that he was intending to 'form a church'. This was a charge constantly laid against Wesley, and indeed, a new church did emerge following his death.[17] However, throughout his writings Wesley denied, time and again, that this was his intention. In his essay, *A Farther Appeal to Men of Reason and Religion* (Part III), Wesley wrote of the Reformers, Luther and Calvin, '... the grand stumbling-block of all was their open avowed separation from the Church; their rejecting so many of the doctrines and practices which the others accounted most sacred; and their continual invectives against the Church they separated from - so much sharper than Michael's reproof of Satan.'[18] The strength of Wesley's opposition to separation is all too plain; Wesley did everything in his power to keep his Methodist Movement within the Church of England.

---

[13] Telford (ed.), *Letters*, III, p. 37, May 1750.

[14] Telford (ed.), *Letters*, III, p. 202; see also *Journal*, III, p. 519, 1 April 1751, where he reports that the disputations of the Baptists, the only time he uses the term, hampered the work at Wednesbury.

[15] Telford (ed.), *Letters*, III, p. 35, 22 May 1750.

[16] Telford (ed.), *Letters*, III, p. 36, 22 May 1750.

[17] For examples of Wesley denying the charge of separatism, see his letters to Dr John Free on 24 August 1758, Telford (ed.), *Letters*, IV, pp. 24-33; to Henry Brooke of 14 June 1786, Telford (ed.), *Letters*, VII, pp. 331-34; and to his brother Charles on 19 August 1785, Telford (ed.), *Letters*, VII, p. 284.

[18] Cragg (ed.), *Works*, II, p. 319.

## A Serious Reply to the Rev. John Wesley

### The Preface

Whatever the nature of the correspondence between Boyce and Wesley, in *A Serious Reply*, Boyce responded to the last two letters he received from Wesley to which he referred constantly, though he did not reproduce them in detail. The *Reply* consisted of five separate pieces of writing: an opening letter (pp. 1-4), the first letter (pp. 5-15), the last letter (pp. 16-133), the work on baptism (pp. 134-83), and a poem entitled 'The True Church' (pp. 185-88). From the preface onwards, the *Reply* was punctuated by assurances from Boyce of his love and affection for Wesley. However, after some 133 pages of constant disagreement with him, these protestations may be questioned. It is evident that the only room in which Boyce could sit comfortably with Wesley was a debating chamber.

Boyce set the tone of the debate in the preface when, writing of the evident success of Wesley in accumulating followers, just like the Pope, Boyce commented,

> But Mr Wesley's being ever so successful in gathering followers, &c does not prove that he is in nothing mistaken; and if he is mistaken, although it should be but in a few things, or even but one thing, it can be no harm in a friendly and affectionate way to tell him of it. And that he is mistaken, greatly mistaken in some things at least, I have I think, if I am not greatly mistaken, evidently made appear.[19]

Although Wesley's *Journal* referred to his overnight stay with Boyce, the collections of his *Letters* contain none of the correspondence to which Boyce referred.

### The Opening Letter

Boyce adopted from the outset what was to become a common ploy throughout the *Reply*. He recalled a statement made by Wesley, with which he wholeheartedly agreed, only to go on to argue that Wesley himself did not agree with it, or rather that Wesley's actions or lack of actions did not prove his agreement. In almost every case the action involved was infant baptism and the lack of action was believers' baptism.

The first such statement was that the Bible was the final arbiter in all matters of faith.[20] Boyce pondered why they could both agree with this statement yet be still divided, and concluded that, despite what men said, they took liberty to interpret the word of God by making such additions and omissions as might suit them. In this particular case it was not baptism that lay at the heart of

---

[19] Boyce, *A Serious Reply*, p. ii.
[20] Boyce, *A Serious Reply*, p. 3.

Boyce's objections. He wrote,

> All therefore that I insist upon, and desire of you is, that you prove by this unerring rule [scripture] of which 'nothing can be abated, nothing softened', nor changed; that the Church of England is the same true Church of Christ; or show me where to find it.[21]

Boyce did not accuse Wesley of believing the Church of England to be the 'one true Church of Christ', but, by challenging him to defend the assertion, he was implying that Wesley did believe it. However, Boyce presented no evidence to substantiate such an implication.

### *The First Letter*

The first letter opened, after an effusive passage in which Boyce declared his love for Wesley, with Boyce agreeing with the Methodist leader that 'God's first design is to save all men'.[22] It was the nature of the design that concerned Boyce. He believed that God had established the means whereby the design was to be carried out and that Wesley had gone beyond the bounds of scripture both in acts of omission and acts of commission. He challenged Wesley as to whether or not he truly in all things followed the example of Paul and the scriptures. Clearly Boyce believed that Wesley did not. He quoted Ephesians 4.5 in support, and asked when Wesley was baptized into the Church of Christ and when he received this one Spirit.

Leaving the question of baptism, Boyce moved on to attack what he considered to be errant teaching on the person and work of the Holy Spirit, stemming from Methodists being enthusiasts who placed too much emphasis on the importance of feelings and experience over and against the Word of God. In particular, he asked if Wesley had received the Holy Spirit by 'prayer and the laying on of hands'.[23] Boyce wrote in conclusion:

> Upon the whole I may safely and without erring conclude, that, let a man pretend to what he will, 'tis certain, he can never be led by the Spirit of God who is not led by the Word of God: for the Word and the Spirit are one: they agree in one: they speak the same thing.[24]

It is perhaps surprising that Boyce did not here or elsewhere make any reference to the occurrence of the physical manifestations that frequented Wesley's revival meetings. Indeed, apart from occasional references to Methodist enthusiasms, there is an almost total silence from contemporary Baptist writers on

---

[21] Boyce, *A Serious Reply*, p. 4.
[22] Boyce, *A Serious Reply*, p. 7.
[23] Boyce, *A Serious Reply*, p. 8.
[24] Boyce, *A Serious Reply*, p. 13.

this subject.

Boyce next took issue with Wesley's assertion that he had found no church which had come as close to the scriptural pattern as his own Methodists. Boyce could only conclude that Wesley in his search had not encountered the Baptists, whom Boyce believed to be the only church to come close to fitting this description. Boyce, however, was so certain of his own convictions that he came perilously close to believing his own denomination to be the one true Church of Christ, with much the same exclusiveness earlier attributed to Wesley. Boyce challenged Wesley to prove his assertion to him from scripture.[25]

## *The Last Letter*

Here Boyce came to the heart of his argument. Whereas the first two letters were four and nine pages long respectively, this final letter spanned 117 pages. It was in essence a defense of believers' baptism against infant baptism. Returning to the theme of the means of salvation, Boyce accused Wesley, as in the first letter, of going beyond the bounds of scripture in the means that he employed. Boyce based his own arguments on Ephesians 4.5, from which he drew his rule of salvation, 'One Lord, one faith, one baptism'. He expanded on this: 'I believe many will be found in heaven, who were never members of Christ's visible church on earth. I believe God is no respecter of persons, but in every nation he that feareth him and worketh righteousness is accepted with him'.[26] This was quite a statement from a mid-eighteenth-century protestant dissenter, and would not have been judged orthodox by many of his evangelical brethren.

Boyce now presented his unease with Wesley's view that no society or denomination might call itself the true church. Rather he believed that the true church was made up of all true believers wherever they might be found.[27] Boyce concluded that this view led to the deduction that there could be no true church this side of heaven; he argued that this had to be an error, as the Word of God clearly taught that the church was an earthly not a heavenly institution. Boyce's argument is not only pedantic but also unfair to Wesley in that what Boyce ended up condemning was not what Wesley had said but what Boyce had extrapolated from Wesley's comments. Boyce concluded, 'Every society of true believers is (say you) a branch of the one true church of Christ. Every society of true believers is (say I) a true church of Christ'.[28] This revealing comment indicates that the difference between Boyce and Wesley here was one of perspective. Wesley was the leader of a movement spawned by the state church with its top-down hierarchy, while Boyce started from the autonomy of the local congregation and looked outwards to the denomination. Put another way,

---

[25] Boyce, *A Serious Reply*, p. 14.
[26] Boyce, *A Serious Reply*, p. 17.
[27] Boyce, *A Serious Reply*, p. 20.
[28] Boyce, *A Serious Reply*, p. 21.

Wesley appeared to define the church as a collective whole, whereas Boyce defined it by its constituent parts. Had Wesley defined his 'societies' as 'churches', that would have opened up a different 'can of worms' which Boyce would have been quick to exploit.

Boyce's letter then took a slightly different tack as he returned to the issue of baptism. From here on, each section of Boyce's argument was preceded by a quotation from one of Wesley's last two letters to him. The quotations that follow in indented italic type are those ascribed by Boyce to Wesley.

*Quotation 1*
*You think the mode of baptism is necessary to salvation, I deny that even baptism itself is so; if it were, every Quaker must be damned; which I can in no wise believe.*[29]

Boyce claimed that what Wesley believed was irrelevant and did not compensate for lack of evidence. Wesley's concern for the Quakers should also be concern for himself for he, having been sprinkled himself as an infant, was no more baptized than they. On the mode, Boyce pointed out that, as their opponents had always called Baptists 'dippers', the terms *baptism* and *dipping* were synonymous. If Wesley insisted that infant baptism was also synonymous with baptism, it had to be also synonymous with dipping, which it unquestionably was not. It made as much sense, Boyce argued, as saying that 'creeping and jumping are two different modes of leaping'.[30] He concluded, 'You make a difference where it is not possible to be made, and part those things which all the world can not put asunder, and join those together which are at the utmost distance from each other'.[31] So Boyce contended that, where baptism was concerned, there was only one complete whole: there were not alternate modes whose validity might be argued.

He then turned in some detail to the question of the 'necessity of baptism'. He had evidently done some research in Wesley's own writings, for he referred to Wesley's *Farther Appeal*. Boyce quoted Wesley as having written:

*Quotation 2*
*We approve of, and adhere to all that we learned when we were children, in our catechism and common prayer book. We hold and ever have done the same opinions we received from our forefathers. We approve both the doctrines and discipline of our church. We agree with you, both in the externals and the circumstantials of religion.*[32]

This was crucial to Boyce's argument. If Wesley truly accepted in their entirety

---

[29] Boyce, *A Serious Reply*, p. 25.
[30] Boyce, *A Serious Reply*, p. 28.
[31] Boyce, *A Serious Reply*, p. 29.
[32] Cragg (ed.), *Works*, II, pp. 134-35.

the thirty-nine articles of the Church of England, Boyce believed that his many arguments with Wesley would be easily won.

Article XXVII concerns Infant Baptism, and Article IX Original Sin. If Wesley truly believed these articles, he believed that by the act of infant baptism a child was made a full member of the Church of Christ with all the privileges that brought (XXVII), and that such baptism was the only means of delivering the child from 'wrath and damnation' (IX). Therefore, argued Boyce, Wesley had to believe in the necessity of baptism. Boyce was turning Wesley's own beliefs against him, for Boyce certainly did not believe in the efficacy of infant baptism or its validity. The logic of this argument was inescapable. The practice of infant baptism had grown up in a world where infant mortality was high and parents wanted the comfort of believing in the salvation of their children. If unbaptized children were damned, then it was infant baptism that made the difference, and so baptism was necessary for salvation. Boyce concluded:

> And now sir, you are I think, brought to this *Dilemma*, viz. You must either allow that baptism is necessary to salvation, or deny that it is necessary to baptize infants. And if you will not allow the former, you must either acknowledge or deny the latter. Acknowledge it you cannot, for that would be allowing what you deny, viz. That baptism is necessary to salvation. And if you deny it, you entirely dissolve infant baptism. How will you find your way out of this labyrinth sir, I do not know, except you renounce your error and embrace the truth.[33]

Boyce next expressed his own views. Baptism, he believed, was unnecessary for those who had never heard the name of Christ, for idiots or for infants. These three he placed in a category of exceptions, as none of them may be held accountable by reason of their lack of knowledge. Boyce's starting point was the belief that baptism as ordained in scripture was primarily about the action of man and not the action of God. Boyce simply contended that such an individual response was in no way present in the act of infant baptism, and without that act of response, baptism could not and did not take place. The response, the necessary pre-condition for baptism, Boyce identified as 'repentance and belief'. Of such action a child was incapable.

Boyce noted also the silence of scripture on the issue of infant baptism and observed, 'Now who can imagine that he who is so great a lover of our souls, would have neglected to appoint every one thing to be done by us as necessary to our or our children's salvation?'.[34] This is a powerful argument: it is one thing to argue we can do a thing because it is not forbidden, but on what real basis may we consider something necessary to salvation, or a means of salvation, on which scripture is silent? In this case, the argument that infant baptism is not required overwhelms the notion that it is not forbidden. Boyce concluded:

---

[33] Boyce, *A Serious Reply*, pp. 31-32.
[34] Boyce, *A Serious Reply*, p. 38.

If Christ has commanded all things necessary to be done by us, but no where commanded us to baptize infants, then infant baptism is not necessary ... If Christ has only commanded penitent believers to be baptized, then surely we must conclude that only such are to be baptized. They [infants] therefore need not be baptized to make them inheritors of the kingdom of heaven, for our Lord has absolutely assured us (and who dare deny it?) they are of that kingdom.[35]

So, having dealt with those for whom baptism was not necessary,[36] Boyce turned to those for whom he considered it to be essential. He wrote, 'Baptism is necessary to all those who repent and believe the gospel, and to them only; for they are the persons commanded to be baptized'.[37] Basing his argument on scripture, Boyce contended that Jesus accepted John's baptism, which he refined in the Great Commission and passed as a command to the Apostles (Matthew 28.19-20).

*Quotation 3*
You say, 'you hold nothing to be (strictly speaking) necessary to salvation, but the mind which is in Christ.'.[38]

Boyce had no trouble agreeing with this statement, but once again, he took issue with Wesley's interpretation and understanding of it. As the mind of Christ made no mention in scripture of infant baptism, Boyce argued that infant baptism could therefore be no part of the mind of Christ: 'Surely he would not have been forgetful or negligent in such a material case as this as some people pretend it is'.[39] It was inconceivable that God would have neglected to inform his beloved sons and daughters of a certain and simple means to ensure the salvation of their own children. Boyce further argued that, if it were not the mind of Christ to baptize infants, then to do so was to act in contradiction to the mind of Christ.

*Quotation* 4
You say, 'They who believe with the faith working by love are God's children'.[40]

Quite right, said Boyce, but in practice, surely this meant that any true child of God would be obedient to all the commands of God, and baptism was a command of God, so why was Mr Wesley not baptized? Boyce quoted from Wesley's own hymns to establish that John Wesley himself taught over and again the importance of being obedient to God in all things. He challenged

---

[35] Boyce, *A Serious Reply*, p. 40.
[36] Boyce said no more about those who had not heard the gospel nor about idiots, perhaps because their fate was not an issue between him and Wesley.
[37] Boyce, *A Serious Reply*, p. 41.
[38] Boyce, *A Serious Reply*, p. 68.
[39] Boyce, *A Serious Reply*, p. 71.
[40] Boyce, *A Serious Reply*, p. 72.

Wesley, while all stood in dispute around him, to rise above it all and show his obedience to God in being baptized.

> You say, 'I do make use (as far as I know) of all the means of grace God has ordained, exactly as God hath ordained them'.[41]

Boyce made a number of comments in response to this, drawing in further remarks by Wesley under the same heading. Boyce conceded he might not be fully aware of the extent of Wesley's knowledge and use of the means of grace, but he was fully aware of his misuse of the means of grace that is baptism. 'I know you make use of the name but not of the thing, as I have already proved'.[42] Here, Boyce returned to the heart of his argument: he did not dispute with Wesley whether infant baptism was a lesser form of baptism or an imperfect copy of the real thing. He disputed that it was baptism at all. He rejected the label of being an Anabaptist (i.e. a re-baptizer) on the grounds that he could not be so, for no baptism had previously taken place.

Then, Boyce turned his attention to the matter of the church as a means of grace. Wesley had written in one letter, 'But here is your grand mistake, you think my design is to form a church. No; I have no such design. It is not my design or desire that any who accept of my help, should leave the church of which they are now members'.[43] Boyce pointed to the reality of the situation for, whatever Wesley's design, it was apparent that people were leaving their churches in large numbers to join his 'societies': 'if this is not forming a church, I should be glad to know what is'.[44]

Boyce next passed to a very interesting comment made by Wesley when he wrote, 'Was I converting Indians I would take every step St Paul took. But I am not; therefore some of those steps I am not to take'.[45] For Boyce, the steps of St Paul were identifiable as preaching repentance and encouraging faith, followed by baptism and receiving the Spirit by the laying on of hands. It was easy for Boyce to infer which part of this method Wesley might not consider necessary for English men and women, most of whom had been baptized as infants. Boyce applied to this the simple logic that had served him so well throughout his polemic. According to the rubric of the catechism, those baptized as infants became fully regenerate members of the Church of Christ so, if infant baptism was as efficacious as the catechism, why was it that so few of those so baptized went on to 'live a life worthy of the Gospel'? And why were those who did invariably those who had a subsequent conversion experience? If infant baptism became efficacious only following a subsequent act of confirmation, what

---

[41] Boyce, *A Serious Reply*, p. 74.
[42] Boyce, *A Serious Reply*, p. 74.
[43] Boyce, *A Serious Reply*, p. 74.
[44] Boyce, *A Serious Reply*, p. 75.
[45] Boyce, *A Serious Reply*, pp. 75-76.

was its initial purpose? Why bother with it in the first place?

By this time, Wesley's relationship with the Church of England was not so much a wound as a festering sore, and Boyce exploited this mercilessly. Historical hindsight might tell us that the rift between the Methodists and the Church of England was inevitable. Wesley was no fool and surely began to suspect that this was so. However, there is no doubt that, from the beginning, he did all he could to keep the movement within the Church of England. Wesley was the dominating figure in the Methodist Revival, a man of immense personal energy and authority, but the revival came to possess a life of its own that Wesley could not wholly control, only influence. On this issue, Wesley was an easy target, possibly an unfair one, and Boyce was not slow to exploit the inconsistencies in his position.

Wesley had written to Boyce, 'I still join with the Church of England so far as I can'.[46] Recalling his total commitment to the catechism in *Farther Appeal*, Boyce wondered on what possible grounds Wesley might be unable to join with them, or they with him. What did the Church of England do that Wesley could not join with, or what did he do that the Church of England rejected? Either way Wesley's claimed adherence to the catechism was undermined.

> What I affirm of the generality of teachers and people of the Church of England I affirm of teachers and people of every other denomination; I mean so far as I know them.[47]

Boyce's comments here illustrated his tendency to extrapolate as negatively as possible from Wesley's remarks. Undoubtedly Wesley encountered good and bad in all denominations, as he did among his own Methodist societies who would appear to be included in the above remark. Boyce's conclusion that Wesley had nothing but 'black and negative' things to say of the Church of England and therefore of all other churches said more about his desire to take and make issue with Wesley than anything else. Clearly, Wesley did not know many Baptists, or else he would surely have excluded them from his remarks, unless they were directed at the Particular Baptists, whose teaching on 'particular redemption' Boyce agreed to be worthy of condemnation.[48]

*Quotation 5*
I do believe the doctrine, worship and discipline (so far as it goes) of the Church of England to be agreeable to the word of God.[49]

Boyce replied to this in some detail, taking doctrine, worship and discipline in turn. Taking doctrine first, Boyce referred to Article XXVII, which says:

---

[46] Boyce, *A Serious Reply*, p. 78.
[47] Boyce, *A Serious Reply*, p. 79.
[48] Boyce, *A Serious Reply*, pp. 81-82.
[49] Boyce, *A Serious Reply*, p. 84.

Baptism is not only a sign of Profession, and a Mark of Difference, whereby Christian Men are discerned from others that be not christened; but it is also a Sign of Regeneration, or New Birth, whereby, as by an Instrument, they that receive Baptism rightly, are grafted into the Church: The Promises of the Forgiveness of Sins and of our Adoption to be Sons of God, by the Holy Ghost, are visibly signed and sealed: Faith is confirmed, and grace increased, by virtue of prayer unto God. The Baptism of young Children is in any wise to be retained in the Church, as most agreeable with the Institution of Christ.[50]

Boyce challenged Wesley once again to justify this Article from scripture. Where did the sprinkling of infants appear as an 'Institution of Christ, did Christ ordain it or the Apostles'? How could all the promises of new birth and regeneration accrue to an infant merely by the sprinkling of water? Boyce was aware of the implication that a child not so sprinkled was damned, but he found in Article IX what was for him a further errant doctrine that lay behind the necessity to justify infant baptism. Article IX states:

Original Sin standeth not in the following of Adam (as the Pelagians do vainly talk), but it is the Fault and Corruption of the Nature of every Man, that naturally is ingendered of the offspring of Adam, whereby Man is very far gone from original Righteousness, and is of his own Nature inclined to Evil, so that the Flesh lusteth always contrary to the Spirit; and therefore in every Person born into this World, it deserveth God's wrath and Damnation. And this infection of Nature doth remain; yea, in them that are regenerated, whereby the Lust of the Flesh {called in Greek, φρόνημα σαρκός, which some expound the Wisdom, some Sensuality, some the Affection, some the Desire of the Flesh, is not subject to the Law of God}. And although there is no condemnation or them that believe and are baptized, yet the Apostle does confess, that Concupiscence and Lust hath of itself the Nature of Sin.[51]

Although Boyce questioned how the mere sprinkling of water upon a child in the absence of repentance and faith might achieve this, it was secondary to his main objective. He was primarily concerned with the validity of the assertion that all human beings were from birth not only tainted by Adam's sin but condemned by it. Where in scripture did God impute Adam's sin to man? That man suffered the consequences of Adam's sin, Boyce did not question, but that was not the same as saying that man was guilty of Adam's sin. Boyce asked, 'How then can we think that the just and righteous God will bring all Adam's

---

[50] Jonathan Warne, *An Attempt to promote true Love and Unity between the Church of England and the Dissenters who are Calvinists, of the Baptist, Independent and Presbyterian persuasions* (London, 1741), p. 26. Cf. also Griffiths Jones *(A Country Gentleman), The Platform of Christ being the General Heads of the Protestant Religion as professed in the Church of England* (London, 1744), pp. 72-76.

[51] Warne, *An Attempt to promote true Love and Unity*, p. 8; cf. Griffiths Jones, *A Country Gentleman*, p. 24. He does not include the passage in {}.

children into this world in a state of wrath and damnation?[52] He thus addressed directly the fear that lay behind the practice of infant baptism, a fear engendered by the Church of England's own Articles of Faith. This fear stemmed from the assertion that all newborn children were guilty of the sin of Adam and, if they died before they came to faith, they would be subjected to God's wrath and condemnation. Faced by such a belief, it was no wonder that God-fearing parents looked to the church for a means of overcoming this fear. For Boyce, that fear was itself totally misplaced. For God to hold a child accountable for the sin of some long-dead forefather was unjust; God did not do this. Moreover, there was nothing in the scriptures to justify the perpetuation of this fear. On the judgement day, all would be called to answer for their own sin, not for Adam's. So Boyce argued that the reason for infant baptism was to deliver children from damnation, but as children were not born damned there was no need to baptize them as infants at all. If accepted, however, this only pushed the matter forward in time. Boyce had not fully solved the dilemma for parents by establishing that a newborn infant was not responsible for the sin of Adam. He was right to say '... we all begin to sin soon enough'.[53] If the ability to sin came soon enough, did the ability to repent and believe come with it? If that first sin subjected the sinner to 'wrath and damnation', and if baptism was necessary to salvation, the parental dilemma remained. Children, perhaps as young as two or three years, were now sinners under condemnation, but were they capable of repentance and belief? Doubtless, they could be encouraged by anxious and loving parents to say the right words at an act of baptism, but that would not satisfy Boyce's concept of believers' baptism. Boyce may have exposed the fear, superstition and prejudice that lay behind the institution of infant baptism, but he had not solved the inherent theological dilemma.

Turning to worship, Boyce passed to a more subjective argument. He noted the irony that the Church of England, that once fought so hard to enforce conformity of worship upon all, was now itself so diverse in its worship. He was especially scathing about the use of songs and of cathedral worship, writing, 'From whence came all your music and your singing boys?'.[54] What scriptural justification was there for singing prayers, for reading set prayers, for frequently repeating the Lord's prayer, and for bowing to the altar, the east, and at the name of Jesus? Boyce was perhaps on thin ice, since the issue of hymn-singing had caused Baptists much anguish in the early part of the eighteenth century. In the late 1780s, Boyce published *Serious thoughts on the present mode ... of singing, etc.*, defending the Old Connexion practice of not singing hymns. It may have been aimed at New Connexion practice which favoured hymn-singing. Dan Taylor replied, rather reluctantly out of respect for his friendship with Boyce, with *A Dissertation on singing in the worship of God:*

---

[52] Boyce, *A Serious Reply*, p. 86.

[53] Boyce, *A Serious Reply*, p. 87, footnote.

[54] Boyce, *A Serious Reply*, p. 91.

*interspersed with occasional strictures on Mr Boyce's late tract entitled: Serious thoughts on the present mode ... of singing, etc.* This brought a further response from Boyce, entitled, *A candid and friendly reply &c.*

Writing of discipline in the Church of England, Boyce displayed a little humour: '... if it be true what a certain clergyman some years ago told me, it will I doubt be somewhat difficult to find it'.[55] Placing his remarks in the context of communion, he again had to tread carefully as this remained a live issue among Baptists. Boyce was a closed-communionist, believing only those with a publicly declared faith in Jesus (i.e. those baptized as believers) should be allowed to take communion. Communion, he argued, was to 'remember Christ', and baptism was for the repentance of sinners. Therefore, only the godly and devout should be admitted to communion. Then, he again returned to infant baptism, which had for him in this debate become the root of all evil. Because the Church of England practised infant baptism, it ended up admitting to communion all manner of men and women whose lives showed no evidence of their supposed regenerate state. Wesley had argued to Boyce that the apostles received communion from the Lord when they were unconverted and that this was justification for his actions.[56] Boyce conceded that they had not received the 'promise of the Holy Ghost' but not that they were not Christians. Wesley's argument was as tangible as Boyce's, perhaps more so. The moment at which the apostles became believers is unclear. The crucial moment for the apostles in the gospels was Peter's declaration on the road to Caesarea Philippi (Mark 8), which might be construed as an act of faith and, therefore, supportive of Boyce's argument. However, if the nature of belief mattered, and if there were an irreducible minimum such as was found in the creeds, it might be said that Peter's declaration was too lacking in content to be discerned as saving faith: the argument would then favour Wesley.

*Quotation 6*
I wish your zeal was better employed than in persuading men to be either dipped or sprinkled. I will employ mine, by the grace of God, persuading them to love God with all their heart, and their neighbours as themselves.[57]

There is no doubt that Wesley found disputing with his own church and with dissenters a thankless, frustrating activity. His low opinion of dissenters was largely due to their propensity toward argument. By commenting on this, Wesley attempted to take the moral and theological high ground, but to no avail. Boyce was far too thick-skinned to be put off. He retorted that nothing could ever induce him to persuade men to be sprinkled, which was not what Wesley was contending for at all. His zeal was reserved for persuading men to

---

[55] Boyce, *A Serious Reply*, p. 93.
[56] Boyce, *A Serious Reply*, p. 99.
[57] Boyce, *A Serious Reply*, p. 103.

repent and be baptized according to the biblical pattern, which did not for a moment prevent him from being just as zealous in persuading them to love the Lord.

> Lastly, you tell me, 'You are convinced I did not write from anger ... but from a zeal for my own opinion and mode of worship'.[58]

No, agreed Boyce, not from anger, but not from personal zeal either. It was the honour of Christ that Boyce believed he was defending and the truth of God's word.

This quotation ended the section of Boyce's work devoted to replying to the letters he had received from Wesley, but it was by no means the end of the matter. Boyce then addressed other matters: first a remark made by Wesley when he visited Boyce at home, and then Wesley's comments on scripture in his *Notes on the New Testament*.

Wesley's comment to Boyce was that 'It could not be proved that our Lord, nor the Eunuch was dipped'.[59] (Matthew 3.1-17; Mark 1.1-11; Luke 3.21-3; Acts 8.26-40). Wesley's supporting argument for this was, according to Boyce, a two-fold one, given verbally when Wesley stayed at Boyce's home: that the Jordan contained insufficient water, and that the language used by the New Testament 'came up out of' may refer not to water but the river-bank. Thirdly, in *Notes*,[60] commenting on Matthew 3.6, Wesley argued that the people who came to John did not possess spare clothing and so would not have been immersed but sprinkled. Wesley's argument was that people stood alongside the river and were sprinkled by John as he passed by. This, however, was a defunct argument from its inception because it allowed for an understanding of baptism alien to the first century. If the apostles had taken from John, and then from Jesus, a form of baptism radically different from the one known to them, this would have been made clear. Reminding Wesley of John 3.23 (which specifically mentions John baptizing where he did because of the amount of water there, a verse Wesley ignored), Boyce crushed the argument about insufficient water for immersion. In respect of clothing, Boyce pointed out that it was well known what John was about and so people would have come prepared. In respect of the eunuch, Wesley commented on Acts 8.38, 'And they both went down - Out of the chariot. It does not follow, that he was baptized by Immersion. The text neither affirms nor intimates any thing concerning it'.[61] Boyce contended that Wesley had translated the Greek to suit his argument: it should be rendered 'went down *into* the water' and not, as Wesley, 'went down *to* the

---

[58] Boyce, *A Serious Reply*, p. 104

[59] Boyce, *A Serious Reply*, p. 108.

[60] John Wesley, *John Wesley's 'Notes on the New Testament'*, ed. John Lawson (London, 1755), p. 9.

[61] Wesley, *Notes on the New Testament*, p. 314.

water'. He accused Wesley also of changing Mark 1.9 to read 'was baptized by John *at* Jordan' rather than *in*.[62] Boyce highlighted the inconsistency he believed existed in Wesley's translation for Philip and the eunuch having gone 'down *to*' the water did not then in Acts 8.39 'come up *from* the water' but, according to Wesley, they 'come up *out of* the water'. Boyce's final argument on this was less complex. Given that Jesus' baptism was not disputed, it rested with Wesley to prove that there existed in the New Testament an alternative mode of baptism to immersion, and that sprinkling was such a mode; he would have to establish that the ancient world knew of such an alternative and that it was widely used in Palestine at the time of Jesus, and would have to provide reasonable grounds for assuming that when the New Testament spoke of baptism it really meant sprinkling.

Finally, Boyce turned to the rubric of the Prayer Book. He quoted: 'If it be certified that a child may well endure it, the priest shall wisely and discreetly dip it into the water'.[63] Arguing that all but the frailest of babies would withstand dipping as prescribed by rubric, Boyce questioned why there was any need for sprinkling, and why the practice of priests was not more consistent with the teaching of the church. In conclusion, he wrote, 'Your own catechism which you so much approve of, and pretend so strictly to adhere to, stands directly opposite to your present practice of sprinkling, and remains like your Rubrics and Fonts, an undeniable witness against you all, that you are gone back from Christ's Ordinance of Baptism and have not kept it'.[64]

Here, Boyce ended his reply to Wesley's last letter, but this was not his last word on the matter. It was followed by *A Serious Reply to what has been objected against the necessity and importance of that divine and heavenly Ordinance Baptism by the people called Methodists in general and more specifically by those whom I have conversed, and with whom I am acquainted.*[65] Under this heading Boyce took a further fifty pages to defend believers' baptism from specific criticisms he had encountered and to look at the teaching of scripture on the subject.

## Conclusion

All this would be of little matter if Gilbert Boyce were a small-minded man of little consequence amongst Baptists of his day, but he was the Messenger of a county where the General Baptist cause was particularly strong. This made him a man of influence not only in Lincolnshire but also on a much larger stage through the long-established, annual, national General Assembly of the General Baptists. The limited biographical material extant shows his standing among

---

[62] Boyce, *A Serious Reply*, p. 127.
[63] Boyce, *A Serious Reply*, p. 131.
[64] Boyce, *A Serious Reply*, p. 133.
[65] Boyce, *A Serious Reply*, pp. 134-83.

General Baptists and his defense of baptism probably had the approval of Particular Baptists, too.

Boyce's comments were the most significant exposition by any Baptist writer of the period on Wesley's practices and beliefs, although Boyce said little about the Methodist Revival itself. He did not discuss Wesley's evangelistic methods, camp meetings, itinerant preachers, nor the wild happenings at meetings that so concerned later writers. The issue of baptism was seen by him as a yawning, unbridgeable chasm between Wesley and the Baptists. For eighteenth-century Baptists, it was believers' baptism that set them apart from other Christians, even from fellow dissenters. They were tenacious in their defence of it and united in their opposition to the abomination that was infant baptism. In other matters, they had common ground with other dissenters, but they had none with the Church of England and little, at this time, with Wesley and his Methodists. The silence of eighteenth-century Baptists on the processes of the revival is deafening: it is as though they had no knowledge of it, or at least no interest in it as something that did not concern them.

CHAPTER 6

# Benjamin Beddome (1717-1795):
# His Life and His Hymns [1]

Michael Haykin

John Newton (1725-1807), the well-known evangelical leader and author of the ever-popular hymn 'Amazing Grace', had the opportunity to meet and hear many of the leading evangelicals of his day. It is intriguing, therefore, to read some remarks that he penned in his diary on 7 August 1776, after he had heard a sermon by a country Baptist preacher by the name of Benjamin Beddome (1717-1795). Beddome's text on that particular occasion was Zechariah 11:12, the verse cited in the Gospel of Matthew with regard to the amount of money Judas Iscariot received for the betrayal of Christ. 'He is an admirable preacher,' Newton observed after hearing the sermon, 'simple, savoury, weighty'. This was not the first time that Newton had heard Beddome preach. The Anglican evangelical had heard him speak the previous year on 2 Corinthians 1:24. Of that occasion Newton later recorded: '[the sermon] gave me a pleasure I seldom find in hearing. It was an excellent discourse indeed, and the Lord was pleased to give me some softenings and relentings of heart'.[2] For one who often heard the greatest preacher of the day, George Whitefield (1714-1770), these words are high praise indeed. But who was Benjamin Beddome and why should his life be remembered today?

---

[1] This paper had its origins in the annual lecture given on 18 February 1998, for The Acadia Centre for Baptist and Anabaptist Studies, Acadia Divinity College, Wolfville, Nova Scotia.
   I wish to acknowledge the tremendous help that Derrick Holmes of Gloucester, England, has given me in this study of Benjamin Beddome's life and hymnody. Thanks are also due to Arie van Eyck, formerly of Shedden, Ontario, for help in procuring a copy of J. R. Watson, *The English Hymn: A Critical and Historical Study* from the library of the University of Western Ontario.
[2] John Newton, *Diary (1703-1805)*, entries for 7 August 1776 and 27 June 1775 (Princeton University Library).

## Baptist Witness in Bourton-on-the-Water

When Newton first heard Beddome, the latter was pastor of the Baptist church in Bourton-on-the-Water, Gloucestershire. Called to this pastorate in 1743, he ministered in this picturesque village, dubbed by some 'the Venice of the Cotswolds', till his death fifty-two years later. The origins of the church lie in the halcyon days of Calvinistic Baptist advance during the period of the Commonwealth, when England was ruled by that quintessential Puritan, Oliver Cromwell (1598-1658). According to the extant minutes of the Midlands [Calvinistic] Baptist Association, representatives of the Bourton Baptists were present at this association's second general meeting on 26 June 1655. How long the church had existed prior to this date, however, is not exactly known. According to one account, it was founded in 1650.[3]

Nonconformity had been a significant force in the village of Bourton and surrounding countryside since the close of the Elizabethan era. During the final years of the sixteenth century, for example, the Puritan preacher, Richard Stock (ca. 1569-1626), was domestic chaplain to a Lady Lane, the lessee of the Bourton manor.[4] Later, in the period of the Commonwealth the village rectory was occupied by Anthony Palmer (1616-1679), who, adopting Congregationalist convictions while at Bourton, was later a friend of John Bunyan (1628-1688). The local gentry were deeply disturbed by Palmer's nonconformity, though, and in 1660 he was forcibly evicted from the rectory. Palmer looked with favour upon those of the Baptist persuasion during his time at Bourton, giving them the opportunity to establish themselves in the village. Palmer eventually made his way to London, where he became one of the city's leading Congregationalists and for a while was pastor of a church made up of both Baptists and Congregationalists.[5]

---

[3] B.R. White (ed.), *Association Records of the Particular Baptists of England, Wales and Ireland to 1660. South Wales and the Midlands* (4 parts; London: The Baptist Historical Society, 1971), 1, pp. 20 & 40 n.9; C. R. Elrington and Helen O'Neil, 'Bourton-on-the-Water', in C. R. Elrington (ed.), *A History of the County of Gloucester* (London: Oxford University Press, 1965), VI, p. 47. For a history of the church, see Thomas Brooks, *Pictures of the Past: The History of the Baptist Church, Bourton-on-the-Water* (London: Judd & Glass, 1861).

[4] 'Stock, Richard', *The Compact Edition of the Dictionary of National Biography* (2 vols; London: Oxford University Press, 1975), II, p. 2012; Derrick Holmes, 'The Early Years (1655-1740) of Bourton-on-the-Water Dissenters who later constituted the Baptist Church, with special reference to the Ministry of the Reverend Benjamin Beddome A.M. 1740-1795' (Certificate in Education Dissertation, St Paul's College, Cheltenham, 1969), p. 3; Elrington and O'Neil, 'Bourton-on-the-Water', p. 47.

[5] R. L. Greaves, 'Palmer, Anthony' in R. L. Greaves and Robert Zaller (eds.), *Biographical Dictionary of British Radicals in the Seventeenth Century* (3 vols; Brighton, Sussex: The Harvester Press, 1982-1984), III, pp. 2-3; Holmes, 'Early Years', pp. 6-8.

The story of Baptist witness in the village for the eighty years following the departure of Palmer is shrouded in obscurity.[6] What we do know of the situation bears out Beddome's description of the Bourton Baptist cause before his coming to the village in 1740 as one in which the church had been 'for a long time...unsettled and divided'.[7] With the coming of Beddome to the village, however, this long period of uncertainty for the Baptists in Bourton was at an end.

### Benjamin Beddome: his Early Years, 1717-1740

John Beddome (1674-1757), Benjamin's father, was the Baptist minister of Alcester Baptist Church, Warwickshire, at the time of his son's birth. Like many other Calvinistic Baptist churches of this period, the Alcester church drew its membership from a wide radius, including meetings at Bengeworth, near Evesham in Worcestershire, and Henley-in-Arden, Warwickshire, six or so miles to the north of Alcester.[8] John Beddome had come to this church in 1697 from the Baptist congregation that met in Horsleydown, Southwark, London, where the pastor was the renowned Benjamin Keach (1640-1704), one of the seventeenth-century fathers of the Calvinistic Baptist denomination.[9]

In 1711, the Alcester church took on Bernard Foskett (1685-1758) as co-pastor to the elder Beddome.[10] Foskett would later became the first principal of Bristol Baptist Academy and exercise a powerful influence upon the course of certain sections of the Calvinistic Baptist community during the mid-eighteenth century.[11] Within a year of Foskett's arrival at Alcester, the two pastors had reconstituted the church on the basis of a confession of faith which British Bap-

---

[6] For a helpful discussion of the available evidence, see Holmes, 'Early Years', pp. 8-19.
[7] *Letter to Prescot Street Baptist Church, 22 November 1750* [in Thomas Brooks, 'Ministerial Changes a Hundred Years Ago', *The Baptist Magazine* 51 (1859), p. 427].
[8] Christopher Stell, *An Inventory of Nonconformist Chapels and Meeting-houses in Central England* (London: HMSO, 1986), p. 226.
[9] *Henley-in-Arden Church Book*, [p.5] (Warwick City Record Office, Warwickshire). I am indebted to James Renihan of the Institute of Reformed Baptist Studies, Escondido, California, for a photocopy of this page. On Keach, see Michael A. G. Haykin, *Kiffin, Knollys and Keach: Rediscovering Our English Baptist Heritage* (Leeds, England: Reformation Today Trust, 1996), pp. 82-97; and especially Austin Walker, *The Excellent Benjamin Keach* (Dundas, Ontario: Joshua Press, 2004).
[10] *Henley-in-Arden Church Book*, p. 5.
[11] For a fine study of Foskett's contribution to Calvinistic Baptist life, see Roger Hayden, 'Evangelical Calvinism among eighteenth-century British Baptists with particular reference to Bernard Foskett, Hugh and Caleb Evans and the Bristol Baptist Academy, 1690-1791' (PhD thesis, University of Keele, 1991), pp. 110-82, now published in a revised form as *Continuity and Change: Evangelical Calvinism among Eighteenth-Century Baptist Minsters Trained at the Bristol Academy, 1690-1791* (Chipping Norton: Baptist Historical Society, 2006).

tist historian, Roger Hayden, has described as 'a closely argued, biblically attested statement of orthodox Christian belief in a Calvinistic form'.[12] By early 1713 they had also led the Alcester congregation to affirm the rightness of singing hymns at the church's public worship. The stand that John Beddome took in this matter is not without significance, for it meant that young Benjamin was exposed at an early age to hymn-singing and thus a foundation was laid for his extensive hymn-writing during his ministry at Bourton.

Whether or not hymns could be sung in worship was an issue upon which Calvinistic Baptists had been sharply divided since the early 1690s.[13] At the heart of this debate was John Beddome's home church, where the pastor, Benjamin Keach, had occasionally introduced hymns into the worship of the congregation since the mid-1670s. But it was not until a church meeting on 1 March 1691, that a large majority of the members voted to have a hymn sung following the service every Sunday. Yet, there were some in the church who felt that this practice was an unscriptural innovation. That March they left the church and formed themselves into a new cause that met at Maze Pond. In the articles of faith that the founders of the Maze Pond church drew up in February 1694, it was explicitly stated that congregational singing was 'a gross error equall with common nationall Sett forme Prayer'.[14]

Prominent among these dissidents was Isaac Marlow (1649-1719), a wealthy jeweller, who became the leading opponent of the practice of congregational singing. In the course of the hymn-singing controversy, which ran from 1690 to 1698, Marlow wrote no less than eleven books that dealt with the issue.[15] The heat generated by the controversy may be discerned to some degree by the terms that the two sides tossed at each other. Marlow tells us that he was labeled a 'Ridiculous Scribbler', 'Brasen-Forehead', 'Enthusiast', i.e. fanatic, and 'Quaker'. But Marlow could give as good as he got. He viewed his opponents as 'a coterie of book burning papists' who were seeking to undermine the Reformation, for, as far as he was concerned, they were endorsing a practice that had no scriptural warrant at all.[16] These acerbic remarks by both sides in the debate indicate that the division over hymn-singing was no trivial matter. It rent the London Baptist community in two, and, in the words of Murdina MacDonald, 'effectively destroyed the capacity of the Calvinistic Baptists as a

---

[12] Hayden, 'Evangelical Calvinism', p. 114. Hayden includes this confession of faith as an appendix to his thesis on pp. 366-75.

[13] For an excellent discussion of the early stages of this controversy, see Murdina D. MacDonald, 'London Calvinistic Baptists 1689-1727: Tensions within a Dissenting Community under Toleration' (D.Phil. Thesis, Regent's Park College, University of Oxford, 1982), pp. 50-66.

[14] MacDonald, 'London Calvinistic Baptists 1689-1727', p. 88. For the early development of the Maze Pond cause, see pp. 83-108.

[15] For a list, see MacDonald, 'London Calvinistic Baptists 1689-1727', pp. 387-91.

[16] MacDonald, 'London Calvinistic Baptists 1689-1727', pp. 62, 72-73, 74.

whole to establish a national organization at this time'.[17]

In 1714 John Beddome married Rachel Brandon, a wealthy heiress and a descendant of Charles Brandon, the first Duke of Suffolk, who was brother-in-law to Henry VIII. Benjamin, the first of five children to survive infancy, was born three years later. When Beddome was seven years of age, his father left the Midlands to accept a call to the Pithay Church, Bristol. At the time, there were two Calvinistic Baptist congregations in the city: Broadmead, where John Beddome's life-long friend, Bernard Foskett, had become pastor in 1720, and the larger Pithay Church, which contained 500 or so members in the early 1720s. For many years, the Pithay had been pastored by Andrew Gifford, Sr (1642-1721), the intrepid evangelist of the West Country. Upon Gifford's death, his son, Emmanuel, had become the senior pastor, but he only survived his father by two years. Possibly acting on the advice of Foskett, this large church approached the elder Beddome about assuming the pastorate. His acceptance in 1724 necessitated the removal of his family to Bristol in the summer of that year.

Although he regularly sat under his father's preaching in the Pithay as he was growing up, Benjamin showed little interest in the things of Christ, and understandably his parents were deeply concerned about his state. In fact, not until he was twenty years of age did God's Word strike home to his heart, and his parents see the fruit of many years of prayer for their son's conversion. On 7 August 1737, a visiting preacher to the Pithay by the name of Ware spoke on Luke 15:7 ['I tell you that in the same way there will be more rejoicing in heaven over one sinner who repents than over ninety-nine righteous persons who do not need to repent', KJV]. So deeply was Beddome affected by the sermon that for some time afterwards he would be in tears while his father preached, and he would hide himself in one of the galleries so that his weeping would not be widely observed.[18] Beddome would later generalize his experience thus in one of his hymns:

> Faith, 'tis a precious grace,
> Where'er it is bestowed;
> It boasts of a celestial birth,
> And is the gift of God.
>
> Jesus it owns as king,
> An all-atoning priest,
> It claims no merit of its own,
> But looks for all in Christ.

---

[17] MacDonald, 'London Calvinistic Baptists 1689-1727', p. 69.
[18] S. A. Swaine, *Faithful Men; or, Memorials of Bristol Baptist College and Some of its Most Distinguished Alumni* (London: Alexander & Shepheard, 1884), p. 43.

> On him it safely leans,
> In times of deep distress;
> Flies to the fountain of his blood,
> And trusts his righteousness.[19]

Soon after his conversion, Beddome was led to consider pastoral ministry. He spent a couple of years in theological training under the tutelage of Bernard Foskett. Then, in 1739, he moved to London to continue his studies at the Fund Academy in Tenter Alley, Moorfields, where the independent John Eames (d.1744) was the theological tutor. Possibly the only layman ever to hold the theological chair in an eighteenth-century Nonconformist academy, Eames was an esteemed scientist who had a very high reputation as a tutor and was once described by the hymnwriter Isaac Watts (1674-1748) as 'the most learned man I ever knew'.[20]

It was during this sojourn in London that Beddome became convinced of the necessity of believer's baptism. He was baptized by Samuel Wilson (1702-1750), the pastor of Prescot Street Baptist Church, and received into the membership of this church in October 1739. At the time of his baptism, his father, in many ways Benjamin's spiritual mentor, wrote to him to express his joy about the step that his son was taking. 'I am pleased to hear that you have given yourself to a Church of Christ', he wrote, 'but more, in that I hope you first gave up yourself to the Lord to be his servant, and at his disposal'.[21] Early the following year the London church took steps to formally recognize God's hand on Benjamin's life for pastoral ministry and to set him apart for that work. The elder Beddome, though, felt that the Prescot Street church was moving far too quickly. As he informed his son: 'I am sorry Mr Wilson is in such a hurry to call you to the ministry'. Nevertheless, the father seems to have accepted the fact and told his son: 'The Lord will help you to make a solemn dedication of yourself to him, and enter on the work of the Lord with holy awe and trembling'.[22]

Beddome's father continued to give his son sage counsel up until his death in 1757, deeming 'nothing unimportant that stood related to the ministry, and might therefore either help or hinder its success'.[23] The younger Beddome's preaching in his early years, for instance, was quite different from that which

---

[19] *Hymns adapted to Public Worship, or Family Devotion* (London, 1818), #165, 'Faith the Gift of God.'

[20] Alexander Gordon, 'Eames, John', *Compact Edition of the Dictionary of National Biography*, I, p. 598. On the influence of Eames on Beddome, see Holmes, 'Early Years', pp. 22-24.

[21] Cited Brooks, *Pictures of the Past*, p. 23.

[22] *Letter to Benjamin Beddome, 21 May 1740* (cited in Brooks, *Pictures of the Past*, p. 23).

[23] Brooks, *Pictures of the Past*, p. 24.

Newton admired in the 1770s. The tone of his preaching was often strident and harsh, and his sermons far too long. John Beddome thus told his son in a letter that he wrote on 17 May 1742: 'If you deliver the great truths of the gospel with calmness, and with a soft, mellow voice, they will drop as the gentle rain or dew. For the good of souls, then, and for your own good, be persuaded to strive after this'. A few weeks later, he again urged him: 'soften your voice, and shorten your sermons ...Let two hours be the longest time you spend in the pulpit at any place'![24]

## Ministry at Bourton-on-the-Water, 1740-1795

Beddome first visited Bourton-on-the-Water in the spring of 1740. Over the next three years, he laboured with great success in the Bourton church. Significant for the shape of his future ministry was a local revival that took place under his ministry in the early months of 1741. Around forty individuals were converted, including John Collett Ryland (1723-1791), a leading Baptist minister in the latter half of the eighteenth century.[25] It may well have been this taste of revival that made Beddome a cordial friend to those who were involved in the evangelical revivals of the mid-eighteenth century, men like George Whitefield and the Mohegan Indian preacher, Samson Occom (1723-1792),[26] and that gave him an ongoing hunger to read of revival throughout British society on both sides of the Atlantic.[27] Within a year of the Bourton awakening, for instance, Beddome had purchased a copy of Jonathan Edwards' *The Distinguishing Marks of a Work of the Spirit of God* (1741), which would have given him a

---

[24] *Letters to Benjamin Beddome, 17 May and 6 August 1742* (cited in Brooks, *Pictures of the Past*, pp. 24-25).
[25] William Newman, *Rylandiana: Reminiscences Relating to the Rev. John Ryland, A.M.* (London: George Wightman, 1835), p. 3. On Ryland, see also James Culross, *The Three Rylands: A Hundred Years of Various Christian Service* (London: Elliot Stock, 1897), pp. 11-66. Ryland has been primarily remembered for the withering rebuke that he gave to the young William Carey (1761-1834) when the latter surfaced the question of whether or not missionary endeavour was incumbent upon the church of their day. This is a shame, for he was, in his own right, a great figure in eighteenth-century English Baptist history and is deserving of a better reputation.
[26] For Beddome's association with Whitefield, see Geoffrey F. Nuttall, 'George Whitefield's "Curate": Gloucestershire Dissent and the Revival', *The Journal of Ecclesiastical History* 27.4 (October 1976), pp. 382-84. Samson Occom seems to have been converted under the preaching of James Davenport around 1740, prior to Davenport's period of fanaticism [W. DeLoss Love, *Samson Occom and the Christian Indians of New England* (Boston/Chicago: The Pilgrim Press, 1899), p. 34]. Occom preached at Bourton in April 1767, during an extensive trip that the Native American evangelist made to Britain (Hayden, 'Evangelical Calvinism', p. 152).
[27] Hayden, 'Evangelical Calvinism', p. 152.

marvellous foundation for thinking about and labouring for revival.[28]

From the time that he arrived in Bourton to July 1743, Beddome divided his time between the Bourton church and the Baptist cause in Warwick, some thirty miles to the north. Eventually, in July 1743, the Bourton church extended an invitation to Beddome to become what they called their 'teaching elder'. Readily acceding to their request, he was ordained on 23 September of that year. When Beddome became the pastor of this congregation, it consisted of about eighty members spread out over a radius of twenty-five miles in a considerable number of villages and hamlets around Bourton.[29] This would have meant a significant amount of travelling for Beddome, as well as for members of his flock and that on roads often well-nigh impassable during the winter and spring. In 1768, Arthur Young (1741-1820), an important agriculturalist who wrote a number of travel narratives, described the main road from Burford to Gloucester, which was only a few miles south of Bourton, as 'the worst I ever travelled on; so bad that it is a scandal to the country'.[30]

Beddome himself chose to live in nearby Lower Slaughter, where he resided till his engagement in 1749 to Elizabeth Boswell (1732-1784), the daughter of Richard Boswell (d.1783) and his wife Hannah (d.1765). Richard, a wealthy jeweller in Bourton, was also one of the deacons of the Baptist church.[31] In view of his upcoming marriage, Beddome decided to relocate to Bourton. A large manse was subsequently built that year for a cost of £324 17s 6½d, the bulk of which was raised by the members and adherents of the Bourton church. Beddome himself gave close to £31. The cost of the manse was no small sum, especially in view of the fact that the previous year the church's building had been enlarged and repaired and that this alone had cost £118.15.6. Today, the manse is a local hotel and pub, with the latter recalling its first owner in its name, the 'Beddome Bar'. These two projects, including further repairs to the church building in 1750, put a considerable strain upon the church's finances, and would be one of the reasons that Beddome resisted attempts to draw him away from Bourton to other pastorates.[32]

The early years of Beddome's ministry saw great numerical growth in the membership of the church. Between 1740 and 1750, the church membership

---

[28] Beddome's own copy of this book may be seen in the Angus Library, Regent's Park College, University of Oxford. On the title page Beddome has written the date 'Apr. 1742,' which would indicate either the date that he purchased the book or the date by which he had read it.

[29] John Rippon (ed.), 'Rev. Benjamin Beddome, A.M. Bourton-on-the-Water, Gloucestershire', *Baptist Annual Register* (4 vols; London, 1790-1802), II, p. 322.

[30] Cited David Rollison, *The Local Origins of Modern Society: Gloucestershire 1500-1800* (London/New York: Routledge, 1992), p. 58.

[31] On the Boswell family, see Holmes, 'Early Years', p. 60 n.137.

[32] See Benjamin Beddome, *Letter to Prescot Street Baptist Church 22 November 1750* (Brooks, 'Ministerial Changes', p. 427).

more than doubled. By 1751, it stood at 180.[33] Describing the state of the church members in 1750, Beddome could thus declare: 'my labours have been, and are still, in a measure, blest unto them, above a hundred having been added since my first coming amongst them'.[34] Derrick Holmes offers explanations for the success of Beddome's ministry during his first ten years at Bourton.[35] There were a number of good men active as deacons and in the leadership of the church during this period, including Beddome's father-in-law, Richard Boswell. Then, Beddome had the ability to preach in a manner fully comprehensible to his village congregation. Robert Hall, Jr (1764-1831), himself no mean preacher, noted that as a speaker Beddome was 'universally admired for the piety and unction of his sentiments, the felicity of his arrangements [of sermons], and the purity, force, and simplicity of his language'.[36] Finally, Beddome was thoroughly convinced that vital Christianity was a matter of both heart and head. And, like others in the Reformed tradition of which his denomination was a part, Beddome found the method of catechizing helpful in matching head knowledge to heart-felt faith.[37] In fact, when John Rippon came to write his obituary of Beddome, he observed that 'one considerable instrument' of the latter's success at Bourton during the 1740s had been his use of catechetical instruction.

Catechisms had been central to the Calvinistic Baptist movement from its inception in the 1630s.[38] For example, the celebrated John Bunyan produced a catechism for his church in 1675 entitled *Instruction for the Ignorant*.[39] The following decade, Hercules Collins (d.1702), the pastor of Wapping Baptist Church, London, later the Prescot Street Church where Beddome was set apart for pastoral ministry, put into print *An Orthodox Catechism* (1680), a Baptist version of the Heidelberg Catechism. The most widely used catechism among the Calvinistic Baptists, though, was the one commissioned by a General Assembly of the denomination which met in London in June 1693. William Collins (d.1702), the pastor of the Petty France Church in the capital, was asked

---

[33] Brooks, *Pictures of the Past*, p. 50.
[34] *Letter to Prescot Street Baptist Church, 22 November 1750* (Brooks, 'Ministerial Changes', p. 427).
[35] Holmes, 'Early Years', pp. 60-61.
[36] 'Recommendatory Preface to a Volume of Hymns' [*The Works of the Rev. Robert Hall, A.M.* (6 vols; New York: Harper & Brothers, 1852), II, 456].
[37] Hayden, 'Evangelical Calvinism', p. 259.
[38] For the importance placed on catechetical literature by the early Nonconformist tradition, see Richard L. Greaves, 'Introduction' to John Bunyan, *Instruction for the Ignorant, Light for Them that Sit in Darkness, Saved by Grace, Come, & Welcome, to Jesus Christ*, (Oxford: Clarendon Press, 1979), pp. xxxiii-xliii.
[39] George Offer (ed.), *The Works of John Bunyan* (3 vols; Glasgow: Blackie and Son/London: John Hirst, 1861-1862), II, pp. 675-90.

to draw it up,[40] but it would appear that Benjamin Keach was mainly responsible for it.[41] This catechism, formally called *The Baptist Catechism* but popularly known as *Keach's Catechism*, was primarily a Baptist revision of the *Presbyterian Shorter Catechism* (1648) and was still being reprinted well into the nineteenth century.[42]

During these early years of his ministry, Beddome used *The Baptist Catechism* extensively but clearly felt that the questions and answers of this catechism needed to be supplemented by further material. So he composed what was printed in 1752 as *A Scriptural Exposition of the Baptist Catechism by Way of Question and Answer*, which basically reproduced the wording and substance of the catechism drawn up by Keach but added various sub-questions and answers to each of the main questions. *The Scriptural Exposition* proved to be fairly popular. There were two editions during Beddome's lifetime, the second of which was widely used at the Bristol Baptist Academy, the sole British Baptist seminary for much of the eighteenth century. In the nineteenth century it was reprinted once in the British Isles and twice in the United States, the last printing being in 1849.

The success that attended his ministry, though, occasioned other churches to desire his services. In 1744, for instance, a Baptist congregation in Exeter approached him about becoming their pastor.[43] His father also repeatedly tried to woo Beddome to the Pithay church in Bristol but to no avail. 'I wish from my heart', he wrote on 28 October 1748, 'the Lord would incline you to come to this city'. Despite his father's offer of a 'comfortable income', the inducement of 'an abundant harvest of souls', and the heart-wringing plea that it 'would be a great comfort to your poor mother to sit under your ministry', Beddome did not see his way clear to leave Bourton.[44]

Two years later, the church in which he had been baptized and which had set him apart for pastoral ministry made an even stronger attempt to secure Beddome's ministry after their pastor, Samuel Wilson, died. The letters that passed back and forth between Beddome, the Bourton congregation, and the Prescot Street Church in London between November 1750 and February 1751 make for fascinating reading.[45] The leadership of the metropolitan congregation were

---

[40] Joseph Ivimey, *A History of the English Baptists* (4 vols; London: n.p., 1811-1830), I, p. 533; II, p. 397.

[41] J. Barry Vaughn, 'Benjamin Keach' in Timothy George and David S. Dockery (eds.), *Baptist Theologians* (Nashville: Broadman Press, 1990), p. 66.

[42] For a recent printing of the catechism, see *The Baptist Catechism*, rev. Paul King Jewett (Grand Rapids: Baker Book House, 1952).

[43] John Collett Ryland, Mss. Notebooks (1744-1745), entry for 25 June 1744 (cited Hayden, 'Evangelical Calvinism', p. 131).

[44] John Beddome, *Letter to Benjamin Beddome 28 October 1748* (cited in Brooks, *Pictures of the Past*, p. 30).

[45] A full copy of these letters may be found in either Brooks, 'Ministerial Changes', pp. 425-29, 482-87 or his *Pictures of the Past*, pp, 32-47. The bulk of the letters may also be

convinced that if Beddome were ministering in London, he would soon be 'ornamental and serviceable in the common cause of religion in a far greater degree than his present retired situation can possibly admit' and that he himself would become 'a celebrated minister of the New Testament of Jesus'. While the Prescot Street Church leaders were prepared to admit that their hopes for Beddome's ministry in the capital might not be fulfilled, they were confident that 'probability' was on their side. They believed this since Beddome's 'labours ...have been wonderfully blest for the restoring of decayed religion, the increasing of the church with members, and the raising up gifts for the help of other churches, some of which are already fixt as pastors'.[46] These reasons say much about the way God had blessed Beddome's ministry during the 1740s. The reference to pastors sent out by the Bourton church would undoubtedly include John Collett Ryland, who went to Warwick in 1750, Richard Haynes (d.1768), who served the Baptist congregation in Bradford-on-Avon, Wiltshire, from 1750 until his death eighteen years later,[47] and John Reynolds (1730-1792), who eventually ended up as pastor of the Cripplegate Baptist Church, London.[48]

In their response to this argument by the London church, the deacons of the Bourton cause, which included Beddome's father-in-law, Richard Boswell, were quick and right to point out that 'usefulness consists not in preaching barely to a very great auditory, but in honouring religion by serving God and our generation in that post in which He sets us'.[49] The Bourton deacons thus firmly, though lovingly, refused to agree to the London church's request.

Beddome was in full agreement with the decision of his congregation. He had read 'the judicious Dr Owen', i.e. John Owen (1616-1683), on the subject and found that the seventeenth-century Puritan divine regarded as lawful only those pastoral changes which occur 'with the free consent of the churches concerned'. Beddome had also sought advice from 'many ... friends in this part of the country, both ministers and private Christians', who, 'almost with one

---

found in Kenneth Dix, ' "Thy Will Be Done": A Study in the Life of Benjamin Beddome', *The Bulletin of the Strict Baptist Historical Society* 9 (1972) [this article occupies the bulk of the *Bulletin* and is lacking pagination].

[46] Prescot Street Baptist Church, *Letter to Bourton Baptist Church, 3 February 1751* (cited in Brooks, 'Ministerial Changes', p. 483).

[47] For an account of Haynes' ministry, see Robert W. Oliver, *Baptists in Bradford on Avon. The History of the Old Baptist Church Bradford on Avon 1689-1989* (Bradford on Avon: Old Baptist Chapel, Bradford on Avon, 1989), pp. 7-8.

[48] For an account of Reynolds' ministry, see Hayden, 'Evangelical Calvinism', pp. 155-56. The Prescot Street leaders were bold enough to suggest that if Beddome came to London, Reynolds could be appointed in his place [Benjamin Beddome, *Letter to Prescot Street Baptist Church, 24 February 1751* (?) (cited in Brooks, 'Ministerial Changes', p. 486)].

[49] Bourton Baptist Church, *Letter to Prescot Street Baptist Church, 24 February 1751* (cited in Brooks, 'Ministerial Changes', p. 484).

voice', urged him to stay at Bourton unless his people freely consented to his departure. Moreover, Beddome noted, if 'the prospect of greater usefulness is in itself a sufficient plea' for a pastor to relocate, then it would be well-nigh impossible for a smaller congregation ever to retain a pastor for any length of time. The Bourton pastor would have been willing to consider the invitation if his congregation had been agreeable. However, 'as they absolutely refuse it, the will of the Lord be done. ... I would rather honour God in a much lower station than that in which he hath placed me, than intrude myself into a higher without his direction'.[50] The London church, though, would not take no for an answer. They made a renewed attempt to obtain Beddome in December 1751. Like their earlier attempts, it too was without success.[51]

During the 1750s and the first half of the 1760s, the numerical growth of the church began to slow. In 1751, the total number of members stood at 180. Between 1752 and 1754, none were added to the church, and fifteen members were lost through death. In 1755, though, there were twenty-two individuals who came into the membership of the church by baptism. Another year which saw a large accession to the church was 1764, when twenty-eight new members were added. But a good number must have died since the mid-1750s, for in that year the membership stood at 183. The next thirty years of Beddome's ministry, though, actually saw decline in the church membership. Between 1765 and 1795, 53 new members were added by conversion and baptism. But in this same period, 105 of the members died, 12 were dismissed to other Baptist works, and 2 were excluded. Thus, by 1795, the year that Beddome died, the church had 123 on the membership roll, sixty less than in 1764.[52] It is quite clear from letters that Beddome wrote on behalf of the church to the local Baptist association during the last three decades of his ministry that he lamented this lack of growth. The size of the congregation maintained its own, probably around five or six hundred, to the end of his life, but that vital step of believer's baptism leading to full church membership was taken by far fewer in the final three decades of his ministry than in the first two and a half.[53] Thus, the poignant prayer of Beddome in the church's 1786 letter to the association: 'Come from the 4 winds O Breath & breathe upon these slain that they may live. Awake O Northwind & come thou South, blow upon our Garden that the Spices may flow out'.[54] Nevertheless, there is no hint that Beddome thought of

---

[50] Benjamin Beddome, *Letter to Prescot Street Baptist Church, 24 February 1751* (?) (cited in Brooks, 'Ministerial Changes', pp. 485-86).

[51] Brooks, *Pictures of the Past*, pp. 48-49.

[52] Brooks, *Pictures of the Past*, pp. 50, 55.

[53] See these letters in the *Bourton-on-the-Water Church Book 1719-1802*, pp. 232-317. For the fact that the size of the congregation listening to Beddome maintained its own during the final years of his life, see the letters for 15 May 1785 and 4 June 1786 (*Bourton-on-the-Water Church Book 1719-1802*).

[54] *Bourton-on-the-Water Church Book 1719-1802*. The punctuation has been added.

ever abandoning his post.

These decades were also fraught with earthly trials. In 1762, he wrestled with what a fellow Baptist pastor, Daniel Turner (1710-1798), termed 'a nervous disorder, attended with spiritual darkness and distress'.[55] Three years later, his eldest son, John, died at the age of fifteen.[56] A second son, Benjamin, died in 1778 of what Rippon calls 'a putrid fever'. It is notable that the very day on which the younger Benjamin died, his father, little suspecting the news he would receive the next morning, wrote the following hymn to be sung at the close of the morning service that day:

> My times of sorrow, and of joy,
> Great God, are in thy hand;
> My choicest comforts come from Thee,
> And go at thy command.
>
> If thou should'st take them all away,
> Yet would I not repine;
> Before they were possess'd by me,
> They were entirely thine.
>
> Nor would I drop a murmuring word,
> Tho' the whole world were gone,
> But seek enduring happiness
> In Thee, and Thee alone.
>
> What is the world with all its store?
> 'Tis but a bitter-sweet;
> When I attempt to pluck the rose
> A pricking thorn I meet.
>
> Here perfect bliss can ne'er be found,
> The honey's mix'd with gall;
> Midst changing scenes and dying friends,
> Be thou my all in all.

Six years later a third son, Foskett, drowned in the Thames at Deptford. His dear wife had died earlier that year.

From the mid-1770s on, he began to suffer from gout and experience tre-

---

[55] Daniel Turner, *Letter to Benjamin Beddome, 4 September 1762* ['Spiritual Darkness', *The Baptist Magazine* 7 (1815), p. 9].
[56] For the following details of Beddome's sons, see Rippon (ed.), 'Rev. Benjamin Beddome', pp. 323-25.

mendous difficulty in walking.⁵⁷ Eventually, it got to the point that he had to be carried to the church, and he would preach to his congregation seated. Despite his physical infirmities, though, Beddome simply refused to give up preaching. At the heart of this refusal lay a deeply-held conviction about the vital importance of preaching. What Michael Walker has said of the nineteenth-century British Baptist community is equally true of Beddome and many of his fellow Calvinistic Baptists in the eighteenth century: they regarded the pulpit as 'a place of nurture, of fire and light, from which words gave wings to the religious aspirations of the hearers, bringing them...to the gates of heaven'.⁵⁸

## The Hymnody of Benjamin Beddome

At the time of Beddome's death in 1795, almost his sole publication was his *Scriptural Exposition*. In the years that followed, though, a good number of his sermons were published, as was a volume of 830 hymns. It is noteworthy that close to one hundred of these hymns were still appearing in hymnals at the end of the nineteenth century, though today, only a handful are still being sung. Robert Hall, Jr spoke for many of his fellow Baptists when he said of Beddome's gifts as a writer of hymns: 'Mr Beddome was on many accounts an extraordinary person. ...Though he spent the principal part of a long life in a village retirement, he was eminent for his colloquial powers...as a religious poet, his excellence has long been known and acknowledged in dissenting congregations'.⁵⁹

Beddome did not write his hymns with the intention of ever getting them published. He was in the habit of preparing a hymn to be sung at the close of the morning worship service, which would pick up the theme of his sermon, a practice that prompted Horton Davies to describe Beddome as an 'indefatigable sermon summarizer in verse'.⁶⁰ However, he did allow thirteen of his hymns to be published in a hymnal edited by fellow Baptists, John Ash (1724-1779) and Caleb Evans (1737-1791), in *A Collection of Hymns Adapted to Public Worship* (1769). Twenty or so years later, thirty-six of them appeared in the first edition of John Rippon's *A Selection of Hymns from the Best Authors* (1787). It was more than twenty years after his death that Robert Hall, Jr supervised the publication of the entire collection of 822 hymns and eight doxologies.

In the preface to this collection, Hall notes that Beddome's hymns were in-

---

⁵⁷ Thomas Purdy, *Letter to John Sutcliff, 11 April 1775* (*Sutcliff Papers*, Angus Library, Regent's Park College, University of Oxford).
⁵⁸ *Baptists at the Table: The Theology of the Lord's Supper amongst English Baptists in the Nineteenth Century* (Didcot, Oxfordshire: Baptist Historical Society, 1992), p. 7.
⁵⁹ 'Recommendatory Preface', *The Works of the Rev. Robert Hall*, II, pp. 456-57.
⁶⁰ *Worship and Theology in England* (3 vols; Grand Rapids/Cambridge, U.K.: William B. Eerdmans Publ. Co., 1996 [1961]), III, p. 136.

debted to his 'acquaintance with the best writers of antiquity'.[61] But as J. R. Watson points out in his splendid work *The English Hymn*, Beddome is also quite familiar with various eighteenth-century hymnwriters, and occasionally borrows from them.[62] For instance, a portion of Beddome's 'The Importance of Prayer' is clearly dependent on John Newton.

> Prayer is the breath of God in man,
> Returning whence it came;
> Love is the sacred fire within,
> And prayer the rising flame—
>
> It gives the burdened spirit ease,
> And soothes the troubled breast;
> Yields comfort to the mourners here,
> And to the weary rest.[63]

Lines two and four in the second verse are all but identical with two from John Newton's 'How sweet the name of Jesus sounds', where, instead of prayer, it is the name of Jesus that

> …makes the wounded spirit whole,
> And calms the troubled breast;
> 'Tis manna to the hungry soul,
> And to the weary rest.[64]

Given the sermonic link of the vast majority of Beddome's hymns it is not surprising to find that many of them are strongly doctrinal. 'God in Christ Jesus' is a good example.

> In the dear person of his Son,
> The Father stands revealed;
> And he who truly knows the one,
> The other has beheld.
>
> In Christ as in a glass we see,
> Unawed and undismayed,
> The glories of the Deity,

---

[61] 'Recommendatory Preface', *The Works of the Rev. Robert Hall*, p. 456.
[62] *English Hymn*, 199.
[63] Beddome, *Hymns*, #405.
[64] For this dependence of Beddome on Newton, see Carey Bonner, *Some Baptist Hymnists from the Seventeenth Century to Modern Times* (London: The Baptist Union Publication Department, 1937), p. 29.

Transcendantly displayed.

> Here mingled beams of truth and grace,
> In all their beauty shine;
> Angels and saints enraptured trace
> The vision so divine.[65]

This admirable clarity of doctrinal expression is never divorced, though, from an experiential focus. In 'View of Christ's Sufferings', for instance, both are obvious.

> Jesus, when faith with fixed eyes,
> Beholds thy wondrous sacrifice,
> Love rises to an ardent flame,
> And we all other hope disclaim!
>
> With cold affections who can see
> The thorns, the scourge, the nails, the tree;
> Thy flowing tears and dewy sweat,
> Thy bleeding hands, and head, and feet!
>
> Look saints, by faith, and view his side,
> The breach how large, how deep, how wide!
> Thence issues forth a double flood,
> Of cleansing water, pardoning blood. ...
>
> Thus could I ever, ever sing,
> The sufferings of my Lord and King;
> With growing pleasure spread abroad,
> The mysteries of a dying God.[66]

The second stanza seems very indebted to a hymn like Isaac Watts' 'When I survey the wondrous Cross', in which the so-called 'Father of English Hymnody' urges the singer of this hymn to

> See from his head, his hands, his feet,
> Sorrow and love flow mingled down...

Yet, the appeal to affection in Beddome's hymn has closer parallels to the hymnody of a William Cowper (1731-1800) or a Charles Wesley (1707-1788). As Watson incisively notes, 'Beddome is a link between two traditions, the Old

---

[65] Beddome, *Hymns*, #258.
[66] Beddome, *Hymns*, #60.

Dissent of Watts and the pre-Romantic intensity of the Evangelicals'.[67]

Among the few of Beddome's hymns still being sung today is the one which begins 'Father of mercies, bow thine ear'.[68] It is a prayer for those called to the preaching of God's Word.

> Father of mercies, bow Thine ear,
> Attentive to our earnest prayer;
> We plead for those who plead for Thee,
> Successful pleaders may they be!
>
> Clothe, Thou, with energy divine,
> Their words, and let those words be Thine;
> To them Thy sacred Truth reveal;
> Suppress their fear, enflame their zeal.
>
> Teach them aright to sow the seed,
> Teach them Thy chosen flock to feed;
> Teach them immortal souls to gain,
> Nor let them labour, Lord, in vain.
>
> Let thronging multitudes around
> Hear from their lips the joyful sound,
> In humble strains Thy grace adore,
> And feel Thy new-creating power.
>
> Let sinners break their massy chains,
> Distressed souls forget their pains;
> Let light thro' distant realms be spread,
> Till Zion rears her drooping head.

The final line of this hymn is an excellent commentary on the general state of the Calvinistic Baptist cause in Great Britain for much of the eighteenth century, the backdrop against which Beddome faithfully exercised his ministry.

The Baptist Zion was 'drooping'. From possibly as many as 300 congregations in 1689, the denomination had shrunk to around 220 Calvinistic Baptist churches in 1715. By the 1750s, probably the nadir of the decline, there were only about 150 churches. During this period, the Baptists were largely an inward-looking denomination concerned primarily with the preservation of their own ecclesiological heritage and somewhat lukewarm when it came to evangelism. In the final two decades of the century, however, the Baptists experienced a genuine reviving. This influx of fresh life transformed them into a body that

---

[67] *English Hymn*, p. 202.
[68] Beddome, *Hymns*, #700.

was outward-looking, vitally involved in vigorous evangelism at home and abroad.

The story of this reviving has been told elsewhere,[69] but there is little doubt that Beddome had a hand in it. The example of his faithful ministry, which sought to pass on the lineaments of orthodox Christianity, his encouragement of younger men like John Sutcliff (1752-1814),[70] who played a central role in the revival, his evangelical catholicity—he was not afraid to associate with men like Whitefield when a good number of his contemporaries had grave doubts about the Anglican evangelist—and his hymns all helped to clear away stumbling-blocks in the pathway of revival. Consider for a moment the influence of his hymnody.

As Beddome's fellow Baptists sang stanzas like the final one in the hymn that we have been briefly considering, 'Father of mercies, bow thine ear', their hearts would have been drawn to reflect on the need of their churches to be engaged more fully in evangelism. In particular, the line 'Let light thro' distant realms be spread' would have been a great rebuke to the parochialism of many Baptist congregations. Another hymn reflecting on the fact that the British people had in their possession the Scriptures, 'God's divine revelation', is just as pointed:

> Ye British Isles, who have this word,
> Ye saints who feel its saving power,
> Your efforts join with one accord,
> To send it forth to every shore.[71]

Equally direct and terse are these lines:

> Lord, send thy truth to every land,
> Let pagans feel its mighty power.[72]

> Let Europe's sons to India's shores,
> This sacred volume send.[73]

Thus, Beddome's life and hymnody played their own small part in the revival of the Baptist community to which he devoted his ministry. It was very

---

[69] See, for example, Michael A.G. Haykin, *One Heart and One Soul: John Sutcliff of Olney, His Friends and His Times* (Darlington, Co. Durham: Evangelical Press, 1994), passim.

[70] For Beddome's influence on Sutcliff, see Haykin, *One heart and One Soul*, pp. 58, 95-97, 120.

[71] Beddome, *Hymns*, #679, stanza 5.

[72] Beddome, *Hymns*, #689, stanza 4.

[73] Beddome, *Hymns*, #692, stanza 4.

much a ministry between the times—those times of Baptist advance in the seventeenth century and those of revival in the final couple of decades of the eighteenth century. Nevertheless, his life and ministry are an eloquent example of the truth of those concluding lines in George Eliot's *Middlemarch*: 'That things are not so ill with you and me as they might have been, is half owing to the number who lived faithfully a hidden life, and rest in unvisited tombs.'

CHAPTER 7

# Daniel Turner and a Theology of the Church Universal

Paul S. Fiddes

### A Vision of the Church Universal

'We denominate ourselves a *Protestant Catholic Church* of Christ, desirous to live in peace and love with all men.' This striking phrase appears in the church covenant of what is now New Road Baptist Church in Oxford, and dates from 1780 when the existing congregation of Protestant Dissenters in Oxford, composed of Presbyterians, Baptists and a few Methodists, was reconstituted as a church with a new covenant.[1] Although Baptists were in a slight minority in the group of 1780, being perhaps five of the thirteen women and men who put their names to the covenant,[2] the congregation was always served after that date by Baptist ministers. There are many interesting features about their covenant, in which the members receive one another into full communion and membership, regardless of their convictions on baptism, but in this paper I want to focus on the phrase, 'Protestant Catholic Church of Christ'.

There is, as we shall see, good evidence for the hand here of Daniel Turner, minister of Abingdon Baptist Church from 1748 to his death in 1798.[3] He not only witnessed the New Road Covenant with five other local ministers but

---

[1] The earliest printed form of the covenant appears in Daniel Turner, *Charity the Bond of Perfection. A Sermon, The Substance of which was Preached at Oxford, November 16, 1780, On Occasion of the Re-establishment of a Christian Church of Protestant Dissenters in that City; with a Brief Account of the State of the Society, and the Plan and Manner of their Settlement* (Oxford, 1780), pp. 20-22.

[2] Evidence for this account is given in Paul S. Fiddes, 'Receiving One Another. The History and Theology of the Church Covenant, 1780' in Rosie Chadwick (ed.), *A Protestant Catholic Church of Christ. Essays on the History and Life of New Road Baptist Church, Oxford* (Oxford: Alden Press, 2003), pp. 68-71.

[3] Daniel Turner (1710-98) is aptly commemorated by a monument in Abingdon Baptist Chapel, reading 'The Scholar, the Poet, the Christian'. A widely respected Calvinistic Baptist minister, he published poems, sermons, theology, and works on English grammar; he was also well known for his hymns, four appearing in the Bristol *Baptist Collection* (1769) and eight in *Rippon's Collection* (1787).

preached the sermon on the occasion of the public re-opening of the chapel, which followed the signing of the covenant, on Thursday 16 November 1780. The sermon, on the theme *Charity the Bond of Perfection*, was subsequently published with an introduction by Turner describing the circumstances of the re-establishing of the church, an appendix containing a copy and a short explanation of the church covenant, and a postscript containing a defence of 'mixed communion'. Turner's account in this pamphlet implies that he played a large part in the composition of the covenant, with such expressions as 'we thought it necessary...', and E.A. Payne judges simply that the covenant was 'no doubt drafted by Turner himself'.[4]

It is Daniel Turner's vision of the church universal that lies at the heart of the covenant. He gives us a picture of this as a 'grand common temple' in the introduction to his sermon on the re-establishing of the congregation of Oxford Dissenters:

> We do not mean to set up this little Society in *Opposition* to *any* other Protestant Church in *particular*; nor as a *Separation* from the Church of CHRIST in *general*, but as an *Addition* to it, connected with it in the *Bonds of Christian* CHARITY - a small hallowed Porch annexed to that grand common *Temple, which is the Habitation of* GOD *through the Spirit...*[5]

Earlier in his introduction to the sermon, Turner had used the expression 'true *Protestant Catholic* Spirit' with regard to finding benefactors for a fund to support poor congregations, 'whether of the Established Church, or the Dissenters' (an appeal that was partly answered, we might observe, in the setting up of a trust by Abraham Atkins to support Baptist congregations that practised open or mixed communion). The term 'Catholic' here of course means 'universal', and the phrase 'Protestant Catholic' means most obviously 'belonging to all Protestant churches' or 'a Protestant church belonging to the whole Church'; but, as we shall see, Turner's thought reaches out to a vision of the whole 'Church of Christ' which finally transcends in its universality even its Protestant and Reformed members. This is echoed in the New Road Covenant, in which the phrase 'to hold the communion of Saints with all Protestant Churches' is followed by '*and* such as love our Lord Jesus Christ in sincerity'.[6] It is a rhetoric that in its progression to a *non-specific* nature constantly seeks to escape labels. The ecumenical thrill that the phrase 'Protestant Catholic' gives to the modern ear is not, then, completely misleading.

In his earlier book, *A Compendium of Social Religion* (1758), Turner provides a description of the relation of the local church to the church universal which is a remarkably clear and rigorous analysis, belying the common accusa-

---

[4] Turner, *Charity*, p. 23. Ernest A. Payne, *The Baptists of Berkshire Through Three Centuries* (London: Carey Kingsgate Press, 1951), p. 81.
[5] Turner, *Charity*, pp. vii-viii.
[6] Turner, *Charity*, p. 22.

tion that Baptists have no ecclesiology. He begins with a threefold definition of the word 'church', which has considerable interest for ecumenical discussion today. First, church in its full and proper sense means 'the real or *invisible catholic* or universal *church*; part of which is triumphant in heaven, and part militant on earth.'[7] This is the '*whole number of real saints and peculiar people of God* who sincerely love and obey him'. Second, church means 'the *apparent* or *visible catholic* church', which is 'the whole body of those that make any visible profession of a religious regard to the revealed will of God', even though some may have only 'the form of godliness' and not its 'real power'.[8] This will administer a shock to those who think that the approved Baptist view of the church universal is that it is simply invisible, and to be contrasted with a visible church that appears only on the level of the local gathered congregation.[9] Regarding the church universal as purely invisible and mystical makes it a concept safely insulated from any demands for fellowship between churches. But Turner is clear that the church universal becomes visible on earth, visibility meaning (he explains) 'what falls under human cognizance and judgement'.[10] In the third place, he says, the term 'church' sometimes means a 'particular visible gospel church', denoting 'only one particular society of christians ... usually meeting for divine worship in one place'.[11] With this meaning of church, Baptists are of course familiar, and Turner says that the rules and observations he is making in his book 'principally refer' to this dimension of the church.

However, his observations are certainly not *confined* to the local church, and it is his attempt to describe coherently the relationship between the 'invisible catholic Church', the 'visible catholic church' and the 'particular visible church' which puts him, in my view, in the front rank of Baptist ecclesiologists. Turner proposes that every true particular church is a part of the 'universal church' or 'general body called by that name',[12] and it is clear that by this he does not mean the invisible but the *visible* catholic church. So he can portray the newly-established Dissenters' church in Oxford as a 'small porch' added to the 'great temple' which the Spirit of God indwells. It is also clear that he means that every true local church belongs *as a church* to the visible catholic church; it is not just the members individually who belong to an invisible

---

[7] Daniel Turner, *A Compendium of Social Religion, or the Nature and Constitution of Christian Churches, with the Respective Qualifications and Duties of their Officers and Members ... Designed as an Essay towards reviving the primitive Spirit of Evangelical Purity, Liberty, and Charity, in the Churches of the Present Times.* (London: John Ward, 1758), p. 2.

[8] Turner, *Compendium*, pp. 3-4.

[9] An influential voice here was Augustus Hopkins Strong, *Systematic Theology* (Philadelphia: Griffith & Rowland, 1909), pp. 887-91.

[10] Turner, *Compendium*, p. 4, note.

[11] Turner, *Compendium*, pp. 5, 4.

[12] Turner, *Compendium*, p. 7, note, 3dly.

catholic church or mystical body of Christ, though that is of course true. Two issues arise immediately from this proposal: (1) what is a true particular church within the visible catholic church, and (2) what is the practical effect of belonging to the visible catholic church? Turner does not shirk these issues, though to grasp his vision it is necessary to combine the main text and the extensive footnotes of the *Compendium*, as well as to place other of Turner's writings alongside it.

On the first point, Turner is reasonably satisfied with the description in the nineteenth of the Thirty-Nine Articles of the Church of England, that a true particular gospel church is 'a congregation of faithful men [sic] in which the true word of God is preached, and the sacraments duly administered, according to Christ's ordinances'. This, he judges, is 'not very different' from his more expansive definition:[13]

> What *I* should call *essentials* to the constitution of a particular visible church – are – The profession of – repentance towards God – sincere obedience to his laws – faith in Christ as the only Saviour – the hopes of pardon and eternal life, through his mediation and sacrifice, – submission to his word, as the sovereign infallible rule of religious faith and practice – with the public worship of one God, through one Mediator, by one Spirit, in the reverent use of the word, prayer, praise, and the two sacraments, or positive institutions, (viz.) Baptism and the Supper of the Lord.[14]

We should notice that Turner includes the practice of both sacraments as essential to the nature of a true particular church. That is, he regards baptism as a 'church ordinance' or 'initiating ordinance', in distinction from other Particular Baptists who were able to argue for mixed communion between those baptized as believers and as infants on the basis that baptism was simply a personal sign of devotion to Christ, and was not fundamental to the constitution of the church.[15] For Turner, by contrast, baptism is 'necessary to a regular entrance into [the] visible church',[16] is one element by which a particular church is 'formed',[17] and is the act 'by which we are first *formally* incorporated into the

---

[13] Turner, *Compendium*, p. 7, note, 1st.

[14] Turner, *Compendium*, pp. 5-6, note.

[15] This was the view taken by Turner's friend Robert Robinson, in his pamphlet *The General Doctrine of Toleration Applied to the Particular Case of Free Communion* (Cambridge: Francis Hodson, 1781), pp. 29-31, 45, following the Particular Baptist tradition of John Bunyan, *Differences in Judgment about Water-Baptism No Bar to Communion* (London: John Wilkins, 1673), pp. 28-30.

[16] Turner, *Compendium*, p. 27, note.

[17] Turner, *Compendium*, p. 16: as 'the same common sign or token of devotion'. Cf. p. 63.

visible church, or body of Christ.'[18] Turner must and can recognize paedobaptist Protestant congregations as true churches of Christ on the basis of *both* word and sacrament. How he does this I want to leave for a moment, but we should notice that he makes a distinction at this point between essence and form: 'where the *essentials* are held, though there be defects in the form, it is to be esteemed a *true* though not an *orderly* church.'[19]

All true particular churches, defined as above, are part of the visible catholic church. So what of the second main issue: what are the practical implications of this belonging? Turner concludes that churches which are part of the universal church 'have *all* the same common head, faith, laws, powers, priviledges, – and therefore, though differing in lesser matters, and not authoritatively subject to one another, *may* and *ought* to hold the Communion of Saints with each other, as the means of preserving and cherishing the common unity of the universal Church.'[20] The language of several churches having the 'same head' [Christ] and 'same laws' is reminiscent of the London Confession of 1644,[21] even to the extent of noting that the distribution of the one church into distinct communities is only for the 'convenience' of edification and worship.[22] But the London Confession was addressing churches of the same (Baptist) faith and order within the city; Turner is referring explicitly to *all* true gospel churches. In other words, he envisages the same principle which unites Baptist churches ('association')[23] as being extendable to all churches. Thus, he declares, 'every regular member and every minister of the word, in any particular church, is in fact a member and minister of the church universal.'[24]

In practical terms, this membership becomes visible in several aspects. *Members* have the right to fellowship in all churches,[25] and ought to share the Lord's Supper together ('commune with each other');[26] if disciplined by a particular church they remain members of the 'real catholic church' and can be properly accepted by another particular society.[27] *Ministers* have the right to minister within other churches 'upon all proper occasions', which Turner later spells out as the authority to preach, administer the sacraments and assist at

---

[18] Turner, *Compendium*, p. 120, note. The term 'formally' opens up some theological space, perhaps for children nurtured in the church and as yet unbaptized.

[19] Turner, *Compendium*, p. 5, note 2.

[20] Turner, *Compendium*, p. 8, note, 3dly.

[21] The Particular Baptist 'London' Confession of 1644, Art. XLVII, reprinted in William Lumpkin (ed.), *Baptist Confessions of Faith* (Valley Forge: Judson Press, 1959), pp. 168–69; this is virtually identical to article 38 of *A True Confession* (1596), in Lumpkin, *Baptist Confessions*, p. 94.

[22] Turner, *Compendium*, p. 9, note, 4thly, 3d.; cf. *Compendium*, p. 119.

[23] See Turner, *Compendium*, p. 35: 'synod or association ... for advice and counsel'.

[24] Turner, *Compendium*, p. 8, note, 3dly.

[25] Turner, *Compendium*, p. 8, note, 3dly.

[26] Turner, *Compendium*, p. 139.

[27] Turner, *Compendium*, p. 75, note, 2d.

ordinations 'elsewhere'.[28] Churches ought to recognize each other as true churches of Christ, seek advice from one another, receive members from one another when recommended, and transfer their members into membership with each other.[29] This picture of intercommunion and inter-changeability of ministry seems remarkably like the vision of 'reconciled diversity' of the modern ecumenical movement. Like that vision of visible unity, Turner is also describing what *is* partly the case now (a visible catholic church only partly one) and what *ought* to be the case (making the visible unity more evident to the world). What a visible catholic church should look like does not, however, for Turner include either an episcopal or presbyterian form of government, which he considers to have no clear scriptural support. For all that, however, he is willing to recognize those local congregations who do have this form of government now as true gospel churches, since what matters is that 'all things be done decently and in order', and 'the meer *form* and *manner* of doing [things decently and in order] cannot be of that *vast* importance, some people imagine'.[30]

Although Turner appeals to the established church in the matter of an open table, or what he calls 'catholic communion', he cannot have had strong hopes of cooperation from the Church of England in issues of interchangeability of ministry and membership. His extension of the association principle beyond those of Baptist persuasion is, however, the background for a proposal he made in December 1772; writing to a friend in London (Joshua Thompson, a fellow Particular Baptist minister), he proposed a plan for a Union of all Dissenters. He regrets that such a union is only likely to be acceptable 'in respect of the *external* polity and conduct of the Dissenters as a body' (my italics). He desires such a union to be 'of a more spiritual nature' but thinks that this will be prevented by the 'well meant Zeal so intemperate and indiscreet' of its participants.[31] In his home area of Oxfordshire and Berkshire, Turner apparently made a start on this enterprise by fostering associations of ministers which included Baptists, Independents (later Congregationalists) and Presbyterians.[32]

Before we turn to further detail of the implications of a visible catholic church, we must not forget the all-embracing context of church in its fullest sense, which was for Turner the invisible catholic church, the 'whole number of real saints ... the mystical Body of Christ, given him by the Father before the

---

[28] Turner, *Compendium*, p. 8, note, 3dly; p. 60 n. 2.

[29] Turner, *Compendium*, pp. 116-17.

[30] Turner, *Compendium*, pp. 11-12, note, (4).

[31] Letter to Joshua Thompson, Abingdon Decr. 18 1772. The letter is in the Essex Record Office, and was brought to my attention by Stephen Copson.

[32] This is implied by Turner's comment on the association of ministers at Henley, in Daniel Turner, *The gathering of the People to Christ considered. In a Sermon, preached at Henley-Upon-Thames, at an Association of Ministers, June the 24th, 1794* (Henley: G. Norton, 1794), p. 31.

world began – purchased with his own blood'.[33] It is here that Turner appears to find a place for *individual* believers within the Roman Catholic Church, though the Roman Church, as an institution, he finds to be 'the most inconsistent of all with the scripture account of a gospel church', and so not to be counted as a member of the *visible* catholic church.[34] The invisible church universal also has room within it for 'many true and proper members of the church, taken in this sense, that are not actually join'd in church-fellowship to any particular christian society'.[35] His reason for this breadth of vision is doubtless in part his Calvinistic conviction about an elect known only to God; but it is probably also grounded in his belief that there is a universal revelation of the Gospel not limited to the life of the visible church, and stemming from an original revelation to Adam and the Patriarchs.[36] Turner's view appears to be that, while only the elect are included in the universal church, some of the elect might hear the address of the Gospel diffused, though imperfectly, through other religions.[37] There seems to be a practical outworking of this in his advice that church members may marry partners who are not members of any particular society, but who 'appear to fear God.'[38] The distinction between the invisible and visible catholic church in Turner's mind thus appears to be this: the invisible church is made up of all redeemed individuals, whereas the visible catholic church is made up of those who explicitly confess their faith, *together with* the particular Christian societies or local churches to which they belong.

## Implications of the Vision: Ministry and the Lord's Supper

If we explore a little more the implications of belonging to the visible catholic church, we might begin with the claim that a minister of any particular gospel church is a minister of the 'church in general'. This gives a pastor the right, thinks Turner, to 'minister to any other' church in word and sacrament – with its consent, of course. This includes, as we have already seen, the authority to assist at ordinations elsewhere'.[39] This latter point fits in with Turner's belief, along with most General and Particular Baptists of his period, that pastors should be ordained only by other pastors (i.e. elders or bishops) after choice by

---

[33] Turner, *Compendium*, p. 2.

[34] Turner, *Compendium*, p. 13, n. 4.

[35] Turner, *Compendium*, p. 2, note.

[36] Daniel Turner, 'Letters on the Nature of Religion, VIII. On Universal Revelation' in *Essays on Important Subjects in Two Volumes*, (2 vols; Printed for the Author: Oxford, 1787), I, pp. 187-99. Cf. Letter from Daniel Turner, dated 14 June 1782, Abingdon; MS in Angus Library, Oxford, FPC C.55. 'The heathen have it [the Gospel] by tradition from the first parents of mankind' (p.2).

[37] Turner, 'Universal Revelation', pp. 93-95.

[38] Turner, *Compendium*, p. 102.

[39] Turner, *Compendium*, p. 60, note 2.

the whole congregation.[40] Ordinations by the people should only happen on exceptional occasions. The reasons that Turner gives for ordination of pastors by pastors are: that this is in accordance with the pattern of ministry in the New Testament; that it prevents unqualified pretenders being loosed upon the churches; and that it is in accord with 'the dignity and authority of the office'.[41] He does not, we notice, explicitly advance another theological argument which would be consistent with his understanding of ministry – that ministers who represent the church in general should be ordained by representatives of a wider church life than the local church alone.

However, there is an interesting conjunction of ideas that tends in this direction. Alongside presbyteral ordination he sets the need for a 'succession' of ministers in the church. Of course, he opposes any view of apostolic succession in which ordained ministers are supposed to be ordained by bishops standing in a literal line of unbroken succession from the Apostles. But he still affirms *a* succession: 'as some official power and authority, is of divine appointment, to continue in the church, till the whole be perfected; so there must of necessity be a succession of persons qualified for it.' What is 'essential' to such a succession seems to Turner to be entirely dependent 'upon the preference of Christ' and the gifts and graces of his Spirit, but it will include an 'orderly exercise of power he has given [the church] for the appointment ... of such qualified persons'.[42] Such a succession is provided, he notes, not only in the sphere of the particular church, but also 'in the whole body' – which must mean the church universal.[43] There are elements here of a theology of ministry that Turner does not appear explicitly to link up – ordination of elders by elders, an orderly succession, and the place of local ministry within the 'general ministry' of the church universal. Perhaps it would be no great step to link these aspects together, to create a Baptist view of ministry that would have wide echoes on the current ecumenical scene.

The most extended account of the visible catholic church appears, however, in Turner's plea for what he calls 'catholic communion' in the long Conclusion to his *Compendium*. For Baptists this is the issue of 'open' or 'mixed communion', that is whether Christians baptized only as infants are to be received at the table alongside those baptized as believers. In writings other than the *Compen-*

---

[40] The General Baptist Assembly, meeting at Horsley Down, 26 May 1702, held that 'the ordination of Elders by Elders [is] of Divine Institution'; in *Minutes of the General Assembly of the General Baptist Churches in England,* ed. W.T. Whitley (2 vols; London; Kingsgate Press for the Baptist Historical Society, 1909), I, p. 70. John Gill among Particular Baptists gave theological weight to this practice in his *Body of Divinity*, II, bk.3, p. 265, although (unlike Turner) he regarded the pastor as commissioned to officiate only in the local church where he was a member.
[41] Turner, *Compendium*, pp. 43, 48.
[42] Turner, *Compendium*, p. 35, second note.
[43] Turner, *Compendium*, p. 36, note.

*dium,* Turner explicitly argues with his fellow Particular Baptists for such mixed communion.[44] The interest of the *Compendium* is that he takes a broader vision, and appeals to *all* churches, not just Baptist ones, to place on one side their 'disputable niceties', 'punctilious peculiarities' and 'lesser disputable modes of religion'[45] that have no basis in scripture, in order to accept one another in sharing the Lord's Supper. This is in line with his concern to describe the relation of all particular churches to the church in general, or to the visible catholic church. The actual dispute among Baptists about open communion is implied, but never directly addressed; it can, for instance, be glimpsed between the lines in the statement – to which we must return – that the Bible says:

> ... a great deal, about our common union in Christ ... as being all his children by the same faith; as professedly devoted to him by the same baptism (at least as to what is essential to that purpose).[46]

Turner presents open communion as the central way of maintaining the unity of the universal church. Sharing in the Lord's Supper is the necessary sign of the 'visible' unity of the whole church of Christ 'in the bonds of peace and love'. Though the Christian church is, 'because of the great numbers of its members', dispersed into 'many distinct societies', since these are all under Christ as one head 'they are to be considered but as parts of the same whole; composing one intire spiritual body'.[47] To preserve their unity in love (says Turner),

> it is absolutely necessary, that, however different and independent in some respects, any of these societies may be, they should be all form'd upon the most catholic and uniting principles, upon the whole: and by some common external means or bond of social unity, maintain (if possible) a visible communion one with another....

This visible catholicity, urges Turner, is best expressed through the Lord's Supper, which 'was intended, amongst other things, to be a standing, visible, external pledge and means, of that divine union and fellowship, all true christians have with Christ, and one another in ONE BODY...'[48] It is 'the common

---

[44] See Daniel Turner (under the name 'Candidus'), *A Modest Plea for Free Communion at the Lord's Table; Particularly between the Baptists and Poedobaptists* (London: J. Johnson, 1772); Turner, *Charity*, pp. 25-8.

[45] Turner, *Compendium*, pp. 125-6.

[46] Turner, *Compendium*, p. 128.

[47] Turner, *Compendium*, p. 119. This echoes the wording of the Particular Baptist 'London' Confession of 1644, art. XLVII, in Lumpkin, *Baptist Confessions*, pp. 168-9. Robert Hall begins his argument, in *Terms of Communion*, pp. 9-14, with the need for the plurality of true churches to be in unity with each other; cf. pp. 105-8.

[48] Turner, *Compendium*, p. 120.

pledge of Christian unity'.[49] So it is the duty of all Christian churches, concludes Turner, to lay the table 'as open as possible to the free access of ALL, who appear to love our Lord Jesus Christ in sincerity'.[50] It is important here to see that open communion is not founded essentially upon individualism and private faith, but on a catholic ecclesiology with a clear concept of the relation of the local church to the whole body of Christ. The sacrament is a visible bond of unity between societies of believers, not only between individual believers.

This becomes clear when Turner urges both the established and dissenting churches[51] to practice 'catholic communion', lest they oblige others to set up 'separate communities; ... thereby dividing ... the *external uniformity* of the *visible catholic church*'.[52] The result of excluding fellow-believers from the Lord's Supper is to force them to create their own particular churches, regarded by Turner as 'dissentient separations' within the union of the body of Christ; such separation, urges Turner, 'is absurd and preposterous' and only excusable when 'through unwarranted impositions, and corruptions intolerably offensive to conscience, it becomes unavoidable.' Speaking *as* a Dissenter, he thinks that failure to practise catholic communion will 'increase and aggravate' 'our at present unavoidable separations'.[53] Frequent meetings together of members from many different Christian societies to celebrate the Lord's Supper will, thinks Turner, 'subdue our mutual prejudices ... and enable us to carry our social unity to the greatest heights of perfection it is capable of, this side heaven'.[54]

## Implications of the Vision: Baptism

The issue of 'catholic communion' raises, for Baptists, the question of baptism. What is to be said about infant baptism, and its relation to sharing in the Lord's Supper, if anything? The question, as we have already seen, also arises from the need to identify churches as true gospel churches within the universal church, whether or not they practise believers' baptism. In the *Compendium*, Turner includes baptism as a mark of the gospel church, but it is remarkable that he does not once identify this as the baptism of believers, or mount any criticism of the baptism of infants. This seems to be in line with his concern to present *particular* Christian churches as part of the *catholic* church. Indeed, he places baptism alongside the Lord's Supper as a mark of visible unity; as the means by which 'we are first formally incorporated into the visible church' it is 'the beginning and foundation of this external communion'. Turner, however, drops a

---

[49] Turner, *Compendium*, p. 123.
[50] Turner, *Compendium*, p. 121.
[51] Turner, *Compendium*, p. 133.
[52] Turner, *Compendium*, p. 135.
[53] Turner, *Compendium*, p. 143.
[54] Turner, *Compendium*, p. 139.

strong hint in the *Compendium* about the way he is approaching the subject, as he often contrasts the 'essentials' of a Gospel church with 'mere modes of faith and worship' or 'non-essential modes of religion' and 'non-essentials to the Christian profession'.[55] This contrast between the essence and the form of religion is recalled in his phrase that members of all gospel churches are 'professedly devoted to Christ by the same baptism (at least as to what is *essential*)'.[56] Turner is implicitly arguing that the essence of baptism appears in all true churches, whether they baptize children or only believers.

In other writings, Turner picks up this contrast more explicitly. What is 'non-essential' is not baptism itself, but the mode or subject of baptism – that is, whether it is offered to infants or more mature disciples, whether by immersion or sprinkling. Turner writes in his piece on *Charity*:

> Our Paedobaptist Brother pleads, 'That he believes that he is rightly baptized – that if he is mistaken, it is an Error of his Head, not of his Heart ... That it ... does not affect the Institution itself, which he reveres, but only the Subject and Mode of it – That he ... feels in his Conscience the same obligations to Holiness of Life, which are the Essentials of Baptism...'[57]

This quotation also displays another aspect of the situation: the paedobaptist *believes* he is baptized, and there is a need to respect the 'sacred right of private judgement'. Though the notion of 'private judgement' has an Enlightenment ring to it, recalling a humanistic confidence in the light of reason and a subjective individualism, it is also rooted in the statement of Paul in Romans 14:5, 'let all be fully persuaded in their own minds'. This in turn is placed in the context of divine judgement: 'for we shall all stand before the judgement seat of Christ' (v. 10). 'Private judgement' thus meant, for open-communion Baptists, that every person's conscience should be respected because, in the last resort, all must answer for their convictions and decisions to their master, Christ:[58] 'Who art thou that judgest another man's servant? To his own master he standeth or falleth' (Rom. 14:4).

Writers on open communion such as Daniel Turner, his friend John Collett Ryland and John Brown of Kettering lay stress on the fallibility of everyone's private judgement, including that of Baptists. Turner, for instance, dares to state

---

[55] E.g. Turner, *Compendium*, pp. 12 note 4, 35 note 2, 123, 125, 128, 135, 143, 148.
[56] Turner, *Compendium*, p. 128.
[57] Turner, *Charity*, pp. 26–27.
[58] Turner, *A Modest Plea*, pp. 5, 11; Robinson, *General Doctrine of Toleration*, p. 39, arguing the connection between duty and benefit; Hall, *Terms of Communion*, pp. 91, 93, 95; *Reply to Rev. Joseph Kinghorn*, p. 346; John Brown (minister at Kettering), *The House of God Opened and his table free for baptists and pædobaptists, who are saints and faithful in Christ* (London: Joseph Brown, 1777), p. 3.

– in the face of some Baptist outrage[59] – that 'it is evident in fact, that the points in Baptism, about which we differ, are not so clearly stated in the Bible (however clear to us) but that even sincere Christians may mistake them. A private opinion therefore, on the one side or the other, can never be justly made an indispensible term of communion at the Lord's Table.'[60] This argument from fallible conscience is a kind of theology of intention. The paedobaptist may be seen as upholding and honouring baptism in his own mind, argues Turner, because he *intends* to have been baptized, and this intention should be respected until eschatological exposure of the truth. In a pamphlet jointly written with John Collet Ryland, *A Modest Plea for Free Communion at the Lord's Table*, he asserts:

> If my Paedobaptist brother is satisfied in his own mind, that he is rightly baptised, he is so to himself; and, while the answer of a good conscience attends it, God will and does own him in it, to all the ends designed by it; so that while he considers it as laying him under the same obligations to holiness in heart and life as I consider my baptism to do me, why should he not commune with me at the table of our common Lord?[61]

Similarly, Turner speaks of the Paedobaptist Brother as having 'an equally just Right' to the Lord's Table because he is 'a Believer in CHRIST, answering in a good conscience to what HE thinks true baptism'.[62] The key question, as opponents of Turner gleefully pointed out, is whether a Baptist can give any objective value to this intention, that is to regard the paedobaptist believer as *actually* baptized, beyond respecting his *view* that he is baptized.[63] Turner's response depends on combining the distinction between the 'substance' and the 'form' of faith and practice with the right of private judgement. Consciences

---

[59] E.g. Abraham Booth, *An Apology for the Baptists. In which they are Vindicated ... Against the Charge of Bigotry in Refusing Communion at the Lord's Table to Paedobaptists* (London: Dilly, Keith, Johnson, 1778), pp. 82–83; Dan Taylor, *Candidus Examined with Candor. Or, a Modest Inquiry into the Propriety and Force of what is contained in a late Pamphlet; intitled, A Modest Plea for Free Communion at the Lord's Table* (London: G. Keith, 1772), pp. 12–14.

[60] Daniel Turner (under the name 'Candidus'), *A Modest Plea for Free Communion at the Lord's Table; Particularly between the Baptists and Poedobaptists* (London: J. Johnson, 1772), p. 7; cf. *Compendium*, p. 125; Turner, *Remarks on a Sermon, Preached at Abingdon, Berks, October 7, 1781, By the Rev. John Neal Lake, M.A., Entitled 'Infant Baptism a Reasonable and Scriptural Service. In a Letter to the Author* (London: J. Buckland, n.d.), pp. 13-14.

[61] Turner, *A Modest Plea*, p. 10.

[62] Turner, *Charity*, p. 23.

[63] E.g. Taylor, *Candidus Examined*, pp. 9, 11; Booth, *Apology for the Baptists*, pp. 59–60; later, Joseph Kinghorn, *Baptism A Term of Communion at the Lord's Table* (Norwich: 1816), p. 88.

can differ about 'non-essentials', which are to do only with form.⁶⁴ So conscientious believers may differ about the 'subject and mode' of baptism because there is a 'substance' to baptism which is deeper than the form. John Brown takes a similar line, arguing that 'Believing Paedobaptists have the same spiritual views of the ordinance of Water-Baptism ... as the Baptists ... so that there is an agreement in the substance, though not in the external mode of it'.⁶⁵

With this threefold argument from conscience, human fallibility and essence, Turner weaves in another, again taken from Romans 14, and with a long precedence in Baptist thinking about open communion: the plain fact is that Christ has 'accepted' his disciples (Romans 14:5), whether baptized as infants as infants or believers, and we should accept them too.⁶⁶ In *A Modest Plea*, Turner asserts, 'it is *undeniably evident* that JESUS CHRIST HIMSELF *does accept of Paedobaptist Christians*, when they remember Him at his table; --- does indulge them the enjoyment of His gracious presence there', and he follows this with the appeal: 'Surely ... if our *Blessed Lord* is pleased so far to overlook their (supposed) mistakes about baptism, why should not *we* do so too?'⁶⁷ We find this last question poignantly echoed and indeed answered in the words of the New Road covenant: 'Christ accepting those on both sides of the question ... we think that we *ought* to do so too'.

Turner himself does not systematically put together his work on the church universal in the *Compendium* with his later writings on open communion. But if we were to do so, we might end up with the following kind of argument. Even if Baptists are right about the *form* of baptism, its subject and mode, yet paedobaptist churches can still be true gospel churches because they have the *essence* of baptism, as a sign of devotion to Christ; they are 'a true but not an orderly church'.⁶⁸ But in fact, Turner would add, Baptists cannot be sure that they *are* right in their interpretation of scripture; while they may and should hold to the form with passionate conviction, not a 'cold indifference',⁶⁹ they must leave final judgement to Christ, as their own judgement is human and fallible. Even more, then, can Baptists acknowledge churches with other baptismal practices as part of the one, visible catholic church.

---

⁶⁴ Turner, *Charity*, p. 17.

⁶⁵ Brown, *House of God Opened*, p. 7.

⁶⁶ E.g. Bunyan, *Differences,* p. 43, 'Christ hath received them'; Henry Jessey, Sermon on Rom. 14.1, 'Such as are weak in the Faith, receive you', printed as an appendix to Bunyan's *Differences in Judgment*, p. 105, 'The Lord has received them'; Robert Hall, *On Terms of Communion*, repr. in Olinthus Gregory (ed.), *The Entire Works of the Rev. Robert Hall* (6 vols; London: Holdsworth and Ball, 1764-1832), II, pp. 93-94, 'all whom Christ has received', p. 104 'those whom we acknowledge Christ to have accepted'.

⁶⁷ Turner, *A Modest Plea*, p. 6.

⁶⁸ Here I combine what Turner says in *Compendium*, p. 5, note, with his distinction elsewhere between essence and form in baptism.

⁶⁹ Turner, *Compendium*, p. 148, note.

## Conclusion: the Essential and the Universal

Turner's vision of the catholic church is bound up with his quest for what is 'essential' in the belief and practice of faith. What is 'of the essence' is also universal. The plea is for all Christians to agree, in charity, on what is essential rather than mere outward form, and so to actualize in a visible way the unity which they have already been given in Christ. This picture of the universal nature of the church seems to owe a debt to two sources – a Baptist tradition of spirituality and an Enlightenment view of reason. As Turner expresses it in *Free Thoughts on the Spirit of Free Enquiry in Religion*, religious enthusiasm is to be united with reason, passionate feeling with critical reflection.[70] The 'essence' of faith is both something to be felt in the heart, and something agreed upon as common by God-given reason.

On the one hand, then, an appeal to the 'essential' is rooted in a warm, vital and inner religion which is part of 'Old Dissent' rather than the new Evangelical Revival. Among Calvinistic Baptists, self-examination was a life-long process. Baptism was an expression of devotion to Christ, and gave rise to never-ending demands to live a holy life. Turner thus argues that if those who have been baptized by sprinkling as infants find that looking back on this event gives rise to a sense of 'obligations to holiness', they are to be respected for this conviction: 'we leave them to their own Judgment and Conduct'.[71] Unlike fellow open-communion advocates among the Baptists, he refrains from ever calling paedobaptists 'unbaptized', since this would be to fail to value their own passionate conviction that they are indeed baptized.[72] But if Christian disciples feel *no* such obligations arising from their baptism as an infant, and at the same time feel that to receive baptism as a believer will 'give real weight to their obligations to Holiness', then 'surely they ought to do so', though 'without any formal Renunciation of the former supposed Baptism'.[73] This Turner believes to be consonant with the response of a 'rational Creature'.[74]

On the other hand, then, Turner invokes the 'plain sober light of simple truth, as it shines in its first principles'.[75] Although firmly distancing himself from Socinian General Baptists, Turner nevertheless exhibits some resonances with them in appealing to a simple faith on which all could agree by reason.[76]

---

[70] Daniel Turner, *Free Thoughts on the Spirit of Free Enquiry in Religion, With Cautions Against the Abuse of it ... Amongst Christians of All Denominations* (Henley: G. Norton, 1793); e.g. pp. 73-75.

[71] Turner, *Remarks*, p. 10.

[72] See Turner, *Remarks*, p. 13.

[73] Turner, *Remarks*, p. 11. Since Turner immediately refutes any suggestion that baptism is repeatable, we must suppose that 'without formal renunciation' means without uncharitable denunciation, which would attack the beliefs of others.

[74] Turner, *Remarks*, p. 10.

[75] Turner, *Free Thoughts*, p. 73.

[76] I am indebted to John Briggs for this suggestion.

Turner thinks that the revelation in the Bible contains 'all the truths necessary ... in such terms of expression, in everything essential, as were best suited to the common sense of mankind'.[77] It was this kind of resort to 'reasonable Christianity' that Grantham Killingworth rejected in criticizing the 'catholic communion' espoused by such Socinian Baptists as James Foster and Charles Bulkley.[78] The appeal that Turner and others make to the 'private judgement' of conscience thus draws both upon the continual act of self-examination in Calvinistic piety and the Enlightenment confidence in human reason. Perhaps both strategies are possible because reason, when turned towards knowledge of God, is never for Turner a purely human enterprise. Indeed, Turner wants to replace the notion of 'natural theology' with 'universal revelation', since he thinks that the Gospel of Christ has been diffused through the world by a revelation of God to humankind far back in antiquity: 'this religion is UNIVERSAL, and has been communicated, more or less to all Nations'.[79] This is consistent with his belief that 'all mankind are under (in several degrees of privilege) the New Covenant' in Christ, though this does not – in his view – contradict a belief that 'the Elect only share in the complete Saving Grace of this Redemption'.[80]

This wider vision of a universal revelation of Christ forms a suitable background to Turner's understanding of the catholic church. The interest and subtlety of his thought is that his vision of the church universal is not only based on what is 'essential' in personal devotion (a Particular Baptist emphasis) and in reason (a new General Baptist emphasis). Were this to be the sum total, we might find Turner's approach too problematic to be useful. In our age, we have become rightly uneasy about the Enlightenment assumption that one can strip 'form' away from a supposed 'substance' in religious practices; we are only too aware of their inseparable cultural and social conditioning. The idea of a substance or essence with universal validity is indeed a component in Turner's thought, but it is woven in with an ecclesiology which is thoroughly Christological. The church universal is the Body of Christ, and every particular church is part of a whole where Christ is the head, where Christ reigns, where the laws of Christ have their universal mandate, and where conscience will come under his final judgement. It is the sovereignty of Christ which is the basis for the 'liberty' of individuals and of particular congregations. Baptism, moreover, is not just a sign of personal devotion to Christ but entrance to both the church particular and the church universal. Turner regards baptism as an initiating sacrament, and as the beginning of the 'outward manifestation' of the

---

[77] Turner, *Free Thoughts*, p. 36.
[78] Grantham Killingworth, *An Examination of the Revd Dr James Foster's Sermon on Catholic Communion, As Published in His First Volume of Discourses on Natural Religion and Social Virtue* (London: M. Cooper, 1750), pp. 37-41.
[79] Turner, 'Universal Revelation', p. 193; cf. p. 195.
[80] Letter, 14 June 1782, p. 4, commenting on Turner, *Remarks*, p. 9.

visible unity of the church universal.[81] By appealing to the 'substance' of baptism held by both Baptists and Paedobaptists, Turner can give real value to *church order* that places baptism before sharing in the Lord's Supper (while still not giving the sequence the absolute authority of a dominical ordinance).[82] It also clears him from the earlier accusation of William Kiffin that those pleading for open communion want a 'non-sacramental Christ'.[83]

We should notice that Turner is not suggesting – as opponents objected[84] – that baptism *itself* is a mere shadow or disposable sign of a universal substance such as faith; rather a particular *mode* and *subject* of baptism is the form which can be distinguished (not separated) from baptism as the substance. It is, admittedly, a weakness that Turner and other open-communionists do not seem to have much more to say about this 'substance' of baptism than devotion to Christ and the call to a holy life. This means that they have no guidance to give in a modern ecumenical situation where Baptists are called not only to respect the baptism of others but to avoid any act which might give the impression of re-baptism. But we should honour Turner's intention of holding all true gospel churches together in the visible catholic church, on the basis of *both* word and sacrament, and it sets all Christians a challenge to work this out in new ways for our own day.

---

[81] Turner, *Compendium*, p. 120 footnote.
[82] Turner, *Charity*, p. 26.
[83] William Kiffin, *A sober discourse of right to church-communion wherein is proved ... that no unbaptized person may be regularly admitted to the Lords Supper* (London: Enoch Prosser, 1681), pp. 42–43.
[84] See e.g. Booth, *Apology for the Baptists*, pp. 135–37, cf. pp. 48–50.

CHAPTER 8

# Andrew Fuller and
# *The Gospel Worthy of All Acceptation*

P. J. Morden

## Introduction

In his book *The Rise of Evangelicalism*, Mark Noll states that a recommendation made to Andrew Fuller (1754-1815), that he should read Jonathan Edwards' philosophical treatise entitled *The Freedom of the Will*, 'led to a critical moment in Baptist history'.[1] The recommendation was made on 3 May 1775, by Robert Hall, Sr, on the day Fuller was inducted as pastor of the Particular Baptist church at Soham.[2] There was little to suggest to those present on this occasion that the events of the day would have any significance beyond that particular area of rural Cambridgeshire. The church at Soham was small, isolated and struggling, in thrall to the theology known as High Calvinism and, in truth, unable to adequately support their new pastor financially. Fuller himself had little by way of formal education, his theological naïvety illustrated by the fact that, in following up Hall's suggestion, he initially obtained the wrong book, one entitled *Veritas Redux*, written by an Anglican Clergyman named John Edwards. But, despite these unpromising beginnings, Fuller would become the premier theologian of the Particular (Calvinistic) Baptist churches, as well as the secretary of the Baptist Missionary Society (BMS) from its inception in 1792 to his death. His discovery of the New England theologian Jonathan Edwards (he eventually obtained a copy of the right book) was to help lead to both these developments.

Firstly, Fuller's reading of *The Freedom of the Will* was crucial in shaping the work on which his own reputation as a theologian largely rests, namely *The Gospel Worthy of All Acceptation*, originally published in 1785. This was a

---

[1] M.A. Noll, *The Rise of Evangelicalism: The Age of Edwards, Whitefield and the Wesleys* (A History of Evangelicalism, 1; Leicester: IVP, 2004), p. 196.
[2] See J. Ryland, Jr, *The Work of Faith, the Labour of Love, and the Patience of Hope Illustrated in the Life and Death of the Late Rev. Andrew Fuller* (London: Button and Son, 1st edn, 1816; 2nd edn, 1818), 2nd edn, pp. 27, 36 for details contained in this paragraph.

seminal book, and contributed significantly to what Michael Haykin has termed a 'profound revitalization' of Particular Baptist life.[3] Secondly, this 'revitalization' included the founding and subsequent growth of the BMS, for which the Edwardsean evangelical Calvinism contained in *The Gospel Worthy* was the theological motor.[4] This paper seeks to map out the development of what became known as 'Fullerism' showing how, in *The Gospel Worthy*, Fuller rejected High Calvinism in favour of a theology which set human responsibility alongside divine sovereignty, and which was deeply indebted to forces associated with the Evangelical Revival. It also offers an assessment of the impact of this theology. In fact, the publication of *The Gospel Worthy*, the event to which Fuller's reading of Edwards made such an important contribution, was not a critical moment in Baptist history alone. It also occupies an important place in the story evangelicalism in Britain, and in the spread of the gospel throughout the globe.

## Fuller in Context

### Fuller's Immediate Context: Soham and High Calvinism

As already noted, the theology which characterised the Soham congregation was that of High or 'hyper' Calvinism. Fundamental to High Calvinism was the belief that the unconverted were under no moral obligation to repent and believe the gospel, because total depravity rendered them incapable of doing so, and they could not justly be held accountable for doing what in reality they were completely unable to do. Following this grim logic to its conclusion meant that what were termed 'indiscriminate exhortations to faith and repentance' could not be addressed to the unconverted in preaching. To do so would be a nonsense, because it could not be the 'duty' of the unregenerate to do 'anything spiritually good'. Reflecting back on High Calvinism later in life, Fuller himself summarized its practical effect: nothing was to be said to 'sinners…inviting them to apply to Christ for salvation.'[5] The first systematic exposition of High Calvinism had been published in 1707 by Joseph Hussey, appropriately entitled *God's Operations of Grace, but no Offers of Grace*. But in mid-eighteenth century Particular Baptist circles it was strongly associated with the views of two London pastors, John Brine and John Gill.[6]

---

[3] M.A.G. Haykin, 'A Habitation of God, through the Spirit: John Sutcliff (1752-1814) and the Revitalization of the Calvinistic Baptists in the Late-Eighteenth Century', *Baptist Quarterly* 34.7 (1992), p. 306.
[4] See P.J. Morden, 'Andrew Fuller and the BMS', *Baptist Quarterly* 41.3 (2005), pp. 134-57, for an analysis of Fuller's role as secretary of the BMS.
[5] Ryland, *Andrew Fuller*, 2nd edn, pp. 31-32.
[6] For Gill's High Calvinism see P.J. Morden, *Offering Christ to the World: Andrew Fuller (1754-1815) and the Revival of Eighteenth Century Particular Baptist Life* (Studies in Baptist History and Thought, 8; Carlisle: Paternoster, 2003), pp. 12-17.

Of these two, Gill was the more significant. His views were mediated through his voluminous published works such as the *Cause of God and Truth*, and he was the favourite theologian of John Eve, pastor at Soham from 1752 to 1771. Eve, an avid reader of Gill, was, according to Fuller, 'tinged with false Calvinism', having 'little or nothing to say to the unconverted'.[7] The congregational life at Soham was characterised by a number of features which often accompanied High Calvinism, namely an insular ecclesiology, antinomianism and theological hair splitting. In 1771, these tendencies combined with disastrous consequences, when Eve was forced to resign following a dispute which Fuller later described as the 'wormwood and gall of my youth'. Eve's mistake was to observe that although people had no power in and of themselves to do anything 'spiritually' good, they did have the power to obey the will of God 'as to outward acts'.[8] As M.R. Watts notes, Eve's High Calvinism had not been consistent enough for the majority of his members.[9] On the day it was suggested that Fuller read 'Edwards on the Will' he was being inducted as pastor of a church which had previously been impervious to the influence of the Evangelical Revival in which Edwards had been a central figure. It is no surprise that when, in December 1779, Fuller sought to introduce 'open offers' of the gospel into his preaching at Soham, he encountered significant opposition from within the church.[10]

### *Fuller's Wider Context: Eighteenth-Century Particular Baptist Life*

To what extent was the Soham church typical of the Particular Baptists in England and Wales as a whole, and to what extent had High Calvinism captured the denomination? A brief discussion of these questions is important for this paper because it effects any assessment of the impact of *The Gospel Worthy* on Particular Baptist life. The dominant view amongst Baptist historians of an older generation (W.T. Whitley stands as an example), was that High Calvinism was almost all-pervasive in the life of the churches for much of the eighteenth century and that this was a period that was analogous to the 'dark ages' for Particular Baptists.[11] But this strain of Baptist historiography has rightly been challenged on a number of fronts. In particular, Roger Hayden has shown that a much more evangelistically minded Calvinism was kept alive during the first half of the eighteenth century through the work of the Baptist Academy in Bris-

---

[7] Ryland, *Andrew Fuller*, 2nd edn, p. 11.

[8] Ryland, *Andrew Fuller*, 2nd edn, pp. 24-26.

[9] M.R. Watts, *The Dissenters*, (2 vols; Oxford: Clarendon Press, 1978 and 1995), I, pp. 459-60.

[10] A.G. Fuller, *Andrew Fuller* (London: Hodder and Stoughton, 1882), p. 168.

[11] W.T. Whitley, *A History of the English Baptists* (London: Charles Griffin, 1923), p. 258.

tol.[12] Other scholars have shown evidence of considerable spiritual life in the regions,[13] and even in London, normally thought of as the bastion of High Calvinism, it has been argued that only a third of the churches were consistently High Calvinist.[14] Moreover, where congregations, like Soham, were weak, to say that their difficulties could be laid entirely at the door of High Calvinism is undoubtedly simplistic. There was a complex matrix of factors, geographical, social and economic, as well as religious, which contributed to decline.[15] The view of eighteenth-century Particular Baptist life represented by Whitley needed to be corrected.

Nevertheless, as Ken Manley states, 'after all this necessary balance has been drawn...the common witness was undoubtedly that by about 1760 Particular Baptists in London and many regions, for whatever reason (and Gill's theology is most commonly cited), evidenced little spiritual vigour.'[16] There is a wealth of evidence to support this broad conclusion. The first half of the eighteenth century saw a significant decline in the number of Particular Baptist churches in England and Wales. The best source of statistical evidence for the number of dissenting congregations is a list largely drawn up between 1715 and 1718 by Dr John Evans, a London Presbyterian minister. Probably, the list is fairly accurate with regard to paedobaptist churches, but Whitley was able to discover a number of Particular Baptist churches not on the Evans list. Whitley suggested there were approximately 220 Calvinistic Baptist congregations in England and Wales in the years between 1715 and 1718, statistics accepted by Watts.[17] Figures for the mid-eighteenth century are largely based on a survey by John Collett Ryland, although, as with the Evans list, the survey is incomplete. Nevertheless, it is clear that the number of congregations had fallen drastically, probably to about 150.[18] Over a period of less than fifty years, therefore, the number of Particular Baptist churches in England and Wales had decreased

---

[12] R. Hayden, 'Evangelical Calvinism Among Eighteenth Century Particular Baptists with Particular Reference to Bernard Foskett, Hugh and Caleb Evans and the Bristol Baptist Academy 1690-1791' (PhD thesis, Keele University, 1991).

[13] See, for example, K. Smith, *The Community of Believers: A Study of Calvinistic Baptist Spirituality in Some Towns and Villages of Hampshire and the Borders of Wiltshire, c.1730-1830* (Studies in Baptist History and Thought, 22; Carlisle: Paternoster, 2005).

[14] R.P. Roberts, *Continuity and Change: London Calvinistic Baptists and the Evangelical Revival 1760-1820* (Wheaton, Illinois: R.O. Roberts, 1989), p. 42.

[15] For the different causes of decline, see the survey in M.A.G. Haykin, *One Heart and Soul: John Sutcliff of Olney, His Friends and His Times* (Darlington: Evangelical Press, 1994), pp. 15-33.

[16] K.R. Manley, *Redeeming Love Proclaim: John Rippon and the Baptists* (Studies in Baptist History and Thought, 12; Carlisle: Paternoster, 2004), p. 2.

[17] W.T. Whitley, 'The Baptist Interest under George I', *Transactions of the Baptist Historical Society*, 2 (1910-11), pp. 95-109; Watts, *Dissenters*, I, p. 498.

[18] A.S. Langley, 'Baptist Ministers in England About 1750 A.D.', *Transactions of the Baptist Historical Society*, 6 (1910-11), pp. 138-57.

by approximately one-third.

To speak, as Manley does, of a lack of 'spiritual vigour' accompanying this numerical decline is, of course, more subjective. But this was certainly how many at the time would have described the life of their denomination. In 1746, Benjamin Wallin, a prominent London pastor, spoke of hearing 'universal complaints of the decay of practical and vital godliness'. Writing again in 1752, Wallin stated his belief that they were living in a 'melancholy day' of 'present declensions' amongst Particular Baptist churches.[19] Even in the west of England, buoyed by the influence of the Bristol Academy, the annual Western Association newsletters still regularly bemoaned the low spiritual temperature of the churches. The letter for 1740 urged readers to acknowledge the prevailing situation and set aside four days in the year ahead for fasting and prayer, at which what had been written could be 'read publicly and pondered by the members'. But twenty years later, it appeared that little had changed. In the 1761 letter, Isaac Hann wrote that he and other concerned ministers were 'almost at a loss to know what we can say further for the stirring up of sleepy professors'. Those who read Hann's words were exhorted to take heed 'lest they sleep the sleep of death'. He went on to plead with his readers: 'Look over the letters which of late years you have had from us ... hearken to the counsel and advice of those who would not cease to warn every one with tears.'[20] Certainly there seemed to have been few ministers who would have disagreed with Daniel Turner of Abingdon in Oxfordshire who, writing in 1769, expressed the view that the spiritual life of the Particular Baptists was markedly 'on the decline'.[21]

To sum up, although there were significant regional variations and pockets of life and growth, much of Particular Baptist life in the middle of the eighteenth century was characterised both by High Calvinism and numerical and spiritual decline. Roger Hayden's thesis is a vitally important contribution to the historiography of the period, but, in my view, he does tend to overestimate the influence of Bristol, as well as underestimating that of the High Calvinist London ministers, which in some parts of the country was all- pervasive.[22] It is hard to disagree greatly with Fuller's own characteristically trenchant assessment of Particular Baptist life at this time. 'Had matters gone on but a few

---

[19] B. Wallin, *The Christian Life, In Divers of its Branches Described and Recommended* (2 vols; London, 1746), II, p. 9; *Exhortations, Relating to Prayer and the Lord's Supper* (London, 1752), pp. 8, 10.

[20] J.G. Fuller, *A Brief History of the Western Association* (Bristol, I. Hemmans, 1843), pp. 40, 44-45.

[21] D. Turner to S. Stennett, cited in E.A. Payne, *Baptists of Berkshire: Through Three Centuries* (London: Carey Kingsgate Press, 1951), p. 79.

[22] For the influence of London High Calvinism in much of the North of England, see J. Fawcett Jr, *An Account of the Life, Ministry and Writings of the late Rev. John Fawcett, DD* (London: Baldwin, Craddock and Joy, 1818), pp. 97-102. In Norfolk and Suffolk the predominance of High Calvinism was even greater.

years longer', he wrote, 'the Baptists would have become a perfect dunghill in society.'[23]

This, then, was the context in which Fuller worked out his new theology. He did not publish *The Gospel Worthy* until after he had left Soham (in 1782) for his second pastorate in Kettering, although he had been working on the manuscript from at least 1781. Finally, in November 1784, with a certain degree of fear and trepidation, Fuller delivered his work to a publisher. As he did so, he offered up the prayer 'that God would bless that to which I am going; namely the printing of my manuscript on the duty of sinners to believe in Christ'. One month earlier, Fuller had confided to his diary his concerns, believing, with good reason, that by publishing he was likely to 'expose himself to a good deal of abuse'. He continued: 'Had I not the satisfaction that it is the *cause of God and truth* I would drop all thoughts of printing.'[24] The phrase 'cause of God and truth' was almost certainly a conscious echo of Gill's major treatise of the same name, highly influential in Particular Baptist life earlier in the century. Fuller was clearly apprehensive about publishing, but *The Gospel Worthy* would in fact outstrip even Gill's work in terms of importance and influence, and Fuller would come to believe that his prayers for God's 'blessing' had been answered.

## *The Gospel Worthy*, First Edition

Fuller began *The Gospel Worthy* by challenging an aspect of High Calvinist theology yet to be discussed in this study, namely its definition of faith. High Calvinists understood faith as being analogous to a person having an 'inner persuasion' of their 'interest' in Christ, something given to them by the Holy Spirit. This gave the person concerned a so-called 'warrant of faith', encouraging them that they were part of the elect, so enabling them to come to Christ. This effectively made faith into a person's subjective, conscious feeling that the Holy Spirit was beginning to work savingly in their life and that the gospel was therefore for them. Against this, Fuller contended that the Bible's definition of faith was quite different. The scriptures consistently represented true faith as being fixed, not on something subjective or 'within' the person concerned, but on something objective or 'without', namely Christ himself. To establish this was extremely important to Fuller, because if faith was someone's belief that they were 'interested' in Christ, then it could not be the 'duty' of the unconverted to believe. Indeed, he stated 'that if this be faith ... the controversy is, or ought to be, at an end ... none but real Christians have any warrant to believe; for it cannot be any man's duty to believe a lie.'[25] Fuller, however, was able to

---

[23] J.W. Morris, *Memoirs of the Life and Death of the Rev. Andrew Fuller*, (1st edn: High Wycombe, 1816; 2nd edn: London: Wightman and Cramp, 1826), 1st edn, p. 267.
[24] Ryland, *Andrew Fuller*, 2nd edn, pp. 131-32.
[25] Fuller, *The Gospel Worthy*, 1st edn, p. 6.

show that faith should be understood differently, as a 'cordial belief of the truth' (i.e. the truth of Christ and his gospel).[26] Because the focus of biblical faith was on something objective it *could*, he argued, be a person's duty to believe. Indeed it *was* a duty, for 'the least thing we can be obliged unto upon any declaration of God is the belief of it'.[27]

Having established this foundation, Fuller marshalled further arguments to show that faith in Christ was the 'incumbent duty' of all who heard the gospel. Central among these was the fact that unconverted sinners were *commanded* to have faith in the scriptures. Indeed, in the New Testament, 'true saving faith [was] enjoined upon unregenerate sinners, as plain as words can express it'. Fuller set out a whole series of texts to support this contention, just one example being John 12.36: 'While ye have the light, believe in the light, that ye may be the children of light,' which he went on to expound:

> The persons to whom this was addressed were such, who though [Christ] had done so many miracles among them, yet believed not on him. Yet it seems they were given over to judicial blindness, and were finally lost. By the light they were commanded to believe in, he undoubtedly meant himself ... and what kind of faith it was that they were called upon to exercise is very plain, for that on their believing they would not have abode in darkness, but would have been the children of light, which is a character never bestowed on any but true believers.[28]

In other words, those who were not believers (and in Fuller's view never became so), were commanded to have saving faith – by Christ himself. Surely to such a command it had been their 'duty' to respond, although in fact they had never done so.

A number of possible objections to Fuller's views, with a focus on those which might be raised by fellow Particular Baptists, were stated and then demolished. The arguments Fuller was putting forward were not inconsistent with, for example, the decrees of God (God's commands, not his secret purposes, are our 'rule of conduct'), or particular redemption (even if not one of the elect, it was still a person's duty to believe what God had revealed). None of the central tenets of Calvinism were in dispute, as Fuller had immediately made clear in his Preface.[29] He saw himself standing in the tradition of older writers, particularly the Puritans, from whom he quoted liberally. His was not a

---

[26] Fuller, *The Gospel Worthy*, 1st edn, pp. 29, 10, where Fuller refers to 2 Thess. 2.13. Cf. the Preface to *The Gospel Worthy*, 1st edn., printed in *The Complete Works of the Rev Andrew Fuller, With a Memoir of his Life by the Rev. Andrew Gunton Fuller* (ed. A.G. Fuller; rev. ed. J. Belcher; 3 vols; Harrisonburg, Virginia: Sprinkle Publications, 3rd edn, 1988 [1845]), II, p. 329.

[27] Fuller, *The Gospel Worthy*, 1st edn, p. 33. Fuller was citing from the Puritan, Stephen Charnock.

[28] Fuller, *The Gospel Worthy*, 1st edn, p. 40, Fuller's italics.

[29] *Fuller's Works*, II, pp. 328-32.

'new scheme', rather a return to the 'good old way'.[30] It was because of this (in addition to natural modesty), that he was later unhappy when the views he expressed in *The Gospel Worthy* came to be dubbed as 'Fullerism' (why not 'Owenism' or 'Bunyanism' he protested?).[31] But there *was* a distinctive eighteenth-century dimension to his argument. As Fuller dealt with further objections he responded to the view that if faith really was the duty of all it could not, at one and the same time, be a sovereign gift of God given to some and not to others. Fuller maintained that faith was both a duty *and* a gift by appealing to a distinction between what he called 'natural' and 'moral' inability, a distinction one will look for in vain amongst the Puritans. Fuller's use of these terms, and the basis for them, are explored later in this paper.

In his conclusion, Fuller came to the two crucial, practical outworkings of his thesis. The first was that there was 'free and full encouragement for any poor sinner to ... venture his soul on the Lord Jesus Christ.' No one need hold back from coming to Christ because they lacked a strong enough 'inner persuasion' that God was at work in their lives. The gospel itself was all the 'warrant' that was needed. Fuller's second conclusion flowed naturally from the first. Christians, especially gospel ministers, should exhort everyone, indiscriminately, to believe in Christ. The New Testament was full of such open 'offers' of the gospel. 'Calls, warnings, invitations, expostulations, threatenings and exhortations, *even to the unregenerate*', were perfectly consistent with Calvinistic belief.[32] Thus Fuller struck, quite deliberately, at the two pillars of High Calvinist 'orthodoxy'. It was the duty of all to believe, and so it was also the duty of ministers to offer the gospel to all. This was the argument which was to have such far reaching consequences, both for Fuller himself and for the Particular Baptist denomination. What had led to this sea-change in his thinking? A range of points need to be considered.

*Reasons for the Change in Fuller's Thinking*

INFLUENCES AT SOHAM AND THE NORTHAMPTONSHIRE ASSOCIATION

In assessing what led Fuller to embrace evangelical Calvinism, a number of factors can be mentioned briefly. Fuller's own conversion experience, an event which occurred without any help or guidance from his pastor, was clearly important. The dispute at Soham which had led to Eve's resignation from the pastorate also caused Fuller to re-examine High Calvinism. Important to note is the fact that, soon after he had become pastor at Soham, on 8 June 1775, Fuller took the congregation into the Northamptonshire Association of Particular Baptist churches. The decision to join was taken by the 'unanimous consent' of the

---

[30] Fuller, *The Gospel Worthy*, 1st edn, p. 138.
[31] Morris, *Andrew Fuller*, 2nd edn, pp. 238-39.
[32] Fuller, *The Gospel Worthy*, 1st edn, pp. 162-63, 166, italics added.

church members, although the implications of the step they were taking would not have been recognised by many of them.[33] The new association had been formed in 1764 and was, according to John Briggs, the 'archetype of the new associations, born out of the Evangelical Revival'.[34] Association life brought Fuller into contact with more men such as Robert Hall, Sr, who held evangelical views. Two of these, John Sutcliff and John Ryland, Jr, Fuller's 'tombstone' biographer, would become very close to Fuller. Both men held to an evangelical Calvinist position (Sutcliff was Bristol trained) and both read the manuscript of *The Gospel Worthy* before publication. By Fuller's own admission, all of these factors were significant in the development of his theological views.[35] But two further influences on Fuller's thinking stand out and deserve a more detailed treatment.

## FULLER'S BIBLICISM

The first of these was Fuller's biblicism. Fuller's resolve to search the scriptures before accepting that something was true was commented on by a number of his biographers.[36] This commitment also appears in Fuller's private papers, particularly in a solemn and private 'covenant' with God discovered by Ryland after his subject's death.[37] The 'covenant' was clearly not intended for publication, or indeed to be seen by anyone but the author. It is dated by Fuller as being written on 10 January 1780, and Ryland believed it was occasioned by Fuller's having read a piece 'written at the time of the controversy between the Calvinistic and Arminian Methodists'.[38] Having read tracts written by both sides, with texts thrown back and forth in support of diametrically opposing views, Fuller was acutely aware of how difficult a thoroughgoing biblicism was in practice. He reflected on how there were many who professed 'to be searching after truth [and] to have Christ and the inspired writers on their side', and he was fully conscious that he was 'as liable to err as other men'. But he was determined to go back to the scriptures, which he regarded as the very 'oracles

---

[33] A. Fuller, 'A Narration of the dealings of God in a way of Providence with the Baptist Church at Soham from the year 1770', Cambridge County Records Office (NC/B – Soham R70/20), p. 25; Morris, *Andrew Fuller*, 1st edn, p. 31. Although Soham was in Cambridgeshire, the Northamptonshire Association accepted churches from neighbouring counties.

[34] J.H.Y. Briggs, *English Baptists of the Nineteenth Century* (A History of the English Baptists, 3; Didcot: Baptist Historical Society, 1994), p. 203.

[35] Ryland, *Andrew Fuller*, 2nd edn, pp. 18-19; 26. I have dealt with these factors more fully in Morden, *Offering Christ to the World*, pp. 27-32.

[36] e.g. Ryland, *Andrew Fuller*, 2nd edn, p. 43.

[37] A. Fuller, 'Sermons…in shorthand, with occasional meditations in longhand (Books 1-5 bound in 1 vol.)', Bristol Baptist College library (G 95 A). Book 3, pp. 2-3, contains the 'covenant'.

[38] See H.D. Rack, *Reasonable Enthusiast: John Wesley and the Rise of Methodism* (Epworth: London, 1989), pp. 198-202.

of God'. At the heart of his 'covenant' was the following passage:

> Let not the sleight of wicked men, who lie in wait to deceive, nor even the pious character of good men (who yet may be under great mistakes), draw me aside. Nor do thou suffer my own fancy to guide me. Lord, thou hast given me a determination to take up no principle at second hand; but to search for everything at the pure fountain of thy word.[39]

This is especially valuable for being heartfelt and private, and also because of the humility before God that it reveals. And there is good evidence to suggest that what was resolved in secret was worked out in public. Of course, an approach to scripture that is free of cultural 'presuppositions' is not possible and Fuller did not achieve this. His reading of scripture was influenced by his temperament, his background and his times. But the writing and subsequent publication of *The Gospel Worthy* is evidence in itself that Fuller was able to submit his theological system to a rigorous biblical critique and revise it accordingly, at great personal cost. In this he displays a characteristic that was one of the hallmarks of the Evangelical Revival. Fuller's biblicism was undoubtedly influenced by growing evangelical convictions. The process which led to the writing of *The Gospel Worthy* cannot be understood if what Michael Haykin terms Fuller's 'transparent desire to be true to the Scriptures' is forgotten.[40]

THE INFLUENCE OF JONATHAN EDWARDS

A further factor to consider was Fuller's use of Jonathan Edwards, as noted at the beginning of this paper. This further highlights the evangelical influences on *The Gospel Worthy*. Fuller's discovery of a variety of Edwards' works, as well as books by other New England theologians, needs to be seen in context. The eighteenth century had seen the establishment of strong links between evangelicals on different sides of the Atlantic (the friendship between Edwards and George Whitefield being a prime example). Susan O'Brien states that 'through an exchange of ideas and materials Calvinist revivalists ... built a "community of saints" that cut across physical barriers.'[41] In addition to the regular exchange of letters there was, from the 1740s onwards, a shared literature which included Revival narratives and theological works. A central figure in this transatlantic network was John Erskine[42] of Edinburgh with whom, by

---

[39] Ryland, *Andrew Fuller*, 1st edn, pp. 203-204.

[40] M.A.G. Haykin, *The Armies of the Lamb: The Spirituality of Andrew Fuller* (Classics of Reformed Spirituality, 3; Dundas, Ontario: Joshua Press, 2001), p. 17.

[41] Susan [Durden] O'Brien, 'A Transatlantic Community of Saints: The Great Awakening and the First Evangelical Network, 1735-1755', *American Historical Review* 91 (1986), p. 813.

[42] M.A. Noll, 'Revival, Enlightenment, Civic Humanism, and the Evolution of Calvinism in Scotland and America 1735-1843', in G.A. Rawlyk and M.A. Noll (eds), *Amaz-

the early 1770s, Fuller's friends, Ryland and Sutcliff, were in contact. It was via this route that Fuller started to receive works that originated in America, although many were now in the form of British editions, published in Scotland. These included Edwards' *Life of David Brainerd* and other biographies of those who had been missionaries amongst the Native Americans.[43] In the Preface to *The Gospel Worthy*, Fuller, referring to himself in the third person, commented directly on the influence these books had on him:

> Reading the lives of such men as Elliot, Brainerd, and several others, who preached Christ with so much success to the American Indians, had an effect on him. Their work, like that of the apostles, seemed to be plain before them. They appeared to him, in their addresses to those poor benighted heathens, to have none of those difficulties with which he felt himself encumbered. These things led him to the throne of grace, to implore instruction and resolution.[44]

Fuller had access to these works, at least by the early 1780s and probably earlier.[45] Clearly, he was impressed by the practical vitality of what he was reading; indeed, he was deeply moved by the sacrificial efforts of these pioneers. Further reflection convinced him that what men such as Brainerd had done was biblical, that they were indeed standing in the tradition of the apostles by freely offering the gospel whilst he himself was 'encumbered' in his own preaching. Thus, his changing theological stance was influenced by works that were descriptive of evangelical action.

Fuller probably read the Edwards' work which was to have the most impact on *The Gospel Worthy* in 1777, two years after Hall, Sr's original recommendation.[46] *A Careful and Strict Enquiry into the Modern Prevailing Notions of the Freedom of Will* was originally published in 1754.[47] The treatise (which was written to combat Arminian views) was, as already noted, largely philosophical rather than theological (the first reference to Jesus Christ does not occur for 175

---

*ing Grace: Evangelicalism in Australia, Britain, Canada and the United States* (Grand Rapids: Baker, 1993), p. 77.

[43] J. Edwards, *The Life of David Brainerd*, in *The Works of Jonathan Edwards*, vol. 7, ed. N. Pettit (London and New Haven: Yale University Press, 1985 [1749]).

[44] *Fuller's Works*, II, p. 329; cf. Ryland, *Andrew Fuller*, 2nd edn, p. 90.

[45] Fuller probably read Edwards' *Life of Brainerd* in early to mid-1781. See Fuller to J. Sutcliff, 28 January 1781, 'Typescript Andrew Fuller Letters', transcribed by E.A. Payne (4/5/1 and 4/5/2), Angus Library, Regents Park College, Oxford (4/5/1): 'I cannot tell how you come to think of my having had Brainerd's life. I have never seen it.' Hayden's comment that 'no doubt Sutcliff remedied' the situation, is surely reasonable. See Hayden, 'Evangelical Calvinism and the Bristol Baptist Academy', p. 363.

[46] Ryland, *Andrew Fuller*, 2nd edn, p. 36.

[47] For the text see J. Edwards, *The Freedom of the Will*, in *The Works of Jonathan Edwards*, vol. 1, ed. P. Ramsey (New Haven: Yale University Press, 1957 [1754]), pp. 135-440.

pages, taking the text from the Yale edition).[48] Doubtless in part because of this, Edwards' publishers thought it necessary to raise subscriptions for the work prior to printing, so to insure themselves against serious loss. Significantly, forty-two of the original 298 subscribers were from Scotland.[49] Edwards' argument, as summed up by Stephen Holmes, was that 'the freedom human beings possess, when properly understood, is not inconsistent with our actions being predictable or indeed necessitated – not incompatible fundamentally with predestination.'[50] The will 'is simply that by which the mind chooses anything', and these choices are always determined by the strongest motive 'in view of the mind'.[51] Holmes uses an image of some traditional balancing scales to illustrate Edwards' point. We have a series of inducements to act one way or another, and what we judge to be the strongest set of inducements will *inevitably* determine which way the scales will tip (i.e. what choices we make). Put another way, although a person could correctly be described as 'free' because they possessed a will, the will itself was *not* free because (contrary to what Arminians believed or implied), it had no self-determining power. As Edwards put it: 'The will itself is not an agent that has a will: the power of choosing, itself, does not have the power of choosing.'[52] Something always causes an act of the will.

It was in expanding on his notion of cause that Edwards developed a distinction between what he termed natural and moral inability, a distinction which was to be absolutely crucial to Fuller.[53] The most relevant section was Part 1, Section 4, headed 'Of the distinction of Natural and Moral Necessity and Inability'.[54] No one could respond to the gospel without the electing grace of God and the regenerating work of the Holy Spirit. But this helplessness was not because of a lack of any 'natural' powers. Rather, a person's inability was wholly of the 'moral' or 'criminal' kind. To return to the image of the scales, there were not enough inducements (as far as the unregenerate mind was concerned) to tip the balance in favour of a positive response to the gospel. All had the natural powers to respond, but the unregenerate person would always refuse to do so. If someone did not respond, therefore, they were still criminally culpable.

---

[48] As noted by Stephen Holmes, *God of Grace and God of Glory: An Account of the Theology of Jonathan Edwards* (Edinburgh: T. & T. Clark, 2000), p. 153. The distinction between theology and philosophy was less sharply drawn in Edwards' day.
[49] As noted by Ramsey in his introduction to *The Freedom of the Will*, p. 7, n. 7.
[50] Holmes, *God of Grace*, p. 151. See pp. 151-54 for Holmes' reading of Edwards' work, from which I have drawn.
[51] Edwards, *The Freedom of the Will*, p. 137.
[52] Edwards, *The Freedom of the Will*, p. 163.
[53] For an excellent discussion of the relationship between Edwards and Fuller see C. Chun, 'A Mainspring of Missionary Thought: Andrew Fuller on "Natural and Moral Inability"', *American Baptist Quarterly* 25.4 (2006), pp. 335-49.
[54] Edwards, *The Freedom of the Will*, pp. 156-62.

In the Preface to *The Gospel Worthy* Fuller made the following comments, continuing to write in the third person:

> He had read and considered, as well as he was able, President Edwards's Inquiry into the Freedom of the Will, with some other performances on the difference between natural and moral inability. He found much satisfaction in the distinction; as it appeared to him to carry with it its own evidence – to be clearly and fully contained in the Scriptures ... The more he examined the Scriptures, the more he was convinced that all the inability ascribed to man, with respect to believing, arises from the aversion of his heart.[55]

In the main body of his work, Fuller regularly showed his debt to Edwards. This is not just true in the chapter, 'General Observations on Natural and Moral Inability', but at many other points, too. For example, in the section where Fuller drives home his main practical conclusions, he makes heavy use of this key distinction.[56] In an earlier passage, he deals with one objection to his view of 'duty faith', that people have 'no power to believe', by saying that:

> Men want power to do this [i.e. believe in Christ] no more than they want power to do everything else that is really good, even so much as to think a good thought. But if this be not the duty of men, then the Almighty had no reason to complain as he did, when he looked down upon the children of men, that none of them did good, no not one. Moreover, I wish what has, or may be said on the subject of natural and moral inability, to be taken as an answer to this objection.[57]

Edwards allowed Fuller to hold together strict Calvinism (no one would come to Christ without the regenerating work of the Holy Spirit) and applied, evangelistic preaching (all had the *natural* powers to come even though, because of *moral* or *criminal* inability, they would not, apart from the Spirit's work). Because their inability was not natural, it was their duty to believe, and, consequently, Fuller's duty to preach. This line of argument is absolutely fundamental to *The Gospel Worthy*. If Fuller had not been reading 'Edwards on the Will' together with other writers who derived their arguments from this work, it is hard to see how *The Gospel Worthy* could have been published. I agree, therefore, with E.F. Clipsham who believes that Edwards was 'probably the most powerful and important extra biblical influence' on Fuller. Indeed, the distinction between natural and moral ability 'became one of the foundation stones' of his doctrine.[58] Hall's suggestion that Fuller read Edwards had certainly been a 'critical moment' in the development of Fuller's thought.

---

[55] *Fuller's Works*, II, p. 330.
[56] Fuller, *The Gospel Worthy*, 1st edn, pp. 172-84, especially p. 186.
[57] Fuller, *The Gospel Worthy*, 1st edn, pp. 152-53.
[58] E.F. Clipsham, 'Andrew Fuller and Fullerism: A Study in Evangelical Calvinism', *Baptist Quarterly* 20.1-4 (1963); '1. The Development of a Doctrine', pp. 110-11.

As David Bebbington states, Jonathan Edwards 'stands at the headwaters' of eighteenth-century evangelicalism.[59] The evidence that he shaped Fuller's argument so decisively is just one factor defining *The Gospel Worthy* as an evangelical tract. Fuller's use of Edwards is also one factor marking out *The Gospel Worthy* as being influenced by certain aspects of Enlightenment thought, for Edwards was undoubtedly an Enlightenment figure. Influenced by the English philosopher John Locke, his attention to epistemology, that is the theory of knowledge, was typical of the spirit of the times.[60] Edwards aimed to show that 'Calvinistic notions of God's moral government' were consistent with 'the commonsense of mankind',[61] 'commonsense' being, as George Marsden notes, one of 'the great touchstones' of eighteenth-century thought.[62] Crucial to Edwards' argument in *The Freedom of the Will* was that God does not compel people to behave in a manner contrary to their wills. Bebbington summarizes: 'Free acts are not forced though they are caused. This was to contend that human beings are part of an ordered universe, but to hold that nevertheless they are responsible for what they do. Edwards was reinterpreting the sovereignty of God as an expression of the law of cause and effect.'[63] Fuller's use of *The Freedom of the Will* indicates that *The Gospel Worthy* was influenced by aspects of the cultural mood and intellectual climate of the age.

## Reactions to The Gospel Worthy

Fuller had correctly foreseen the negative way *The Gospel Worthy* would be received by some. In the wake of publication, Ryland recorded that Fuller had to contend with many 'ignorant people' who 'began to raise an outcry against the book and its author; charging him and his friends with having forsaken the doctrines of grace, and left the good old way.'[64] This comment refers in the main to High Calvinist opponents from within Fuller and Ryland's own denomination. But there were also others in the wider Christian world who thought that Fuller had not gone far enough in modifying his theology. As a result of his decision to go to print, Fuller would be engaged in controversy for the rest of his life.

---

[59] D.W. Bebbington, *Evangelicalism in Modern Britain: A History from the 1730s to the 1980s* (London: Unwin Hyman, 1989), p. 6.
[60] See Rack, *Reasonable Enthusiast*, p. 163; Bebbington, *Evangelicalism*, p. 48. The degree to which Edwards was or was not influenced by Locke is discussed by Ramsey in his introduction to Edwards, *The Freedom of the Will*, pp. 47-64.
[61] J. Edwards to John Erskine, 7 July 1752, *Jonathan Edwards: Letters and Personal Writings* in *The Works of Jonathan Edwards*, vol. 16, ed. G.S. Glaghorn (London and New Haven: Yale University Press, 1998), p. 491.
[62] G.M. Marsden, *Jonathan Edwards: A Life* (Yale University Press: New Haven & London, 2003), p. 437.
[63] Bebbington, *Evangelicalism*, p. 64.
[64] Ryland, *Andrew Fuller*, 2nd edn, p. 132.

HIGH CALVINIST OPPOSITION TO *THE GOSPEL WORTHY* IN PARTICULAR BAPTIST LIFE

Much of the opposition to *The Gospel Worthy* came from High Calvinists, and much of it was both petty and personal. Pride of place goes to Rushden Baptist Church, ten miles to the south of Kettering, and its pastor William Knowles. One of the Rushden members, a Mrs Wright, had moved to Weekley, a village immediately to the north of Kettering. She started to attend Fuller's church, but when she asked to come into membership in 1785, Rushden refused to provide the normal letter of transfer because, as Knowles informed her, 'the church at Kettering had gone off from their former principles'.[65] The Kettering deacons wrote to Rushden on 7 August 1785, protesting 'that we know of no one principle relating to the doctrines of grace which we feel in the least inclined to give up'. They asked the church at Rushden to 'consider the matter again'. Two months later, they had received no reply, prompting them to write again, in stronger terms. The Rushden Baptists eventually responded in December, again refusing to provide a letter of 'dismission' for Mrs Wright and accusing the Kettering church of 'lording it' over them. The real root of the problem was freely acknowledged in the church book at Kettering:

> That there are differences in sentiment between us and the church at Rushden, is true. We consider the doctrines of grace as entirely consistent with a free address to every sinner, and with an universal obligation on all men where the gospel is preached to repent of their sins, and turn to God through Jesus Christ. They think otherwise, and it is simply on account of this difference that they have disowned communion with us.

Described as 'a timid character', Mrs Wright was reluctant to transfer membership without a formal dismissal from Rushden, despite the Kettering church now being ready to receive her without a letter of transfer. It was not until 1796, two years after the death of Knowles, that such a letter was provided. J.W. Morris mentioned a congregation close to Kettering which refused to have any dealings with Fuller or 'allow any of their members to have fellowship with his church' for seven years. Probably, he was referring to Rushden, although doubtless there were other candidates.[66]

A number of High Calvinists published pamphlet replies to *The Gospel Worthy*. Two in particular, both written from a High Calvinist perspective by Particular Baptists, are important because Fuller responded to them in print. These were by William Button and John Martin, both of whom were London pas-

---

[65] See 'The Church Book of Kettering Baptist Church (The 'Little Meeting'), 1773-1815', Fuller Baptist Church, Kettering, pp. 84-95, 106, for information and quotations in this paragraph. The relevant entries are for 28 July, 17 August, 6 November, 22 December 1785 and 26 February 1796. Cf. the use made of some of the same material by Haykin, *One Heart and Soul*, pp. 150-51.

[66] Morris, *Andrew Fuller*, 2nd edn, p. 271.

tors.⁶⁷ In his responses, Fuller restated his basic arguments again, something he was able to do with vigour.⁶⁸ These disputes show the gulf that had now opened up between Fuller and his High Calvinist opponents. Fuller was also drawn into dispute with the leader of the New Connexion of General Baptists, Dan Taylor, who held evangelical Arminian views, and with Abraham Booth, another London pastor who, although he was not a High Calvinist, was wary of some of Fuller's emphases. The dispute with Taylor, who initially responded to *The Gospel Worthy* using the pseudonym 'Philanthropos', would, in particular, leave its mark on the second edition of *The Gospel Worthy*.⁶⁹

## *The Gospel Worthy*: Second Edition

1801 saw the publication of a new edition of *The Gospel Worthy*. In his 'Advertisement' to the book, Fuller made it clear he had made a number of significant changes to his original work, stating that 'corrections and additions form a considerable part of this edition ... it would be inexcusable to have lived all this time without gaining any additional light ... upon the subject.'⁷⁰ In fact, although the essential argument remained the same, it was a thoroughly revised and expanded work (in terms of style alone there were numerous alterations), and the extent of the differences between the two editions has not always been recognized.⁷¹ Focusing on two of the most important changes helps summarize the movement in Fuller's thought that had taken place between 1785 and 1801.

### *Fuller's Change of Views on the Atonement*

First of all, it should be noted that Fuller incorporated some significant modifications ('concessions' as Dan Taylor's biographer, Adam Taylor, had called them),⁷² to his views concerning the death of Christ. In the course of his disputes with Taylor, Fuller had changed his mind on the extent of the atonement. Fuller was now arguing that the particularity of redemption consisted 'not in the degree of Christ's suffering (as though he must have suffered more if more

---

⁶⁷ W. Button, *Remarks on a Treatise Entitled The Gospel Worthy of All Acceptation* (London, 1785); J. Martin, *Thoughts on the Duty of Man Relative to Faith in Jesus Christ...* (London, 1788-91).
⁶⁸ *Fuller's Works*, II, pp. 417-458; 716-736.
⁶⁹ For more on these disputes see Morden, *Offering Christ to the World*, pp. 52-102.
⁷⁰ From the 'Advertisement to the Second Edition', *The Gospel Worthy*, in *Fuller's Works*, II, p. 328.
⁷¹ R.W. Oliver, 'The Emergence of a Strict and Particular Baptist Community Among the English Calvinistic Baptists, 1770-1850' (PhD thesis, CNAA [London Bible College], 1986), pp. 115-16, is helpful in tracing the development of Fuller's thought on the atonement.
⁷² A. Taylor, *Memoirs of the Rev Dan. Taylor* (London: Baynes and Son, 1820), pp. 178-82.

had been finally saved) ... but in the sovereign purpose and design of the Father and the Son.' The sufferings of Christ, he continued, 'are of infinite value, sufficient to have saved all the world, and a thousand worlds, if it had pleased God ... to have made them effectual to this end.'[73] Fuller was now locating the particularity of redemption in the application of the atonement or, more precisely, 'in the design of the Father and the Son, respecting the persons to whom it shall be applied'.[74] This enabled Fuller to continue to speak of a 'special design' in the death of Christ, because those to whom the atonement would be applied had been decided in the purposes of God 'before time'. Nevertheless, Fuller's view of the atonement could now properly be called 'general'. As he stated: 'if all the inhabitants of the globe could be persuaded to return to God in Christ's name, they would undoubtedly be accepted by him.'[75]

Consequently, in the second edition of *The Gospel Worthy*, Fuller completely rewrote the section on particular redemption.[76] In the first edition, he had written that there was 'no necessity' for someone to have a 'particular interest in Christ's death, in order to make trusting him his duty'. Fuller used an illustration of a man condemned for treason. Was it not right, Fuller reasoned, for the man to admit his guilt and ask 'his prince' for mercy, not knowing how that plea might be received? There would be no other course of action he could take. Similarly, it was the duty of the sinner to 'cast his soul on Christ for mercy, determined either to be saved by him or to perish at his feet'.[77] This echoed Fuller's own conversion experience, and he supported his argument with quotations from the Calvinist writers Coles, Ridgely, Witsius and Owen.

In the second edition, this line of reasoning was abandoned completely, together with most of the quotations (which Taylor had attacked as proving nothing). The atonement, Fuller now argued, was not 'a literal payment of a debt'. If it was, then it would be inconsistent, not only with 'indefinite invitations' but also with 'free forgiveness of sin', for sinners in the scriptures were directed to apply for forgiveness as 'supplicants rather than claimants'.[78] Christ's sacrifice was applied, by God's sovereign wisdom, to some and not to others, and so there was still, a 'peculiarity of design in the death of Christ'. But there was no inconsistency between maintaining both that there was this special design and also that there was a universal obligation to believe, an inconsistency which

---

[73] Fuller, *Reply to Philanthropos*, in *Fuller's Works*, II, pp. 488-89.

[74] From a 'Conversation with a friend at Edinburgh, on the subject of Particular Redemption, in 1805', recorded by Morris, *Andrew Fuller*, 2nd edn, p. 311.

[75] Fuller, *Reply to Philanthropos*, in *Fuller's Works*, II, p. 506.

[76] See Fuller, *The Gospel Worthy*, 1st edn, pp. 132-39; *The Gospel Worthy*, 2nd edn, pp. 373-75 in *Fuller's Works*, II, for the relevant sections.

[77] Fuller, *The Gospel Worthy*, 1st edn, pp. 132-33.

[78] This of course reflects Fuller's own conversion experience. Cf. the comments of M.A.G. Haykin, 'Particular Redemption in the Writings of Andrew Fuller (1754-1815)' in D.W Bebbington (ed.), *The Gospel in the World: International Baptist Studies* (Studies in Baptist History and Thought, 1; Carlisle: Paternoster, 2002), p. 117.

would have been present if Christ's death had not been, in some sense, for all.

Taylor had continued to press him in this area, even after he had made these changes, but Fuller now felt sure of his ground:

> If God, through the death of his Son, has promised salvation to all who comply with the gospel; and if there be no natural impossibility as to a compliance, nor any obstruction but that which arises from aversion of heart; exhortations and invitations to believe are consistent; and our duty, as ministers of the gospel, is to administer them.[79]

The distinction between natural and moral inability, as the ground for asserting that saving faith was the duty of all, had been maintained. Even more crucially, so had the ground on which the gospel could be offered to all. Once again, Fuller probably had some help from Jonathan Edwards in coming to these conclusions.[80] Fuller had also come into contact with the writings of other American theologians from the New England (New Divinity) school, disciples of Edwards such as Joseph Bellamy, Samuel Hopkins and Edwards' son Jonathan Edwards, Jr, who went beyond Edwards in abandoning strict Calvinism and openly adopting a Grotian, or moral government view of the atonement. Fuller went some way towards adopting some 'moral government' language in his own works.[81]

### An Increased Emphasis on Evangelism

Practical considerations to do with gospel preaching were never far from the surface in Fuller's theology, and the second important difference between the first and second editions of *The Gospel Worthy* was a new note of boldness, indeed of urgency, as he pressed the practical consequences of his thesis on his readers. In the first edition, there were several notes of caution sounded in the main concluding section, 'Inferences from the Whole'.[82] One example in particular can be cited. Fuller had made it clear that:

> It is not intended here to vindicate all the language that has been addressed to unconverted sinners, nor all the principles of those whose practice it has been to address them. Doubtless there have been extremes in these as in other things, and many who have used them have been very wide of the truth as to sentiments on other subjects; but a sober use of such means is nevertheless to be retained.

Fuller followed this up with some detailed comments on what he termed the

---

[79] Fuller, *The Gospel Worthy*, 2nd edn, in *Fuller's Works*, II, pp. 373-74.
[80] Compare, for example, the statements from Fuller's *Reply to Philanthropos* just cited (Fuller's Works, II, pp. 488-89, 506) with *The Freedom of the Will*, p. 435.
[81] Morden, *Offering Christ to the World*, pp. 89-92.
[82] Fuller, *The Gospel Worthy*, 1st edn, pp. 163-84.

'order' of addressing exhortations to the unconverted. Concerned to guard against careless evangelistic preaching, he urged that a gospel minister should, amongst other things, first 'labour to convince them of the evil of their sin', together with 'the awfulness and equity of their condemnation'. Hearers should also be exhorted to 'pray to God for an interest in his salvation'.[83] But, as with the section on Particular Redemption, in the second edition these pages were to be completely rewritten.

Fuller's approach in 1801 was to jettison the paragraph quoted above and drastically shorten and alter his comments about the order of addressing the unconverted. In fact, none of the sentences cited above from 'Inferences from the Whole' survive in the corresponding chapter in the second edition, entitled 'Concluding Reflections'. Fuller quickly listed the need to preach about subjects such as 'the just requirements of the law' and the 'impossibility of being justified by works' as a precursor to gospel preaching. But the central point he wanted to make was that although 'these representations [were] proper and necessary', there was a danger that ministers would be too reticent in preaching the gospel to their hearers. The truth was that it was 'never unsafe' to introduce the gospel. He continued by using an illustration from the Napoleonic wars: 'Divine truths are like chain shot, they go to together, and we need not perplex ourselves which should enter first; if anyone enter, it will draw the rest after it.'[84]

The reference to 'chain shot' was to the practice of connecting two cannon balls with a chain before firing both at the enemy with the aim of causing maximum damage. The image may have been alarming, but Fuller's point was clear enough. It was not necessarily that Fuller was repudiating everything that he now left out of *The Gospel Worthy*, as he made clear in his 'Advertisement' to the second edition. Rather, there were other things which appeared to be more 'immediate'. Fuller had experienced much in the years 1785 to 1801, in addition to the theological disputes referred to earlier. These years had seen the development of his own thoroughly evangelistic pastoral ministry, and the formation of the BMS, with Fuller as the very active secretary. By 1801, he was clear that the need of the hour was not caution – rather, it was committed gospel preaching. Throughout this period, Fuller's views were shaped by evangelical forces (e.g. Edwards), and driven by evangelical concerns (a desire to safeguard the theological basis for offering the gospel to all). Bebbington speaks of those whose 'eagerness for converts had the effect of modifying the theology of a section of Evangelicalism'.[85] Fuller certainly fits this pattern. His overriding concern now was that Christ should be offered to all.

---

[83] Fuller, *The Gospel Worthy*, 1st edn, p. 164.
[84] Fuller, *The Gospel Worthy*, 2nd edn, in *Fuller's Works*, II, pp. 391-92.
[85] Bebbington, *Evangelicalism*, p. 9.

## The Impact of *The Gospel Worthy*

### *The Impact of* The Gospel Worthy *on Particular Baptist Life*

Fuller's contemporaries recognised his importance as a theologian. Ryland, a significant thinker in his own right, considered Fuller 'the most judicious and able theological writer that ever belonged to the Baptist denomination'.[86] Joseph Ivimey, writing soon after Fuller's death, believed that the Kettering pastor enjoyed a high and, in many ways, 'unrivalled station' as the denomination's theologian.[87] These are just two of many comments that could have been cited. Undoubtedly, there were other factors at work weaning the Particular Baptists away from High Calvinism. As already noted, the influence of the Bristol Academy needs to be borne in mind, as do the importance of other published works which attacked the basic tenets of High Calvinism. In particular, the minister who had originally recommended Edwards to Fuller, Robert Hall, Sr, produced the influential *Help to Zion's Travellers* (1781), a work which challenged High Calvinism with some success.[88] But *The Gospel Worthy* was without doubt the most important and most developed statement of evangelical Calvinism the denomination produced, helping to crystallise the thinking of some who were already moving in the same direction as Fuller, as well as influencing many more who were as yet uncertain. Ryland wrote of how an older minister who initially opposed *The Gospel Worthy*, Joshua Thomas, 'came over to Mr Fuller's views at last'.[89] He would have been one of many. In 1797, a group of deacons in a Baptist Church in Hull wrote to the evangelical Baptist pastor Joseph Kinghorn. The Hull church wanted Kinghorn to help them to find a minister and specified the sort of man they were looking for. Amongst other things, they were clear that he was to be a 'lively, zealous and affectionate preacher' and 'orthodox'. The letter has a marginal note explaining the meaning of 'orthodox'. It says 'of Mr Fuller's sentiments'.[90] Fuller's triumph in writing *The Gospel Worthy*, and then effectively defending its central arguments, was considerable.

### The Gospel Worthy *and the Revival of Particular Baptist Life*

Consequently, Fuller and the treatise for which he was best known occupies a

---

[86] Cited by Clipsham, 'Development of a Doctrine', p. 99.

[87] J. Ivimey, *A History of the English Baptists* (4 vols; London: Hinton, Holdsworth & Ball, 1811-30), IV, p. 532.

[88] See R. Hall, Sr, *The Complete Works of the Late Robert Hall* (ed. J.W. Morris; London, 1828), pp. 47-199, for the second edition.

[89] Ryland, *Andrew Fuller*, p. 131.

[90] Cited by A.H. Kirkby, 'The Theology of Andrew Fuller in its Relation to Calvinism' (PhD thesis, Edinburgh University, 1956), p. 11. The letter is dated 23 March 1797, from three Deacons at George Street Baptist Church in Hull. Kinghorn was pastor of St Mary's Baptist Church, Norwich. The original is held in the archives at St Mary's.

central place in the story of the revival of Particular Baptist life which took place at the end of the eighteenth century. That such a revival was taking place is attested by a number of sources. In 1793, Fuller wrote a letter detailing 'the state of religion in Northamptonshire'.[91] This firstly indicated the triumph of Fuller's own brand of evangelical Calvinism amongst Particular Baptists in the county. Out of twenty-one churches, there were four or five who embraced 'what is called the High Calvinist scheme', including the Rushden church pastored by William Knowles. But the rest, according to Fuller, made 'no scruple' about openly 'exhorting' people to believe the gospel. The county with which both Gill and Brine had been associated in their ministerial careers was now coming down decisively on Fuller's side. Ministers could and should offer the gospel openly and freely to all.[92] But the letter also indicated something else. The churches which embraced what Fuller here termed 'Moderate Calvinism' were growing. Fuller spoke of a 'readiness discovered in many parts of the county for hearing the gospel', and of a 'considerable increase' among the churches. Indeed, he could be more specific, stating that: 'Seven or eight new churches have been raised amongst [us] within the last 20 years.' There is no reason to doubt the figures Fuller gave, particularly as he expected his correspondent, possibly a General Baptist layman, to publish them. Together with the number of people regularly coming to hear Fuller in Kettering (where congregations were often a thousand strong),[93] these figures indicate that something significant was taking place.

Nor was this growth confined to Northamptonshire. The 1790s saw the publication of several volumes of John Rippon's *Baptist Annual Register*, which provides what Nuttall describes as a 'fine contemporary record of [English Particular Baptist] churches'.[94] The formation of such a comprehensive survey was in itself an indicator of the health and confidence of the denomination. In Volume One of the *Register* (covering the period from 1790 to the first part of 1793), there were 326 churches listed; in Volume Three (which covered 1798-1801), 361 churches were recorded by Rippon.[95] These figures can be compared with those quoted at the beginning of this paper, which suggested that in the 1750s there were only 150 Calvinistic Baptist churches in England and

---

[91] G.F. Nuttall, 'The State of Religion in Northamptonshire (1793) by Andrew Fuller', *Baptist Quarterly* 29.4 (1981), pp. 177-79. All quotations and information in this paragraph and the next, unless otherwise stated, are from Fuller's letter and Nuttall's introductory remarks. Fuller was writing here of the churches within the county of Northamptonshire, not the Northamptonshire Association as a whole.

[92] G.F. Nuttall, 'Northamptonshire and the Modern Question: A Turning Point in Eighteenth-Century Dissent', *Journal of Theological Studies* 16.1 (April, 1965), pp. 101-23.

[93] Ryland, *Andrew Fuller*, 2nd edn, pp. 246, 383.

[94] G.F. Nuttall, 'The Baptist Churches and Their Ministers: Rippon's Baptist Annual Register', *Baptist Quarterly* 30.8 (1984), pp. 383-87.

[95] John Rippon, *The Baptist Annual Register* (4 vols; London: Dilly, Button and Thomas, 1793-1803), I, pp. 8-13; III, pp. 3-40.

Wales (in Rippon's surveys the Welsh churches were counted separately and do not appear in the figures quoted above). If these statistics are even approximately right (the complete accuracy of the 1750s figure is open to some question), then something of great significance was happening. The late-eighteenth century was, of course, a time of rapid population increase, but this was certainly outstripped by the growth of the Particular Baptist churches.[96] In addition to his figures, in Volume Three of the *Baptist Annual Register,* Rippon also provided extensive notes on many of the congregations listed. Page after page reveals that many churches were experiencing 'considerable additions', facing 'the pleasing necessity' of enlarging their meeting houses and were increasingly involved in village preaching.[97] It is surely correct to say that a revitalization of Particular Baptist life in England was taking place and that Fuller's theology had been an important catalyst for growth.

Nevertheless, Fuller's triumph was not complete. Older High Calvinists would continue to reject 'duty faith', and their criticisms would be taken up by a new generation. Key leaders of the nineteenth-century Strict Baptist movement such as William Gadsby and J.C. Philpot were scathing in their condemnation of Fuller. For Gadsby, Fuller was 'the greatest enemy the church of God ever had, as his sentiments were so much cloaked in the sheep's clothing'. Fuller was blamed for the erosion of true Calvinistic principles amongst the Particular Baptists, for opening the door to mixed communion and, along with it, Arminianism.[98] This view has some supporters today,[99] but Kenneth Dix's verdict is fair, and deserves to be quoted in full:

> The Strict Baptists did not treat Fuller with the respect he deserved as the leading Baptist theologian of his day. There was a failure to accept Fuller's testimony of his commitment to 'strict Calvinism', or of the very gracious way he wrote of his opposition to mixed communion principles. There were certainly times when Fuller made statements which might have been construed as a departure from the particularist position, but this was not the case. His belief in an atonement that was sufficient for all men but efficacious only for the elect, offended high-Calvinists, but he never gave up the seventeenth-century confessions. Andrew Fuller was no more responsible for any shift from orthodox Calvinism in the nineteenth century than the men who framed the 1677 Confession could be held responsible for the path taken by some of their opponents into the chilling winds of high-Calvinism.[100]

---

[96] Bebbington, *Evangelicalism*, p. 21.
[97] Rippon, *Baptist Annual Register*, III, pp. 5-9.
[98] K. Dix, *Strict and Particular: English Strict and Particular Baptists in the Nineteenth Century* (Didcot: Baptist Historical Society, 2001), pp. 37 n., 103.
[99] See especially G.M. Ella, *Law and Gospel in the Theology of Andrew Fuller* (Eggleston, Co. Durham: Go Publications, 1996), *passim.*
[100] Dix, *Strict and Particular*, pp. 269-70.

This is an assessment with which I heartily concur. Certainly nineteenth-century Strict Baptists regarded Fuller as their *bête noire*, and so an analysis of his theology is important in any description of the emergence of the Strict and Particular Baptist Community.[101] But the nineteenth-century shift away from what Fuller termed 'strict Calvinism' was far more attributable, as Ian Sellers states, to 'the tide of nineteenth-century opinion [which] was running against religious particularism of any form'.[102] Those who laid the 'blame' for the erosion of Calvinistic distinctives amongst the Particular Baptists at Fuller's door were wrong. Rather than abandoning Calvinism and opening the door to Arminianism, Fullerism actually opened the door to expansive gospel ministry by allowing increasing numbers within the Particular Baptist denomination to hold together strict Calvinism and invitational gospel preaching. That he was able to do this so successfully was a large part of his genius as a theologian.

## Conclusion

Ernest Payne, seeking to summarize Fuller's theological contribution to Particular Baptist life, stated: 'It was Andrew Fuller's vigorous independent mind which first broke out of the trammels of Hyper-Calvinism and produced in *The Gospel Worthy of All Acceptation* ... a little book destined to effect a theological and practical revolution in most of the Calvinist [i.e. Calvinistic Baptist] churches.'[103] For once, Payne, normally such a careful historian, overstates his case. As noted, there were a number of Particular Baptists who had never accepted the High Calvinism typified in the works of Gill and Brine, and there were a number of others who were already embracing views similar to Fuller's by the time *The Gospel Worthy* was published. Nevertheless, once all the necessary caveats have been made, there is ample evidence to support Noll's claim that its publication was indeed a 'critical moment'. It was probably at the beginning of the nineteenth century that the term 'Fullerism' decisively entered the theological vocabulary of the Particular Baptists, appearing as early as 1804 in pamphlets such as *A Blow at the Root of Fullerism* and *Fullerism Defended* to describe the Edwardsean evangelical Calvinism which was increasingly the hallmark of the denomination. As Geoffrey Nuttall points out, its coining and subsequent acceptance by friend and foe alike 'points to a remarkable achievement'.[104] The revival in Particular Baptist life bears the unmistakable stamp of

---

[101] Oliver, 'Emergence of a Strict and Particular Baptist Community', p. 119.

[102] I. Sellers, 'John Howard Hinton, Theologian', *Baptist Quarterly* 33.3 (1989), p. 123. Evangelical Calvinism would enjoy a significant resurgence at the end of the nineteenth century in the person of C.H. Spurgeon.

[103] E.A. Payne, *College Street Church, Northampton, 1697-1947* (London: Kingsgate Press, 1947), p. 22.

[104] Morris, *Andrew Fuller*, 2nd edn, pp. 238-39; Nuttall, 'Northamptonshire and the Modern Question', p. 101.

*The Gospel Worthy*, and its publication was a 'watershed' in Baptist history, as well as being an important landmark in the history of Christianity in the modern world.

# CHAPTER 9

# Caleb Evans and the Anti-Slavery Question[1]

Roger Hayden

### A Baptist View of Civil Liberty

In a sermon titled *The Remembrance of Former Days*, preached in Broadmead on 5 November 1778, Caleb Evans spoke of what he understood by 'civil liberty' in these terms,

> Liberty from arbitrary confinement at the mere will of a superior independent of law and justice, liberty from unjust condemnation and death; and liberty to enjoy and dispose of our own property. In every free state, and such, blessed be God, is ours, this liberty is enjoyed, nor can there be true freedom without it. Where an arbitrary tyrant can imprison who he please, without even producing an accusation, or naming the accusers; where he can deprive of life, merely to gratify his resentment and caprice; and where the property of his subjects is at his absolute disposal, not their own: what are such men but poor, abject slaves, who may be rather said to breathe than live; reduced as they are to an equality with brutes, the property and at the disposal of the masters who happen to possess them. A more humiliating state cannot, I think, be conceived off. And yet this, alas, was once the case in too great a degree, with the inhabitants of this land ...

In a footnote, Evans added,

> If any man, or sett of men, over whom I have no legal controll, have the absolute disposal of my property, how can I still be a free-man? ... Even if it should be proved that slavery is preferable to liberty; or that to have our property at the absolute disposal of those over whom we have no control is to be FREE...[2]

---

[1] This article is the text of a paper given by Rev Dr Roger Hayden, when President of the Baptist Historical Society to the Society's Day Conference at Bristol Baptist College on 13 May 2000, and subsequently published in the *Baptist Quarterly*, 39.1 (2001), pp. 4-14.

[2] Caleb Evans, *The Remembrance of former days.... 1778* (Bristol: W. Pine, 1778), pp. 13-15.

## Bristol Baptists and the Slavery Issue

In terms of British Constitutional liberty, particularly as it affected the repeal of the Test and Corporation Acts at home and the right of tax-paying American colonists abroad to have representation in the British parliament, Caleb Evans was a campaigner. His published works and his activity within the larger Bristol Dissenting community has been well researched by James Bradley.[3] However, the nearest Evans came to political action for the anti-slavery movement was when the issue surfaced within the Western Baptist Association in 1788 and, as the Moderator for that Assembly, he signed a resolution to recommend

> earnestly to the members of all our churches to unite in promoting to the utmost of their power every scheme, that is or may be proposed, to procure the *abolition* of a traffic so unjust, inhuman, and disgraceful; and the continuance of which tends to counteract and destroy the operation of the benevolent principles and spirit of our common Christianity.[4]

The 1789 Association Letter contained a copy of Granville Sharp's reply on behalf of the abolitionists, in which Sharp noted that Caleb Evans sent one of his sons to London with the five guineas. The Association's intention had already found its way into the *Bristol Gazette,* 12 June 1788, along with other earlier correspondence and articles arising out of Thomas Clarkson's visit to Bristol in June 1787. Clarkson had a letter of introduction to a Bristol Quaker, Harry Gandy. Gandy's experience of two slave voyages as a young man had brought him into the Bristol Society of Friends who had already been campaigning for abolition for a decade.[5]

Clarkson's view of Bristol attitudes to slavery at this time was, 'every body seemed to execrate it, though no one thought of its abolition'.[6] The issue remained a lively one in the Western Baptist Association, and two more donations of five guineas 'from our little fund' were sent to Granville Sharp and the London Committee in 1789 and 1790, with the issue being commended each year to local congregations for action.[7] Baptist experience then, as now, made it easy to have resolutions passed at the Association annual meeting but difficult to get them on to the agenda of a local congregation for further action.

---

[3] James E. Bradley, *Religion, Revolution and English Radicalism: Non-conformity in Eighteenth-century Politics and Society* (Cambridge: Cambridge University Press, 1990), especially chapters 4-7 for Caleb Evans.
[4] *Western Baptist Association Letter*, 1788, p. 8.
[5] Thomas Clarkson, *The History of the Rise, Progress and Accomplishment of the Abolition of the African Slave Trade by the British Parliament* (2 vols; London, 1808), I, pp. 294-95.
[6] Clarkson, *History*, I, p. 297.
[7] *Western Baptist Association Letter*, 1789, p. 13; 1790, p. 11.

## Divisions within the Broadmead Church

There was no reference to the anti-slavery concern at Broadmead, either in the Baptist or the Independent (Little Church) minute books. The Anti-Slavery issue might be thought to have caught the congregations' attention not only because it was being widely canvassed in the Bristol press[8] and the Western Association but also because of its relevance to an application for membership which came before the church in the spring of 1789. 'Frances Coker, the descendant of African ancestors, gave a most intelligent and pleasing account of the work of God upon her soul and was accepted as a candidate for baptism'. A later hand, probably John Ryland's, added, 'Lived honourably and died comfortably, April 1820'.[9] However, there was no record of the Association's Anti-Slavery issue coming before a regular church meeting prior to the arrival of John Ryland. Other public issues did find a place, for example on 9 April 1789, the church book recorded that 'John Harris, John Page and Mr Lunell to be deputies' to act for the repeal of the Test Act.[10]

A key factor in the lack of response from Broadmead to the abolitionist concern could have been its obsession with the deep divisions in the congregation over the ministry of its associate minister and classical tutor at the Academy, Robert Hall, Jr Hall had been nominated a John Ward scholar and came to Bristol Academy at the age of fourteen in 1778. Caleb Evans had a considerable interest in the young man and prepared him to go on to further studies at King's College, Aberdeen, in November 1781. The young Hall had preached at the Broadmead mid-week service prior to moving to Scotland, and in the summer of 1783, supplied the Sunday ministry at Broadmead. A church meeting of 19 October 1783 invited Hall to become co-pastor with Evans when he finished at Aberdeen in 1785.[11] Hall accepted and in that year also took responsibility for tutoring classics at the Academy as James Newton's health was failing. He was also appointed pastor at the so-called 'Little Church', an independent congregation which had functioned in parallel with Broadmead since 1757.[12] Hall was now twenty-one and Evans forty-eight, the latter at the height of his powers.

Hall's pulpit ministry was popular, and the Broadmead congregation grew; but there were increasing tensions over Hall's doctrinal orthodoxy, his attitude to baptism, and his eccentric bachelor lifestyle. Eventually, he decided to seek a

---

[8] Some references to the press campaign in Peter Marshall, *The Anti-Slave Trade movement in Bristol* (Bristol: Bristol Branch of the Historical Association, 1998, [1968]), pp. 1, 7, 18-20.

[9] *Broadmead Baptist Church Minute Book*, 1779-1817, p. 61. (Bristol Record Office, 30251/M1/3). Hereafter, *Broadmead Minutes*.

[10] *Broadmead Minutes*, p. 62.

[11] *Broadmead Minutes*, pp. 31-32.

[12] *Independent Church Minute Book*, 1757-1818, for 1783. (Bristol Record Office, 30251/M2/1). Hereafter *Little Church Book*.

more congenial pastorate, and his contacts with St. Andrew's Street, Cambridge, were deepened when its ailing minister, Robert Robinson, died in June 1790. Hall went to preach at Cambridge over a six-month period and gave his resignation to Broadmead on 11 November 1790.[13]

Caleb Evans, aware of the tensions over Hall's ministry, affirmed his personal support of Hall, while recognizing that the two Broadmead congregations and the Academy had problems with aspects of his ministry. Hall initially indicated that 'my opinions upon some points of religious and moral speculation are different from those proposed by this Society', and his preference for 'a congregation in which I shall meet with sentiments more congenial with my own and where I shall not be in danger of falling into acts of collusion or incurring the vexations of honesty. I have always endeavoured to avoid the mixing of private passions with religious conduct'.[14] He had come close to Socinian views, and Andrew Fuller and John Ryland, Jr, had both mentioned their concern to Hall, which Caleb Evans would also share because of his own trenchant and published attack on it. It emerged that Hall was 'not a strict Calvinist', but in that respect Evans would have been more sympathetic, having himself espoused a moderated Calvinism which Andrew Fuller had acknowledged in his *Gospel Worthy of All Acceptation* (1785) by quoting Caleb Evans at length on the issue. It had also been claimed he was not a Baptist, an issue about which Hall felt he had been seriously misunderstood. He affirmed that in regard to the subject and the mode he was a Baptist, that he believed infant baptism to be 'a perversion' of the ordinance, but he did not think he could 're-baptize anyone who has been sprinkled in adult age'.[15]

There were those who felt that Caleb Evans had manoeuvred Hall's resignation by suppressing full discussion in the Church Meeting, declining to accept a resolution for Hall's re-invitation to the pastorate for lack of a second, and threatening his own resignation if such a course were followed. That matter came to a head after a series of church meetings in November and December 1790 when an attempt to reconcile the estranged parties took place at the Bristol Mansion House on 18 December prior to a church meeting the following day. John Harris, the senior Broadmead deacon, and Arthur Tozer, the senior deacon of the Little Church stood with Caleb Evans while John Prothero and John James stood with Robert Hall. It was a total disaster with Hall, Prothero, and James making accusations against Caleb Evans, Harris, and Tozer, and then refusing to hear a reply to what they had alleged.

The matter flared up when, in early January 1791, Hall and his supporters circulated their view of events in London. Harris and Tozer believed their own characters, as well as Caleb Evans', had been 'grossly injured by a paper lately sent them and now in circulation in London and other places' by Prothero and

---

[13] *Broadmead Minutes*, pp. 68-70.
[14] *Broadmead Minutes*, pp. 69-70.
[15] J.W. Morris, *Biographical Recollections of Robert Hall*, 1833, p. 72.

James regarding the Mansion House meeting on 18 December 1790.[16] Caleb Evans' account of the special church meeting demanded by Harris and Tozer, which covers ten pages of the Church Book, was his last entry and concluded with his own view of this sad situation. He was deeply hurt by the 'unjust' and 'unprecedented' attacks on his character made by some at Broadmead, complaining that, after thirty-two years of fidelity and success, 'to be traduced, calumniated, vilified, my ministry forsook and the Table of the Lord at which I reside withdrawn from - is treatment which surely could never be suspected to have been given to a Pastor, by a people who had professed to love and honour him'.[17] After affirming his own 'almost unconquerable attachment' to Hall, he then moved to a defence of himself. 'Mr Hall has said in London, to my certain knowledge, that I was capable of *telling* deliberate lyes, that what he had hitherto done was but *milk and water,* but he had pepper and salt in store for me.' Further, Hall said 'he must lye down under a "blasted character" for I have blasted it for him at Bristol thoro'ly, or words to that effect'.[18] Hall's biographers are aware of this clash with Evans, acknowledge his Socinian tendencies, the concern of Fuller and Ryland, the personal support of Evans for Hall, and move speedily to the ministry at Cambridge.

Was it only doctrine and life-style that led to this outburst at the Mansion House? Timothy Whelan's recent article on Hall's support of the abolitionist cause under the assumed name of 'Britannicus' in the *Bristol Gazette* of 7 and 14 February 1788 gives a clear indication of Hall's own strong feelings.[19] Hall concluded his second letter: 'It is by no means my intention to enter into a particular consideration of the *policy* of abolishing the Slave Trade; I think it is best to submit this to the wisdom of the legislature'. This was the position of many Bristolians, and perhaps that of Evans and Harris, but the debate would move on quickly from there. There is no doubt in my mind that the paper's printer, William Pine, would be well aware of Hall's identity as Pine had published and printed at least sixteen sermons, tracts, and books by Caleb Evans since 1771. Hall's opening sentence of his letter to his father on 10 February 1788 told him: 'We have a great deal of talk here about the slave-trade as I understand from your letter you have had too'. It was the talk of the city, and everyone who lived and worked there was caught up in the outcome of the aboli-

---

[16] *Broadmead Minutes*, 25 January 1791. Harris and Tozer's published defence of themselves includes publication of an inter-change of letters between Hall and Evans in Nov and Dec 1790; and then the publication of documents in which Harris and Tozer defend themselves against what they feel to be the serious misrepresentations of Pritchard and James, published 31 January 1791. A copy of this, owned by deacon Paul Nash, has recently been found in the Broadmead Baptist Church Archive, but most importantly there is absolutely no discussion of the slave trade issue in this document.

[17] *Broadmead Minutes*, p. 83.

[18] *Broadmead Minutes*, p. 85.

[19] T. Whelan, 'Robert Hall and the Bristol Slave-trade Debate, 1787-1788', *Baptist Quarterly*, 38.5 (2000), pp. 212-24.

tionists' cause, which particularly included the Broadmead minister, Caleb Evans, and members of the congregation who were engaged in trade, shipping, and sugar.

## Caleb Evans and the Broadmead Elite

Caleb Evans was born in Bristol and grew up in Broadmead, a well-to-do nonconformist community, where his father was the minister. He was sent to London for formal education. While there, he was baptized by Samuel Stennett, minister of Little Wild Street Baptist Church, and received a call to Christian ministry which was confirmed when he was invited to join the Josiah Thomsons, father and son, at Unicorn Yard in London. Evans moved among the 'elite' London Baptist society of the Stennetts,[20] and had as a family friend nearby Andrew Gifford, who collected coins for King George III, lectured for the institution in Sloane Square which became the British Museum, and was a confidant of George Whitefield. When Foskett died, Caleb was invited to join his father, Hugh, at Broadmead and, after an initial hesitation, came back to Bristol in 1759.[21]

Once more, he was among friends who held key roles in the city's commercial and public life. The Pope family was no longer in membership at Broadmead, but Andrew Pope was a generous benefactor. His grandfather, Michael Pope, had bought out Whitson Court when Terrill's widow had died in 1691 and built a second Sugar House at Lewin's Mead, which remained in the Pope family until 1808 when the family moved into banking. Michael was admitted a member of the Merchant Venturers Society on 18 July 1720 and was Sheriff in 1733. Andrew Pope was Master of the Merchant Venturers Society in 1769, Sheriff of Bristol in 1763 and Mayor in 1776.[22] A member of the Little Church, deacon Nathaniel Wraxall, who died in 1786, had been 'swordbearer for the city of Bristol' since 1781.[23] Most important among all these connections for Caleb Evans was John Harris. The Harris family had Broadmead connections going back into the seventeenth century. John was baptized in 1746, and he and Caleb grew up together in the church. John was elected deacon in 1760, just as Caleb came back to Bristol, and for over thirty years, they worked together in

---

[20] See L. G. Champion, 'The Social Status of some 18th century Baptist Ministers', *Baptist Quarterly*, 25.1 (1973), pp. 10-14. See also Champion's *Farthing Rushlight: The Story of Andrew Gifford, 1700-1784*, London, 1961 with Gifford wide ranging contacts with the Royal Court, the British Library, and George Whitefield.

[21] R. Hayden, 'Evangelical Calvinism among Eighteenth-Century Particular Baptists' (PhD Thesis, University of Keele, 1991).

[22] Donald Jones, *Bristol's Sugar Trade and Refining Industry* (Bristol: Bristol Branch of the Historical Association, 1996). See also Bristol Record Society, Vol. 27, 1974, pp. 7-11; and Bristol and Gloucestershire Archaeological Society, Vol. 65, 1944, pp. 1-95 for I.V. Hall's article on Whitson Court Sugar House.

[23] *Little Church Book*, pp. 27, 31.

the leadership of Broadmead with a unity which remained unimpaired despite the distress caused by the young Robert Hall. It was Harris who had taken the initiative in proposing Robert Hall to the church in 1783.[24] In 1776, Harris, a hosier by trade, was appointed a Common Councillor for Bristol, having taken 'the oath appointed, instead of the Oaths of Allegiance and Supremacy and also the oath of a Common Council Man' before the Mayor on 12 September. Harris was Sheriff in 1776 and 1788, and appointed Mayor in 1790. In April 1789, Harris, Page, and Lunnell were appointed deputies by Broadmead to work for the repeal of the Test Act.[25]

A further significant commercial person and councillor was John Bull, Bristol's Sheriff in 1764 and Mayor-elect in 1778, who had to decline appointment because of ill health, though he later served for a short time in 1780. Originally, John Bull was a founding member of the Little Church on 25 December 1757. In January 1766, Bull gave an account of his Christian faith and was accepted for baptism and membership. However, it was then noted in the church book (without any explanation) that he had been privately baptized by Hugh Evans in 1765.[26] When Trustees were required for the newly formed Bristol Education Society, John Bull became the first treasurer, a post he filled until 1783. Another friend of Caleb Evans was Frederic Bull, a London tea merchant and member of Little Prescott Street who became Lord Mayor of London in 1773-74 and an MP from 1773-1784. He contributed £150 to the Bristol Education Society in 1770 and left it a legacy of £1,000.[27] Everything points to Caleb Evans' significant place among the leading political and commercial citizens of Bristol and London. His father, Hugh Evans, had paid four shillings and sixpence to purchase his place as a freeman of the city on 24 January 1735, to which he became entitled by his marriage to Sarah Brown. Caleb followed his father's example and paid the same amount to become a freeman of the city on 9 January 1765, thereby securing, as his father had done, his voting rights in the city.[28]

## Bristol, Sugar, and Slavery

It was impossible to ignore the slave connections for commerce particularly as it related to the sugar trade. Whitson Court, originally created in the 1660s by Ellis and Terrill, with Terrill's son, William, working on the Barbados Plantation at the end of the seventeenth century, was now in the hands of the Pope

---

[24] *Broadmead Minutes*, 19 Oct 1783, pp. 31-32.
[25] Bristol, *Proceedings of the Common Council, 1772-1782*, folio, 126. *Broadmead Minutes*, 9 April 1789, p. 62.
[26] *Broadmead Minutes*, 5 and 7 January 1766.
[27] D.W. Bebbington, 'Baptist MPs in Seventeenth and Eighteenth Centuries'. *Baptist Quarterly*, 28.6 (1980), pp. 245-62.
[28] Bristol Record Office. FC/BD/1/(M) 3, f. 40. FC/BB/1(V)3, f. 11.

family, who employed John Collett as a manager. Collett had a one-tenth holding in the ship *Molly,* which he relinquished in 1752, proof of his business interest depending indirectly on the slave trade; he was noted as a generous benefactor to Broadmead.[29] In the city, there were not large numbers of African slaves because 'the whole purpose of the Triangular Trade was to take goods from Bristol to Africa, slaves from Africa to the West Indies, and cargoes like sugar, tobacco and rum back to Bristol, not to bring African slaves to England'.[30] There are considerable myths about the numbers of black slaves in the city, but the newspapers provide no 'evidence in Bristol of a public auction or for the sale of more than one slave at a time. The picture of the warehouse full of slaves being auctioned on the dockside is entirely unfounded'.[31]

In 1765, Granville Sharp, the reformer and colleague of Clarkson, took up the case of a slave called Somerset, owned by David Lyle. Lyle mistreated Somerset and, when he became ill, abandoned him. Sharp took Somerset in, and the slave recovered, whereupon Lyle demanded him back. 'The whole case came to a head in 1772 when Lord Mansfield found that James Somerset (supported by Sharp), by the fact of having landed in England, became subject to English law which forbade the practice of slave owning. In effect, this meant the abolition of black slavery in the British Isles ... Africans therefore could be welcomed into a church community in their own right...'.[32]

For most Bristolians, it was the Triangular Trade and the obsession with sugar which meant society at large could not fail to have some awareness of the slave trade. Hugh Thomas underlines the close connection between sugar and the slave trade, delineating the eighteenth century as the age of sugar.

> We observe in England the consequences, in the fat faces in the portraits of the beauties and the kings, of the ostlers and the actresses. In 1750, already, 'the poorest English farm labourer's wife tok sugar in her tea'. She baked sweetcakes, and spread treacle on her bread as well as her porridge. Mrs Hannah Glasse's famous first cookery book in England (1747) ... shows that sugar was no longer to be considered primarily a medicine ... The pudding, hitherto made of fish or light meat now embarked on its unhealthy history as a separate sweet course ... How could the supply of sugar be assured? ... the plantations of the West Indies seemed, therefore, the source of all comfort.[33]

Even a minority group of Baptist dissenters knew the craving, and one, at

---

[29] David Richardson, *The Bristol Slave Traders: a Collective Portrait* (Bristol: Bristol Branch of the Historical Association, Reprint, 1997), pp. 14-15.

[30] R. Jones and R. Youseph, *The Black Population of Bristol in the Eighteenth Century* (Bristol: Bristol Branch of the Historical Association, Reprint, 1994), p. 2.

[31] Jones and Youseph, *The Black Population of Bristol,* p. 5.

[32] Jones and Youseph, *The Black Population of Bristol,* p. 9.

[33] H. Thomas, *The Slave Trade: the History of the Atlantic Slave Trade, 1440-1870* (London: Picador, 1997), pp. 263-64.

least, made the connection. William Carey put it into words and drew a conclusion at the close of his *Enquiry into the Obligations of Christians to use means for the Conversion of the Heathens* (1792). The finance for such a project could easily be raised among Baptists.

> Many persons have of late left off the use of *West Indian sugar* on account of the iniquitous manner in which it is obtained. Those families who have done so, and have not substituted anything else in its place, have not only cleansed their hands of blood, but have made a saving to their families, some of sixpence and some of a shilling a week. If this, or a part of this were appropriated to the uses before mentioned, it would abundantly suffice. We only have to keep the end in view, and have our hearts thoroughly engaged in the pursuit of it, and the means will not be very difficult.[34]

## The Organization of the Abolition Movement in Bristol

But, for Baptists at Broadmead, the connection, though known with the head, was not so easily recognized in daily life. For them, it was a blind spot, as their involvement, either directly or indirectly, clouded the issue. Perhaps John Harris was at the heart of the matter since, without doubt, he was the one who shifted his position on the abolition issue in the critical two years 1788-1790.

It was imperative for Clarkson to see the Customs House records if he was to prepare his evidence for Parliament, and this was made possible by Tucker, the Dean of Bristol. Henry Sulgar, the Moravian minister, provided documentary evidence of Africans being killed in Calibar in 1767. The Bristol Quaker, Harry Gandy, provided Clarkson with access to a number of sailors and ships' surgeons who knew the mortality of crews and slaves on the 'middle' passage. Clarkson reported to his London committee in October 1787 that Bristol and other places in the west of England were ready to petition against the trade when the signal was given.[35]

It was on 28 January 1788 that the Bristol abolitionists held their first meeting at the Guildhall and formed a committee to prepare a petition against the trade. Among a variety of clergy, Caleb Evans was one of the prominent dissenting ministers involved, along with Alderman John Harris, a senior deacon at Broadmead. The clergy were also joined by numerous doctors and merchants.

In February 1788, Robert Hall's brilliant attack on slavery was published in the *Bristol Gazette* on 7 and 14 February, and Hall indicated to his parents his intention to publish his pieces in pamphlet form which he hoped to send them in due course. He did not publish them, and it would be more than thirty years before he addressed the issue again, still using a pseudonym. Certainly by

---

[34] *Baptist Missionary Society*, reprint, 1991, p. 111.
[35] Marshall, *The Anti-Slave Trade Movement in Bristol*, provides the basic outline of events given here.

March 1788, it was likely that John Harris had become aware of Robert Hall's views, not least because of the connection between William Pine and Caleb Evans. *Bonner and Middleton's Bristol Journal* of 2 February 1788 indicated that the petition for abolition of the slave trade would be available for signature during the week commencing 9 February. The Bristol newspapers carried correspondence for and against the slave trade through the next few weeks.

### Political Representation and the Case against Abolition

Inevitably, the supporters of the trade began to oppose the abolitionists. A meeting was held at the Merchants Hall on 6 March where it was agreed to petition the Privy Council in London with the views of the Merchant Venturers Society. Some felt the abolitionists' cause would soon be dissipated, but the unexpected introduction of Sir William Dolben's bill to regulate conditions on the slave ships changed that. The bill established the maximum number of slaves to be carried in proportion to the tonnage of the ship – a logistical requirement which seriously threatened the profitability of the trade. James Jones, with nine ships, was Bristol's largest trader, and Dolben's bill meant he would be compelled to reduce his cargoes by a quarter. In London in February 1788, a West India committee of planters and merchants had been formed to oppose abolition. It was a year later, in April 1789, that they requested the support of Bristol merchants to gather petitions opposing abolition.

A large meeting in Bristol on 13 April 1789 began to organize these petitions. Peter Marshall concludes: 'The shift of opinion in Bristol was clearly indicated by the presence on the committee of Alderman Daubeney and Harris who had, in January 1788, supported the initial protest against the trade'.[36] News of this Bristol meeting appeared in Bristol, Bath, and London newspapers. Three petitions against abolition were quickly organized and were in London by the end of April. Henry Cruger, one of the two Bristol MPs, in the absence through illness of Matthew Brickdale, took on the task of presenting the now six petitions against abolition when William Wilberforce opened his parliamentary campaign on 12 May 1789. Cruger had fought and won the parliamentary elections in 1774 and 1784, although he lost his seat in 1780-2. The role of Dissenting ministers in these elections in Bristol is discussed in considerable detail by James Bradley who comments,

> The clergy known for their Tory sympathies voted overwhelmingly against the government candidate in 1754 and for the government in 1774 and 1781, while the Dissenting ministers turned unanimously to the Whig opposition.[37]

It is perhaps surprising that Caleb Evans consistently supported Henry

---

[36] Marshall, *The Anti-Slave Trade Movement in Bristol*, p. 12.
[37] James Bradley, *Religion, Revolution and English Radicalism*, p. 233.

Cruger in each Parliamentary election between 1774 and 1784 in Bristol, and Cruger was still one of the two Bristol MPs in 1790.

Evans' argument with John Wesley over issues related to the latter's ambivalence towards the American Colonies is well rehearsed by Henry Abelove and has already been documented by W.M.S. West.[38] Abelove calls Cruger 'a flamboyant radical ... Born and educated in New York, Cruger came to Bristol while still young and made a reputation there as a merchant, a womanizer, an opponent of the Stamp Act, and a partisan of Wilkes. Campaigning in 1774, he issued a broadside calling for more frequent Parliaments ... favored conciliation with the Americans ... opposed the ministry's policy of tolerating the Catholic of Canada ... and ... believed members of Parliament should vote as their constituents instructed'.[39] James Bradley states that, in the 1774 Parliamentary election, 'the most frequently occurring theme was liberty: in broadside after broadside Burke and Cruger were associated with America, and America, in turn, was associated with civil and religious liberty ... The election literature in favour of Burke and Cruger clearly reinforced the pro-American political orientation of the Dissenting sermons of Caleb Evans'.[40] Bradley further claims that 'When Caleb Evans went to the polls in 1774, 1781 and 1784, he voted for Henry Cruger and his Baptist congregation, almost to a man faithfully followed in his steps!'[41]

In Evans' *Letter to John Wesley and Political Sophistry Detected (1776)*, he said that his political attitudes were based on reason, scripture, and the English constitution. He told his opponent that if he could prove that 'political slavery' was recommended in the Bible, it would shock his feelings and revolt his mind, but he would as a Christian submit to it absolutely.[42] 'Slavery', said Evans, 'considered in its principle, does not depend upon the treatment of the slave, for if he is deprived of his liberty, and is at the disposal of another, he is equally a slave when treated well as when treated ill'.[43]

When Wilberforce opened his abolitionist campaign on 12 May 1789, among the six Bristol petitions against abolition were those from the Corporation and the Merchant Venturers. The West India interest claimed that three-fifths of Bristol's commerce depended upon African and Caribbean trade, and abolition would have dire effects on British shipping, would bring about the

---

[38] Henry Abelove, 'John Wesley's *A Plagiarism of Samuel Johnson*', *Huntington Library Quarterly*, 59 (1997), pp. 73-79; and W. M. S. West, 'Methodists and Baptists in Eighteenth Century Bristol'. *Wesley Historical Journal*, 44 (1994), pp. 157-67.

[39] Abelove, 'John Wesley's *A Plagiarism of Samuel Johnson*', p. 74.

[40] Bradley, *Religion, Revolution and English Radicalism*, p. 214. It was Cruger's 'supposedly treasonous letter to Peter Wikoff' in Philadelphia, July 1774, which cost him the elections in 1780 and 1781, when his opponents re-published Wesley's *Calm Address*, (5,000 copies), for distribution to the electorate. (pp. 216-17).

[41] Bradley, *Religion, Revolution and English Radicalism*, p. 236.

[42] C. Evans, *A Letter to John Wesley* (Bristol: W. Pine, 1775), p. 51.

[43] Bradley, *Religion, Revolution and English Radicalism*, p. 152, quoting Caleb Evans.

closure of Bristol sugar refineries, throwing several hundred out of work, and would bring no improvement to the Negro's life. Therefore, cautious regulation of the trade was the way forward.

Throughout the parliamentary debate, Cruger kept in touch with the Bristol opponents of Wilberforce. He also played an active part in resisting the abolitionist case. On 21 May when Wilberforce proposed that the House go into committee, Cruger spoke in support but only as a means of proceeding to a refutation of the arguments for abolition. Declaring himself to be a supporter of humanitarian causes and an opponent of oppression, he proceeded to demand that 'the cost of ending the trade should not fall on individuals, but the nation ... he argued for gradual regulation leading to abolition, rather than for a "precipitate amputation". The bringing to Africa of internal peace and industry would do more than international agreement to abolish the trade ... For these reasons Cruger proclaimed his support of the petitions he had presented and his intention to vote against Wilberforce's propositions.'[44]

In this oblique manner, Cruger moved in public toward his already privately agreed arrangement with the West Indian group to defeat the bill. Cruger had written to the Bristol Merchant Venturers on 18 May about the tactics to be used in Parliament against Wilberforce, of which his own intervention was a significant part. The Bristol West India Merchants' meeting on 3 June 1789 imposed a tax of 'sixpence per hogshead and puncheon' on all imported articles for a year from 24 April 1789 to finance the costs of opposing abolition, a move which affected all who traded in Bristol through the port. The West India interest in Parliament persuaded the Commons to make their own enquiry into the slave trade, but this did not begin until January 1790.[45] In the 1790 general election, Cruger retired as one of the two Bristol MPs, and his successor, Lord Sheffield, spoke frequently against abolition.[46] Wilberforce sustained his attack, and the 24 and 31 March 1792 editions of *Felix Farley's Bristol Journal* reported abolitionist petitions with over a thousand signatures including many nonconformist ministers and laity. However, both sides were now settled into their positions, and the 'surprise onslaught of 1789 had by 1792 become a phase in a protracted struggle'.[47]

## Concluding Remarks

As the century came to a close, although the abolitionist agitation had aroused moral distaste for the trade, it was the economic crisis of 1793 which broke Bristol's connection with the trade. Of sixty voyages undertaken from Bristol between 1790 and May 1792, twenty-seven were supported in whole or part by

---

[44] Marshall, *The Anti-Slave Trade Movement in Bristol*, pp. 13-14.
[45] Marshall, *The Anti-Slave Trade Movement in Bristol*, p. 15.
[46] Marshall, *The Anti-Slave Trade Movement in Bristol*, p. 17.
[47] Marshall, *The Anti-Slave Trade Movement in Bristol*, p. 18.

those who were reported bankrupt in 1793. Unlike London merchants, Bristol merchants owned their ships, and all were affected. When in 1806 it was finally decided to abolish the slave trade, 'relief was doubtless general in Bristol at the passing of a trade which had once seemed both indefensible and essential: the economics of 1793 had fatally sapped the material strength of the slave trade [from] Bristol'.[48]

It could be that Caleb Evans sincerely welcomed Hall's intervention because he recognized he was too closely involved with members and personal friends whose commercial interests depended both directly and indirectly on the trade. It may have been that Evans, like all people, had a personal 'blind spot'. Whatever Evans' views were on slavery it seems clear that this was not the issue at the root of the disastrous Bristol Mansion House meeting on 18 December 1790. The materials circulated by Hall and his London supporters have not been found. What is clear is that the violent disagreement between himself and Hall, with its considerable fall-out in the congregation, resulted in great personal stress for Evans and his early death in 1791. The disagreement in the congregation continued for some years and resulted in serious problems for John Ryland, Jr, during his Broadmead ministry. Perhaps the final word regarding the congregation's attitude to slavery in the next Broadmead generation, which was led by John Ryland, Jr, should be in the recognition that from its ranks came 'Knibb, the Notorious: the slaves' missionary', as his 1973 biographer, David Wright, called him.

---

[48] Marshall, *The Anti-Slave Trade Movement in Bristol*, p. 24.

CHAPTER 10

# Martha Gurney and William Fox: Baptist Printer and Radical Reformer, 1791-1794

Timothy Whelan

**Dissent in the 1790s Divided over Political Action**

The 1790s was one of the most politically divisive decades in the history of England, especially for Dissenters. Those Dissenters who actively engaged in the political issues of the day, primarily the slave trade debate, the repeal of the Test and Corporation Acts, and parliamentary reform, faced criticism, not only from those who aligned themselves with the established church, but also from many within their own denominations. According to David Bogue and James Bennett, some Dissenters were determined, 'regardless of events ... taking place on the theatre of the world', to pursue their Christian course in relative isolation. Others, however, felt 'themselves bound, because they [were] Christians and citizens of the great republic of human nature, to take an interest in the welfare of all mankind, and promote their highest happiness'.[1] Those Dissenters aligned with the first group questioned political activism and even 'condemned it as contrary to the spirit of the Gospel'.[2] Those in the second group, however, were convinced 'that the laws of God applied to social bodies as well as to individuals'. Consequently, the politically inactive Dissenters of the first group had allowed their rulers to forget this principle, resulting in what those of the second group believed was a loss of individual rights and an increase in political corruption.[3]

By 1790, however, the 'Christian philanthropists' of the second group, enthralled by political events in America and France and the prospects of social and political reform in England, were convinced that 'an era of melioration in the state of society, of liberty to extend the influence of pure religion, and of

---

[1] David Bogue and James Bennett, *History of Dissenters, from the Revolution in 1688, to the year 1808* (4 vols; London: Printed for the Authors, 1808-12), IV, pp. 189-90.
[2] Bogue and Bennett, *History of Dissenters*, IV, p. 190.
[3] Bogue and Bennett, *History of Dissenters*, IV, p. 191.

peace among nations, appeared to be drawing near...'[4] In the aftermath of Edmund Burke's *Reflections on the Revolution in France* (1790), some parts of English society fell into a paranoia that led to confrontation, retaliation, and the rejection of meaningful political reform. 'Liberty', now associated with French Jacobinism, became 'dangerous', despotism and slavery 'harmless', and political reform an unnecessary 'innovation'.[5] Those Dissenters who comprised the first group were content to allow political developments to take their natural course, but those of the second group were vehemently opposed to such passivity in the wake of numerous political actions on the part of the Pitt administration that were clearly detrimental to the freedoms previously enjoyed by Englishmen, especially Dissenters. Utilizing the pulpit and the press, these activists of the second group preached and wrote with 'an enthusiasm of ardour for the cause of liberty which exalted the mind far above its ordinary level...' Convinced that the Pitt administration and the confederated powers of Europe were part of a 'conspiracy against the liberties of mankind' designed 'to spread the triumphs of superstition and priestcraft, to bind the consciences of mankind in adamantine fetters, to prevent the propagation of divine truth, and, in short, – to put the great clock of Europe back five hundred years',[6] these reform-minded Dissenters could no longer remain silent or inactive.

Among these politically active Dissenters, so aptly described by Bogue and Bennett, were numerous Unitarians, or 'rational Dissenters', as they were often called.[7] Besides the Unitarians, a large number of Particular Baptist ministers and laymen, in London and throughout the provinces, made significant contributions—whether by serving on local and national political committees, publishing sermons, leading petition drives, or printing and selling pamphlets – to the political debates of the 1780s and '90s.[8] Among these are such familiar

---

[4] Bogue and Bennett, *History of Dissenters*, IV, pp. 193-94.

[5] Bogue and Bennett, *History of Dissenters*, IV, p. 199.

[6] Bogue and Bennett, *History of Dissenters*, IV, pp. 200-201.

[7] Representative studies of 'rational Dissenters' include H. T. Dickinson, *Liberty and Property: Political Ideology in Eighteenth-Century Britain* (New York: Holmes and Meier, 1977); Albert Goodwin, *The Friends of Liberty: The English Democratic Movement in the Age of the French Revolution* (Cambridge, MA: Harvard University Press, 1979); John Gascoigne, 'Anglican Latitudinarianism and Political Radicalism in the Late Eighteenth Century', *History* 71.1 (January, 1986), pp. 22-38; and Alan Booth, 'Popular Loyalism and Public Violence in the North-West of England, 1790-1800', *Social History* 8.3 (October, 1983), pp. 295-313, who contends that the Unitarian Dissenters were 'the most politically advanced of the sectaries and among the first to embrace the ideals of the French Revolution' (p. 306). Unitarians did not formally become a denomination until after 1806.

[8] The role Baptists played in politics between 1787 and 1800 has received only passing notice by historians of the period. For instance, Raymond Brown, in *The English Baptists of the Eighteenth Century* (London: Baptist Historical Society, 1986), devotes three small paragraphs to the slave trade controversy (pp. 121-22) and only four pages to the

names as Robert Robinson, Caleb Evans, Robert Hall, Samuel Pearce, Abraham Booth, James Dore, John Liddon, John Beatson, and William Ward, to name a few.[9] At least one woman should be added to that list. Though un-

---

political consequences of the French Revolution and its aftermath for Dissenters (pp. 132-36). Generally, studies have been confined to specific locations, such as Norwich, Bristol, Cambridge, and Derby. Examples include C. B. Jewson's 'Norwich Baptists and the French Revolution', *Baptist Quarterly* 24.4 (1971), pp. 209-15; Jewson's *The Jacobin City: A Portrait of Norwich in its Reaction to the French Revolution 1788-1802* (Glasgow: Blackie and Sons, 1975); James Bradley's 'Religion and Reform at the Polls: Nonconformity in Cambridge Politics, 1774-1784', *Journal of British Studies* 23.4 (October, 1984), pp. 545-78, as well as his important study, *Religion, Revolution and English Radicalism: Non-conformity in Eighteenth-Century Politics and Society* (Cambridge/New York: Cambridge University Press, 1990); Roger Hayden's 'Caleb Evans and the Anti-Slavery Question', *Baptist Quarterly* 39.1 (2001), pp. 4-14, as well as his discussion of Caleb Evans's politics in *Continuity and Change: Evangelical Calvinism among Eighteenth-Century Baptist Ministers Trained at Bristol Academy, 1690-1791* (Chipping Norton: Baptist Historical Society, 2006), pp. 136-38; Timothy Whelan's 'Robert Hall and the Bristol Slave-Trade Debate of 1787-1788', *Baptist Quarterly* 38.5 (2000), pp. 212-24; and A. Christopher Smith's 'William Ward, Radical Reform, and Missions in the 1790s', *American Baptist Quarterly* 10.4 (October 1991), pp. 218-44.
[9] Robinson (1735-90), pastor at St. Andrews's Street in Cambridge, the most politically active Baptist minister of the 1770s and '80s, authored numerous political works including *Slavery Inconsistent with the Spirit of Christianity* (1788). Evans (1737-91), pastor at Broadmead in Bristol, exchanged some heated pamphlets with John Wesley in 1775-76 concerning the War of American Independence. He also published several political sermons between 1775 and 1778, as well as helping to create a Bristol auxiliary of Granville Sharp's Society to Effect the Abolition of the Slave Trade. Hall (1764-1831), Robinson's successor at Cambridge, penned two of the most important political works by a Baptist writer in the 1790s – *Christianity Consistent with a Love of Freedom* (1791) and *An Apology for the Freedom of the Press* (1793) – and, like Evans, was a member of the Bristol Abolition Society, contributing two very important letters to the *Bristol Gazette* in February 1788 against the slave trade. Pearce (1766-99), pastor at Cannon Street in Birmingham during the 1790s, penned one of the harshest critiques of the Test Acts during the repeal movement of 1789 and 1790 in his sermon, *The Oppressive, Unjust, and Prophane Nature, and Tendency of the Corporation and Test Acts* (1790). Booth (1734-1806) was greatly appreciated for his sermon, *Commerce in the Human Species* (1792), published on behalf of the London Abolition Committee, as was Dore (1763/64-1825) (Maze Pond, Southwark) and his *Sermon on the African Slave Trade* (1788) and Liddon (1746/47-1825) (Hemel-Hempstead) and his *Cruelty the Natural and Inseparable Consequence of Slavery* (1792), both sermons sold by Martha Gurney. Beatson (1743-98), Baptist minister at Hull, authored two political works in 1778 and 1779 as well as an abolitionist sermon, *Compassion the Duty and Dignity of Man; and Cruelty the Disgrace of his Nature* (1789). Ward (1769-1823), the future BMS missionary in Serampore, besides his activities as a radical newspaper editor in Derby, Stafford, and Hull between 1789 and 1796, also contributed to the debate about the slave

known today, Martha Gurney (1733-1816), through her printing and selling of more than thirty radical political pamphlets and abolitionist tracts, played a major role in raising the consciousness of the English people against the evils of the slave trade and the virtues of political reform. Her period of greatest political activity occurred between 1791 and 1794 when she formed a unique publishing partnership with another radical London Dissenter, the brilliant pamphleteer William Fox, whose *An Address to the People of Great Britain, on the Propriety of Abstaining from West India Sugar and Rum* (1791) became the most widely distributed pamphlet of the eighteenth century.

## Martha Gurney (1733-1816)

Martha Gurney was the daughter of Thomas Gurney (1705-70), a clockmaker by trade, who came to London from Bedfordshire in 1738 and soon began working as a shorthand writer at the Old Bailey. A Baptist from birth, Gurney attended the ministries of John Gill and George Whitefield, and was, like Gill, a 'High Calvinist', taking a great interest in Whitefield's controversy with John Wesley, as evidenced by Gurney's published poems from this period.[10] Thomas Gurney had three children who lived to maturity: Martha (1733-1816), Thomas (1736-1775), and Joseph (1744-1815). Martha Gurney may have learned the printing/bookselling trade from her brother, Joseph (1744-1815), who, after completing his articles in 1766 with George Keith (son-in-law to Gill), opened his own bookshop, first at 39 Bread Street and then at 54 Holborn. Although he continued to operate as a bookseller until around 1780, Joseph Gurney was primarily a shorthand writer. After his father's death in 1770, Joseph took his place as shorthand writer for the Old Bailey. He would later perform the same services for both houses of Parliament, becoming the best-

---

trade and political reform in his pamphlet, *The Abolition of the Slave Trade, Peace, and a Temperate Reform Essential to the Salvation of England* (1796).

[10] W. H. G. Salter (ed.), *Some Particulars of the Lives of William Brodie Gurney and his Immediate Ancestors. Written Chiefly by Himself* (London: Unwin, 1902), pp. 29-30. Thomas Gurney is another eighteenth-century Baptist who deserves closer study. Between 1741 and 1770 he published eight works, including his most famous work, *Brachygraphy, or Swift Writing Made Easy to the Meanest Capacity* (1750), which went through eighteen editions in the eighteenth and nineteenth centuries. Among his other publications, most dealing with contentions between the followers of the Calvinist George Whitefield and the Arminian John Wesley, are *Zeal for the Church: or, the Lamentation of the Cl---gy, Occasioned by the Reverend Mr Whitefield's Return to England* (1741); *Perseverance, a Poem. In Reply to the Reverend Mr Wesley's Poetical Performance, falsely call'd, An Answer to all which the Reverend Mr Gill has Printed on the Final Perseverance of the Saints* (1755); *Poems on Various Occasions* (1759); and *The Nature and Fitness of Things; or, the Perfections of God a Standing Rule to Try All Doctrines and Experience By: A Poem, Humbly Offered to the Consideration of Mr John Wesley, and his Followers* (1770).

known shorthand writer of his day, transcribing and publishing more than eighty state trials between 1770 and 1813.[11]

In the mid-1780s, Joseph moved his family from Stamford-Hill, north of the Thames, to a house in Keene's Row, Walworth, leaving Thomas Craner's congregation at Red Cross Street for the Baptist church at Maze Pond, Southwark, under the ministry of James Dore. Martha Gurney would join the rest of the Gurneys at Maze Pond, and for the next three decades they would be one of Maze Pond's leading families.[12] Joseph's two sons would both become significant figures of their day. John (later Sir John) Gurney (1768-1845) rose to prominence as a defense attorney in several celebrated state trials of the 1790s, including the treason trials of Thomas Hardy and John Horne Tooke (1794) and the conspiracy trials of the United Irishmen James O'Coigly, Arthur O'Connor, and John Binns (1798). He would later serve as counselor for the King's Bench and Baron of the Exchequer. He would also serve as vice-chairman of the General Body of Protestant Dissenters from 1805 to 1816.[13] The younger son, Wil-

---

[11] Edward Starr's *Baptist Bibliography* (25 vols; Rochester, NY: American Baptist Historical Society, 1947-76) attributes only ten works to Joseph Gurney, but he was considerably more active than that. During his lengthy career (1766-1813), Gurney appeared as a bookseller, printer, or transcriber on over 125 publications, including editions of thirty-five religious works by Dissenters and Anglican evangelicals (printed between 1768 and 1780).

[12] According to the *Maze Pond Church Book*, Vol. 2 (1784-1821) (MS., Angus Library, Regent's Park College, Oxford), on 18 April 1785, 'Martha Gurney, (formerly a member of the late M$^r$ Craner's church) [at Red-cross Street] . . . and Miss Elizabeth Gurney [Joseph Gurney's daughter] were proposed for communion . . . their moral characters being well attested to the satisfaction of the Church'. They were received into communion on 5 June 1785 (fols. 43, 45). Rebecca Gurney (1747-1814), Joseph's wife, joined the congregation at Maze Pond on 5 March 1786 (fol. 52), with Joseph joining on 5 August 1787 (fol. 58). W. B. Gurney, their son, would later write, 'The interests of the Church and the happiness of their Pastor were . . . dear to their hearts, and their cooperation was cheerfully given in any plan of usefulness in which the Church and congregation engaged. He [Joseph Gurney] bore a high character, both for talent and integrity, and was highly esteemed by those who knew him best' (Salter [ed.], *Some Particulars*, p. 45).

[13] Bernard Lord Manning, *The Protestant Dissenting Deputies* (Cambridge: Cambridge University Press, 1952), p. 481. An entry in the *Maze Pond Church Book* for 1813 reads: 'Resolved that the special and cordial thanks of this Community be given to M$^r$ John Gurney not only for his services as one of our Deputies but for his prompt, unwearied and disinterested attention to those Cases which come before the Deputation and which affect the civil rights of Protestant Dissenters' (II, fol. 185). As W. B. Gurney noted in his family memoir: 'My Brother entered into public life shortly after the French Revolution, when the efforts made here to repress what was considered the rise of liberty in France, and perhaps in other countries also, created a strong feeling of opposition to our Government on the part of those who were liberal in their views' (Salter [ed.], *Some Particulars*, p. 56). A signed volume of radical political tracts from the 1790s

liam Brodie Gurney (1777-1855), followed in his father's footsteps, becoming the shorthand writer for the House of Commons in 1806, and in 1813, after his father's retirement, the chief shorthand writer for Parliament and the Old Bailey.[14] He became one of the leading Baptist laymen of his day, playing a key role in the formation of the Sunday School Union in 1803 as well as serving for many years as a member of the committee of the Religious Tract Society and as treasurer of both Stepney College (1828-44) and the Baptist Missionary Society (1835-55).[15]

Martha Gurney never married, earning a 'comfortable subsistence, and, ultimately, a small independence'[16] as a printer and bookseller from 1772 to 1813, first at 34 Bell-yard and, after 1782, at 128 Holborn Hill, adjacent to Leather Lane and just opposite Fetter Lane, between Gray's Inn Road and Hatton Garden.[17] As the printing trade continued to grow throughout the eighteenth century, so did the number of women involved, increasing by as much as fifty per cent in the last quarter of the century in London.[18] Martha Gurney's career is indicative of this phenomenon. Her name appears on more than 130 titles, either as printer or bookseller or, in some cases, as both. Besides nine literary titles, Gurney's name appears on fifty titles by writers that span the spectrum of religious thought in England, including Anglicans, Baptists, Independents, Methodists, and Unitarian General Baptists. 'Her dealings were principally in old Divinity and Bibles', her nephew, W. B. Gurney, recalled in his Reminiscences. 'She had at one time the best collection of old and curious Bibles of any one in the trade.

---

once owned by John Gurney, now resides in the Angus Library, Regent's Park College, Oxford, (shelfmark 42.e.15).

[14] W. B. Gurney and Sons (eds.), *A Text-Book of the Gurney System of Shorthand*, 18th ed. (London: Butterworth, 1884), p. 6.

[15] Salter (ed.), *Some Particulars*, pp. 102-11.

[16] Salter (ed.), *Some Particulars*, p. 34.

[17] Martha Gurney does not appear, either as a printer or bookseller, in the early directories compiled by John Pendred (1785) or H. R. Plomer (1922). Gurney does appear in Maxted's *The London Book Trades 1775-1800*, but she is listed only as 'M. Gurney' operating as a bookseller at 128 Holborn from 1790-1805; Maxted seems unaware of both her previous location at Bell-yard and the length of her career. See John Pendred, *The Earliest Directory of the Book Trade in London and Surrounding Environs* (London: Bibliographical Society, 1955); H. R. Plomer, *A Dictionary of the Printers and Booksellers who were at Work in England, Scotland and Ireland from 1726 to 1775* ([Oxford]: Bibliographical Society, Oxford University Press, 1922); Ian Maxted, *The London Book Trades 1775-1800: A Preliminary Checklist of Members* (Kent: William Dawson, 1977), p. 97.

[18] Hannah Barker, 'Women, Work and the Industrial Revolution: Female Involvement in the English Printing Trades, c.1700-1840', in *Gender in Eighteenth-Century England: Roles, Representation and Responsibilities*, ed. Hannah Barker and Elaine Chalus (London and New York: Longman, 1997), p. 85.

Her particular line of business brought her into acquaintance with a great many of the leading ministers and private Christians of different denominations, who were frequently surprised, in conversing with her, at her intimate acquaintance with the best works which she sold. But she had much leisure, and great enjoyment in reading'.[19] Besides publishing sermons of several prominent Dissenting preachers of her day, such as James Dore, Benjamin Kingsbury, Samuel Bradburn, Joseph Swain, Samuel Fisher, and Abraham Booth, she also sold two works by the controversial London poet and polemicist, Maria De Fleury (1753-94), who, like Gurney, was a Baptist, a single woman, and, at times, a bookseller. In collaboration with her brother Joseph, Martha Gurney printed or sold transcriptions of thirty-one trials between 1774 and 1806, including such famous state trials as that of Thomas Paine, Thomas Hardy, Horne Tooke, William Stone, Edward Despard, and Lord Melville; these works, along with her editions of *Brachygraphy*, were her most profitable enterprises.[20] More importantly, between 1788 and 1802 Martha Gurney printed or sold thirty-six radical political pamphlets, of which fourteen vehemently attacked the slave trade.

Although historians have commented upon the work of Joseph Gurney and his son, William Brodie, as Parliamentarian shorthand writers,[21] Martha Gurney's role as a leading Dissenting printer and bookseller has never been noted.[22] Even when her publications have been mentioned and discussed by scholars, Gurney herself has never been recognized. Because historians have, until recently, largely ignored the contributions of women's work during this century, the general assumption has been, unfortunately, to attribute initialed names on title pages to men, not women, which in the case of Martha Gurney has contributed significantly to her obscurity. Consequently, scholars have failed to note certain key facts about 'M. Gurney'—that the appellation represented an unmarried woman who was a member of a Particular Baptist congregation in Southwark and who, between 1787 and 1794, was one of London's leading Dissenting printers and sellers of radical political pamphlets and abolitionist tracts. In fact, she was the *only* woman bookseller/printer engaged in

---

[19] Salter (ed.), *Some Particulars*, p. 34.

[20] Salter (ed.), *Some Particulars*, p. 41.

[21] See Edward Augustus Bond (ed.), *Speeches of the Managers and Counsel in the Trial of Warren Hastings* (4 vols; London: Longman [and others], 1859-61); also W. H. G. Salter, *A History of the Gurney System of Shorthand* (Oxford: Blackwell, [1924]), pp. 1-13.

[22] The best discussion of women printers and booksellers in England during the eighteenth century is Barker's essay 'Women, Work and the Industrial Revolution'. Barker notes that in London some 250 women operated in the printing trades during the eighteenth century, with 70 listed as stationers, 54 as booksellers, 45 as printers and 24 as bookbinders, with a marked increase in the last decades of the century (p. 90). Unfortunately, Barker does not mention Martha Gurney.

such activities at that time.[23]

### William Fox and 128 Holburn Hill

Even less is known today of William Fox, who collaborated with Martha Gurney on sixteen radical political pamphlets between 1791 and 1794. He was a minor bookseller at 128 Holborn Hill from 1773 to 1794,[24] specializing in editions of Shakespeare, Cervantes, Dryden, Congreve, Rowe, Beaumont and Fletcher, Fielding, Samuel Richardson, and James Thomson, as well as such popular works as Edward Wortley Montagu's *Reflections on the Rise and Fall of the Ancient Republicks* (1778), Samuel Johnson's *Lives of the Most Eminent English Poets* (1781), Andrew Kippis's *Biographica Brittanica* (1778,) and the *Universal History from the Earliest Accounts to the Present Time* (1779-81). Like many Dissenters, Fox's interest in the slave trade did not commence in 1791, for in 1785 he collaborated with four other sellers in publishing Thomas Southerne's dramatic version of Aphra Behn's novel, *Oroonoko*, a version that became popular with the abolitionist movement because of its emphasis upon the natural nobility of the African-born prince Oroonoko, who suffers a terrible fate at the hands of his slave-owners in Surinam. Fox appeared on a title page for the last time in 1794 when he joined a consortium of sixteen booksellers in distributing a three-volume reprint of *The Adventurer*, a popular series of essays that originally appeared in 1753.

In 1782, Fox entered into a business arrangement with Martha Gurney, for that year she moved her bookshop from 34 Bell-yard into his quarters in Holborn Hill. They operated as booksellers from the same address until 1794, after which Fox ceases to appear on title pages. He seems to have gone into a semi-retirement in 1788, however, for after that date he appears on only six titles. Gurney remained at Holborn Hill until her death in 1816. The fact that both Fox and Gurney appeared on titles as printer or bookseller between 1782 and 1794 from the same address suggests that they were sharing not only a business location but most likely living quarters as well. Nothing is known, however, about Fox's marital status; he may have become a widower in the early 1780s, which may explain Martha Gurney's arrival at 128 Holborn Hill as both a busi-

---

[23] Though not involved like Martha Gurney in printing pamphlets, Hannah Humphrey of London was a popular printer of broadsides among the anti-jacobins; she was best known for publishing James Gillray's satirical caricatures during the 1780s and '90s. See Barker, 'Women', p. 99.

[24] Plomer lists Fox as being at Holborn only from 1773-77 (*Dictionary*, p. 96). Maxted places Fox at his Holborn address from 1773-83 (*London Book Trades*, p. 84). Fox is listed as a bookseller at 128 Holborn in Lowndes' *London Directory* for 1779 and 1780, as well as in the 1783 edition of the *New Complete Guide to all Persons who have any Trade or Concern with the City of London and Parts Adjacent*. Fox, however, continued to appear on title pages from his Holborn address until 1794.

ness and domestic collaboration, an arrangement beneficial to each party, since both were well past middle age at that point. Her merger with Fox brought a new dimension to 128 Holborn Hill, domestically as well as professionally, for Gurney was both an active printer and seller, whereas Fox had appeared strictly as a bookseller since 1775. By the late 1780s, Martha Gurney had clearly become Fox's superior as a printer and bookseller. Her expertise and opposition to the slave trade provided Fox with the necessary means and stimulus for his distinctive transformation (and in many respects, hers as well) from a minor bookseller into one of the most significant voices in the public debate over the slave trade and political reform in the early 1790s.

Even before his merger with Martha Gurney, William Fox had developed a connection with Joseph Gurney. In 1778, Fox, along with booksellers John Rivington, Charles Dilly, and William Owen, sold Colin Milne's *A Sermon Preached at St. Sepulchre's, London, on Sunday, March 15th, and at the Parish Church of Cheshunt, Herts, on Sunday, October 27th, 1778, for the Benefit of the Humane Society, Instituted for the Recovery of Persons Apparently Dead by Drowning*. Among the 'public-spirited gentlemen' listed at the front of the sermon who donated at least one guinea on that occasion to the Humane Society were William Fox of Holborn (a 'perpetual director' for having donated over 5 guineas) and Joseph Gurney.[25]

It is likely, given the Gurneys' close connections with so many Baptist ministers and laymen, that Fox was also a Baptist, possibly a member of the congregation at Red Cross Street (where the Gurneys worshiped prior to 1785) or a hearer at Maze Pond (where they worshiped thereafter). A search of the available church books, unfortunately, has proved unproductive in locating Fox. One last fact about his life, however, provides further evidence of his connection with the Gurneys and the Baptists at Maze Pond, for in 1794, Fox was elected a member of the Pennsylvania Society for Promoting the Abolition of Slavery, along with seven other English Baptist ministers, including James Dore of Maze Pond. The following year, Joseph Gurney was inducted as a member as well.[26]

The fact that Fox shares little information about himself in his pamphlets is not surprising, for initially he sought anonymity. On the title pages to four of

---

[25] Milne, *Sermon*, pp. 6, 7. Fox had previously sold Hawes's *An Examination of the Rev. Mr John Wesley's Primitive Physic* (1776); he would also sell Thomas Francklin's *A Sermon Preached at St. George's Bloomsbury, on Sunday, March 28, for the Benefit of the Humane Society, instituted for the Recovery of Persons apparently Dead by Drowning* (1779).

[26] Gurney's certificate of membership was dated 25 September 1795. John Gurney, Joseph's son, was also elected a member at the same time. See *Act of Incorporation and Constitution of the Pennsylvania Society, for Promoting the Abolition of Slavery: and for the Relief of Free Negroes Unlawfully Held in Bondage, and for Improving the Condition of the African Race: also, a List of Those who have been Elected Members of the Society* (Philadelphia: Merrihew & Thompson, 1860), pp. 22, 24.

his pamphlets, Fox's name does not appear, the most noteworthy being his first and most widely distributed pamphlet, *An Address to the People of Great Britain*. Given the nature of the political climate between 1791 and 1794, it is understandable that Fox would have been hesitant, in some instances, to attach his name to these pamphlets. The only positive identification of William Fox the bookseller as the author of the *Address* occurs in a footnote in an anonymous pamphlet in which the writer informs his readers that 'the Author of the pamphlet in question is well known to be a Mr F\*\*, formerly an eminent Bookseller in Holborn'. 'This gentleman', the writer adds, 'has been not a little remarkable for the singularity of his opinions in general', implying that Fox had some reputation for his politics prior to his *Address*.[27] By 1794, however, Martha Gurney was frequently listing, either on the title pages or on the back pages of her pamphlets, the majority of Fox's other titles, even those he had published anonymously.[28] Though many within London's Dissenting community may have known the identity of the author of these provocative political pamphlets that filled the shelves of Martha Gurney's bookshop, they would have discovered little information within Fox's pamphlets that would have identified him as anything more than a reform-minded Dissenter.

The chief consequence of this paucity of contemporary references to Wil-

---

[27] Anon, *A Vindication of the Use of Sugar, and other Products of the West-India Islands, in Answer to a Pamphlet entitled Remarkable Extracts, &c* (London: Printed by H. L. Galabin ... for T. Boosey, 1792), p. 9. Peter C. Hogg suggests that the author is Henry Clutterbuck, a member of the Corporation of Surgeons and Surgeon to the Royal Universal Dispensary, who had two other pamphlets in the 1790s printed for Thomas Boosey (*The African Slave Trade and its Suppression, a Classified and Annotated Bibliography of Books, Pamphlets and Periodical Articles* [London: Frank Cass, [1973], p. 170).

[28] Thirteen of Fox's pamphlets can be found at the British Library. Of the remaining three pamphlets, the only known copies of two of them – *On Trials for Treason* (London, [1794?]) and *Poor Richard's Scraps. No. 1* (London, [1 794?]) – can be found at the University of Michigan in a bound volume that contains fifteen pamphlets by Fox, all originally owned by Elizabeth Gurney, Martha Gurney's niece. The MS. 'Table of Contents' for the bound volume is in Miss Gurney's hand, after which she adds, 'all written by William Fox'. The only pamphlet missing in her collection is Fox's *A Summary View of the Evidence Delivered Before a Committee of the House of Commons, Relating to the Slave Trade* (1792). Copies of the remaining pamphlet, *Poor Richard's Scraps*, No. 3 [and no. 4], entitled *On the Excellence of the British Government*, can be found in Miss Gurney's volume at Michigan and at Dr Williams's Library in a volume of pamphlets once belonging to Theophilus Lindsey (1723-1808), Unitarian minister at London's Essex Street Chapel, 1778-93, and a leading political reformer. The British Library, however, incorrectly attributes to Fox the anonymous pamphlet, *An Abridgment of the Evidence Delivered before a Select Committee, in the Years 1790 and 1791, on the Part of the Petitioners for the Abolition of the Slave Trade* (London: J. Phillips, 1791) but that pamphlet was actually composed by Thomas Clarkson (see Fair Minute Books, ADD. MS. 21256, British Library, fols. 17r-26r).

liam Fox the bookseller has been that his pamphlets, unfortunately, have subsequently been attributed to the wrong William Fox. The most common beneficiary has been 'William Fox, Attorney-at-Law', to which the British library attributes all thirteen of its William Fox pamphlets. This William Fox was not hesitant to identify himself in considerable detail on his title pages, one of which describes him as an

> Attorney at Law; a Master in the High Court of Chancery; a Governor of the Gloucester Infirmary; a Freeman by honorary presentation of that city; a Freeman by the like title and by birth of the city of London; a Freeman by honorary presentation and by birth of the Worshipful Company of Grocers; a Governor of the Philanthropic Institution; and one of their Majesties own loyal London Lambeth Naval Volunteers.[29]

William Fox the attorney authored four works between 1796 and 1813, and a cursory reading of his works reveals that he was a devout Anglican, a loyal supporter of the King and the Pitt administration in the 1790s, and an outspoken opponent of political reform and religious dissent.[30] Another individual who has been confused with William Fox the pamphleteer is the well-known merchant and philanthropist, William Fox (1736-1826), for many years a deacon in the Baptist congregation in Little Prescot Street, Goodman's Fields, and founder of the Sunday School Society in 1785.[31] His son, William Fox, Jr

---

[29] William Fox, *A Sailor's Manual of Prayer* (London: Printed for the author ..., 1812).

[30] The attorney's works are *The Friend: A Weekly Essay* (1796), *Remarks on Various Agricultural Reports. Transmitted to the Honourable Board of Agriculture, in the Year 1794* (1796), *A Sailor's Manual of Prayer* (1812), and *Protestant Thoughts on Catholic Claims* (1813). The works of William Fox the bookseller and William Fox the attorney, besides their political differences, can be differentiated sociologically as well by an examination of the printers and booksellers each used and the quality of their publications. Unlike the inexpensive pamphlets produced by Martha Gurney, all four of the attorney's publications were handsomely bound, expensively priced, and sold by the some of London's leading booksellers, many of whom had ministerial connections, such as G. Nicoll and Sons, Pall Mall, booksellers to King George III; J. Debrett; J. Scott of Westminster; the Philanthropic Society, St. George's Fields; and Benjamin White and Son, Fleet-Street.

[31] William Fox, Sr, authored only one brief pamphlet, *Address to the Friends of Evangelical Truth in General; and to the Calvinistic Baptist Churches in Particular*, which appeared in 1797 on behalf of the Baptist Society for the Encouragement and Support of Itinerant Preaching, an organization for which Fox served as treasurer. It was printed in John Rippon's *Baptist Annual Register*, II, [1794-97], pp. 465-70. For more on William Fox, Sr, see Joseph Ivimey, *Memoir of William Fox, Esq., Founder of the Sunday-School Society* (London: G. Wightman, 1831); John Carroll Power, *The Rise and Progress of Sunday Schools: A Biography of Robert Raikes and William Fox*, 2nd ed. (New York: Sheldon and Company, 1868); Ernest Kevan, *London's Oldest Baptist Church* (London: Kingsgate Press, [1933]), pp. 93, 122, 139-42.

(listed in the catalogue of the British Library as 'William Fox, the Younger, of Hackney'), was an author as well, publishing five books between 1796 and 1821, and in some cases, he too has been confused with William Fox the bookseller. The writings of William Fox, Jr, indicate that he was widely read and a gentleman of considerable means, both of which would bespeak his position as the son of the wealthy merchant, William Fox.[32] The inability of historians and archivists to correctly identify William Fox the bookseller and to separate his pamphlets from the writings of the other three William Foxes has led to considerable confusion and historical inaccuracies, much to the detriment of the pamphleteer and his colleague, Martha Gurney, and to the role these two radical Dissenters played in the history of the political reform movement in England in the early 1790s.

### Martha Gurney, William Fox, and the Abolition Movement

Martha Gurney had opposed the slave trade for some time prior to her collaboration with Fox. In fact, her first political pamphlet was *A Sermon on the African Slave Trade*, delivered by her pastor, James Dore (1763/64-1825), in November 1788; it was printed the next month on behalf of the congregation at Maze Pond in conjunction with Granville Sharp's Society for Effecting the Abolition of the Slave Trade.[33] Dore's *Sermon* reflects the inevitable linking that occurred at this time between individuals opposed to the slave trade and those who espoused notions of equality and the natural 'rights of man'. Citing Blackstone's *Commentaries on the Laws of England* and Paley's *Principles of Moral and Political Philosophy*, Dore joined numerous Particular Baptist ministers who decried slavery as a grievous violation of individual rights and Christian charity. His *Sermon* appeared at the end of an eventful year in the annals of the abolitionist movement, a year that included a significant Parlia-

---

[32] William Fox, Jr, authored *Original Pieces: in Verse and Prose* (1796), *Sketches and Observations Made on a Tour through Various Parts of Europe, in the Years 1792, 1793, and 1794* (1799), *Cursory Remarks on a Work entitled Apeleutherus; or, An Effort to Attain Intellectual Freedom. In a Letter to a Friend* (1800), *La Bagatella; or, Delineations of Home Scenery, a Descriptive Poem* (1801), and *The Grecian, Roman, and Gothic Architecture, Considered as Applicable to Public and Private Buildings, in this Country; to which are added, Some Remarks on Ornamental Landscape, Designed to Recommend, and to Introduce a More Correct Taste into the Residences of the Nobility and Gentry of Great Britain* (1821). For more on William Fox, Jr, see Power, *Rise and Progress*, pp. 229-31.

[33] James Dore, *A Sermon on the African Slave Trade*, 3rd ed. (London: Printed for J. Phillips, and sold by J. Buckland, C. Dilly, M. Gurney, and W. Button, 1788). The minutes of the Abolition Committee on 9 December 1788 record a resolution of thanks to the pastor and congregation of Maze Pond 'for their liberal Collection towards the support of the Views of this Society', which amounted to £22.8s.11/2d (Fair Minute Books, ADD. MS. 21255, fol. 73r).

mentary debate on the slave trade that provoked numerous petitions and pamphlets, both pro and con, on the controversial topic.

The congregation at Maze Pond was united in opposition to the slave trade, for a prefatory note mentions that the *Sermon* was printed 'to gratify the wishes of an affectionate people, who are zealous friends to the GLORIOUS CAUSE of UNIVERSAL LIBERTY'. Dore may have been attempting to provoke the London Baptists to begin a more concerted effort in opposition to the slave trade, for Robert Robinson had already preached his sermon on the slave trade the previous February in Cambridge. In a note affixed to his sermon, Dore also reminds his readers that on 14 and 15 May 1788, a group of West Country Baptist ministers had met at Portsmouth Common and passed resolutions condemning the slave trade and recommending their churches 'unite in promoting, to the utmost of their power, every scheme, that is or may be proposed, to procure the Abolition of a traffic so unjust, inhuman, and disgraceful; and the continuance of which tends to counteract and destroy the operation of the benevolent principles and spirit of our common Christianity'.[34] Thus, Dore's *Sermon* and its subsequent distribution by Gurney and the Abolition Committee (which purchased 100 copies 'for the use of the Society') reflects the increasing level of participation by Baptists in the abolitionist movement and a keen awareness that the London Baptists could and should play a major role in this unfolding drama.[35] 'The spirit of the nation is roused', Dore concluded, 'and Parliamentary wisdom will be soon employed in devising means to redress' the evils incurred by the slave trade.[36]

Martha Gurney's 'spirit' was certainly 'roused' by the sermon. Not only was she printing and selling abolitionist pamphlets and sermons, but also, according to her nephew, 'display[ing] openly in her shop the section of a slave ship, with its living cargo stowed for the voyage...'.[37] This was the large fold-out drawing of the slave ship *Brookes* which had been commissioned by the Abolition Committee in March 1789 and published the next month. It soon found its way into nearly every abolitionist home, becoming, like Wedgwood's cameo of the kneeling slave, one of the movement's most powerful symbols.[38] 'Her efforts in this cause', W. B. Gurney says of his aunt, '... brought her to the acquaintance of some of the most intelligent Quakers, who valued her as a coadjutor,

---

[34] Dore, *Sermon*, p. 38.

[35] See minutes for 24 February 1789, *Fair Minute Books*, ADD. MS. 21255, fol. 86v., for more Baptist activities concerning the slave trade debate.

[36] Dore, *Sermon*, p. 32. Brycchan Carey discusses Dore's Sermon, as well John Liddon's *Cruelty the Natural and Inseparable Consequence of Slavery* (1792) (another work sold by Martha Gurney), in *British Abolitionism and the Rhetoric of Sensibility: Writing, Sentiment, and Slavery, 1760-1807* (Basingstoke, UK; New York: Palgrave MacMillan, 2005), pp. 154-56.

[37] Salter (ed.), *Some Particulars*, p. 34.

[38] See *Fair Minute Books*, ADD. MS. 21255, fol. 91r; also Ellen Gibson Wilson, *Thomas Clarkson: A Biography* (Houndsmill, Basingstoke: Macmillan Press, 1989), p. 50.

engaging as she did in the circulation of these pamphlets, not so much as objects of trade as means of promoting the benevolent design'.[39]

Quakers had petitioned Parliament for an end to the slave trade as early as 1783, but no organized effort was launched until the formation in 1787 of Granville Sharp's Society for the Purpose of Effecting the Abolition of the Slave Trade. Joseph Gurney had been a subscriber to the Society from its inception.[40] Through his role as shorthand writer for Parliament, he had immediate access to the proceedings on the slave trade debate in Parliament in 1791 and 1792, giving Martha Gurney a distinct advantage over every other Dissenting printer in London. According to W.H. Gurney Salter, the family historian, because of their reputation for transcribing and printing accurate records of court proceedings, the Gurneys 'gained a good name for difficult work, in, e.g., the trials of Lord Baltimore, the Duchess of Kingston, Lord George Gordon (for the Riots), etc. ... This led to a great increase in their professional work, and they were engaged to take discussions for private parties at the Bar of the two Houses of Parliament, by permission, e.g. on the Slave Trade, and also in some of the Committees'.[41] Consequently, Joseph attended the six Committees in the House in 1791 when they were conducting interviews on the slave trade; he also served as shorthand writer during the debate on the slave trade in the House of Lords in 1792,[42] all of which warranted appreciation from the Pennsylvania Society and the London Abolition Committee as well as providing his sister and William Fox with immediate access to the evidence presented in Parliament during the height of the controversial debates in 1791 and 1792.

---

[39] Salter (ed.), *Some Particulars*, p. 34. Martha Gurney would later sell the Quaker William Allen's stirring pamphlet, *The Duty of Abstaining from the Use of West India Produce; A Speech, Delivered at Coach-Maker's-Hall, Jan. 12, 1792* (London: Printed for T. W. Hawkins, and sold by M. Gurney, 1792).

[40] See 'List of Subscriptions reported to the 11th of September, 1787', in *Society Instituted in 1787, for the Purpose of Effecting the Abolition of the Slave Trade* (London, [1787]).

[41] Salter, *History*, p. 11. W. B. Gurney relates a meeting between Joseph Gurney and the Duke of Clarence during the evidence proceedings in the House that adds further insight into his father's abolitionist stance. The Duke (afterwards William IV) 'had been in early life in the Navy, and the West Indies he had mixed with the planters and the members of the government, and had imbibed notions of the happiness and comfort of the slaves, which led him to think that they had received a benefit in being brought from their own country, and that it was lawful, and even praiseworthy, to bring more. He was on the side of the planters, and one day addressing my father, he said, "I thought from your countenance you were an Abolitionist. I thought you had an Abolition face". The Duke's remark, though not intended as a compliment, was doubtless true, for Joseph Gurney had long been opposed not only to the Slave Trade, but to the institution of Slavery itself' (Salter [ed.], *Some Particulars*, pp. 43-44).

[42] Salter (ed.), *Some Particulars*, pp. 34-35; Salter, *History*, pp. 11, 13.

## Fox's *Address to the People of Great Britain, on the Consumption of West-India Produce*

The efforts of the abolitionists seemed likely to bear fruit in 1791, when a wave of testimony—much of it generated by Thomas Clarkson as a result of his numerous tours of England and Scotland and the major cities involved in the slave trade—came before the Privy Council and the Select Committee in the House of Commons, depicting the horror of the slave trade in Africa, the dreaded 'middle passage', and life on the West Indian plantations. James Phillips's efforts in propagating the vision of the Abolition Committee through the printed word, coupled with William Wilberforce's powerful parliamentary skills, led many to think that the bill for the abolition of the slave trade would finally pass that spring. Despite the overwhelming evidence accumulated by the abolitionists against the slave trade, Wilberforce's motion was defeated on 19 April by a vote of 163 to 88, forcing abolitionists like Martha Gurney and William Fox to take their message directly to the people in the form of sharply worded, inexpensive pamphlets, chief of which was Fox's *Address to the People of Great Britain, on the Consumption of West-India Produce.*[43]

During his years as a London bookseller and in the years immediately following his retirement, Fox says he steered clear of public politics, noting in one of his last pamphlets that he was never a member of a 'Constitutional, or a Corresponding Society, or enlisted under the banners of Parliamentary Reform'.[44] To Fox, the majority of the parliamentary reform plans presented between 1780 and 1792 resembled primarily 'the vileness, and corruption, of the assemblies they harangued'; as a result, it was 'preferable to leave them in possession of the powers they possessed, than risk the peace of the community by attempting to rescue it from their hands'.[45] However, after the defeat of the slave trade bill

---

[43] The *Address* underwent several variations in its title during twenty-six editions. The 1st and 2nd editions bore the above title. The 3rd edition was changed to *An Address to the People of Great Britain, Proving the Necessity of Refraining from Sugar and Rum, in order to Abolish the African Slave-Trade*; the 4th-6th editions were titled *An Address to the People of Great Britain, on the Utility of Refraining from the Use of West India Sugar and Rum*; the 7th-26th editions exhibit the title for which the work is best known today, *An Address to the People of Great Britain, on the Propriety of Refraining from the Use of West India Sugar and Rum*. An edition printed in Hull bore the title *A Call to the People of Great Britain, to Refrain from the Use of West India Sugar and Rum*. Editions in Sevenoaks and Chester were combined with another anonymous pamphlet, *A Short Account of the African Slave Trade*. James Phillips appeared as seller with Martha Gurney on the first four editions; on the 5th edition, Gurney appeared with William Darton; on the 6th-13th editions, Gurney appeared as first seller, along with Thomas Knott and Charles Forster; on the 14th-26th editions, Gurney appeared alone on the title page. Editions of the *Address* were also printed in Sheffield, Newcastle, Sunderland, Birmingham, and Leeds, as well as in Wales, Ireland, Scotland, and America.

[44] William Fox, *On Trials for Treason*, (London: M. Gurney, [1794?]), p. 4.

[45] Fox, *On Trials for Treason*, p. 5.

in the spring of 1791, Fox was compelled to enter the public debate. Sometime in August or September of that year he published the *Address*, with James Phillips (1745-99), the primary printer for the London Abolition Committee, and Martha Gurney as sellers—an indication of Gurney's stature within the abolitionist community even before she began her collaboration with Fox. In less than a year, the *Address* went through twenty-six English editions, with contemporary estimates of 250,000 copies sold or given away, far eclipsing Paine's *Rights of Man* and Burke's *Reflections on the Revolution in France* as the most widely distributed pamphlet of the eighteenth century.[46]

Fox begins his *Address* by noting how ironic it is that England, which boasts of its freedom and benevolence, should be traversing the globe to enslave other peoples. To Fox, the wealth and power produced by the slave trade can only be reduced by boycotting the produce of slavery. In what would be his most controversial statement, Fox accused every user of West Indian sugar of 'participat[ing] in the crime. The slave-dealer, the slave-holder, and slave-driver are virtually the agents of the consumer, and may be considered as employed and hired by him to procure the commodity'.[47] Thus, the consumer becomes an

---

[46] Martha Gurney provided several clues to the *Address*'s total circulation on the title pages of its various editions. A note attached to the 10th edition stated that 50,000 copies of the pamphlet had been printed in the first four months of circulation. A note to the 13th edition declared that the phenomenal circulation of the *Address* 'affords the most flattering hopes of the plan proposed being extensively adopted and producing very important effects: to further them a trivial price is affixed, that those who approve the Pamphlet may be more generally enabled to promote its circulation'. If Gurney printed 5,000 copies per run (as indicated above), by the 26th edition she would have printed 130,000 copies. Numerous other printings, some without her approval, were carried out in 1791 and 1792. Along with these printings were the private printings paid for by various individuals, such as the wealthy manufacturer and abolitionist, Josiah Wedgwood, who ordered 2000 copies at the bequest of Thomas Clarkson. When all these printings are added together, William B. Gurney's claim that Fox's *Address* reached a circulation of 250,000 copies seems more than feasible. Ian Christie estimates that Paine's *Rights of Man* sold over 200,000 copies as well. William St. Clair, however, believes such estimates of Paine's work 'defy credibility when compared with what is recoverable from archival sources'. He estimates the total distribution of Paine's pamphlet at slightly more than 20,000 copies, with 30,000 copies of Burke's *Reflections* sold by the 1840s. He also offers a more conservative estimate of Fox's *Address* at 100,000 copies, which still makes it the most widely distributed pamphlet of the century. See Salter (ed.), *Some Particulars*, p. 35; E. L. Griggs, *Thomas Clarkson: The Friend of Slaves* (London: Allen and Unwin, 1936), p. 69; Ian Christie, *Wars and Revolutions: Britain, 1760-1815* (Cambridge, MA: Harvard University Press, 1982), pp. 225-26; William St. Clair, *The Reading Nation in the Romantic Period* (Cambridge: Cambridge University Press, 2004), pp. 561, 583, 623-24.

[47] William Fox, *An Address to the People of Great Britain, on the Propriety of Refraining from West India Sugar and Rum*, 11th ed. (London: M. Gurney [and two others], 1791), p. 3.

accessory, not only to robbery, but in a figurative sense, to cannibalism as well, for Fox believed that 'every pound of sugar used' was the equivalent of 'consuming two ounces of human flesh'.[48] Fox proposed that if the average British family, which used five pounds of sugar a week, would abstain for a period of twenty-one months, each family would prevent the murder of one slave; eight families over the span of nineteen years would prevent the murder of 100 slaves, and '38,000 would totally prevent the Slave Trade to supply our islands'.[49] The reduced use of sugar would also sink its market price, thus lessening the need for more slaves in the West Indies.[50]

Fox was convinced that a sufficient number of individuals abstaining from sugar for just a few years 'would destroy the Slave Trade to the West-India Islands, bring fresh land into culture, and place the slaves in such a situation, that they must rapidly increase'.[51] Like many of the abolitionist writers of the day, Fox was not afraid to present in graphic detail the 'three endemic diseases' the typical West-Indian slave was daily subjected to—'hunger, torture, and extreme labour'.[52] As a result, the very character of Englishmen—as Christians, humanitarians, and lovers of freedom—was at stake in this issue. Since Parliament was 'not only unwilling, but perhaps unable, to grant redress', Fox urged the English people

> To abstain from the use of sugar and rum, until our West India Planters themselves have prohibited the importation of additional slaves, and commenced as speedy and effectual a subversion of slavery in their islands, as the circumstances and situation of the slaves will admit: or till we can obtain the produce of the sugar cane in some other mode, unconnected with slavery, and unpolluted with blood.[53]

If those who professed the national religion were unwilling to rise up and support the boycott, Fox was convinced that 'the various denominations of dissenters', such as the Baptists, Independents, Quakers, and even the Methodists,

---

[48] Cannibalism was often linked with slavery, both verbally and pictorially, in abolitionist literature of the 1790s. See Deirdre Coleman, 'Conspicuous Consumption: White Abolitionism and English Women's Protest Writing in the 1790s', *English Literary History* 61.2 (Summer, 1994), pp. 341-62.

[49] Fox, *Address*, p. 5. These figures used by Fox were quoted in numerous country papers. William Ward, at that time editor of the *Derby Mercury* and an ardent abolitionist, inserted the passage (which he had borrowed from the *Bath Chronicle*) in his newspaper on 10 November 1791.

[50] Thomas Clarkson claimed that by the last quarter of 1791, Britain's sugar revenue had fallen by £200,000. See Katherine Farrar (ed.), *Correspondence of Josiah Wedgwood 1781-1794* (London: Women's Printing Society, 1903-1906), p. 193.

[51] Fox, *Address*, pp. 4-5.

[52] Fox, *Address*, pp. 5-6.

[53] Fox, *Address*, pp. 8-9 (emphasis by Fox).

'will think it at the least, as requisite to dissent from the national crimes, as the national religion'.[54]

The success of Fox's *Address* was extraordinary, spawning one of the most strident pamphlet wars of the 1790s. Thomas Clarkson noted that Fox's pamphlet, along with William Bell Crafton's *A Short Sketch of the Evidence, Delivered before a Committee of the House of Commons, for the Abolition of the Slave-Trade; to which is added, a Recommendation of the Subject to the Serious Attention of People in General* (1792), another pamphlet printed and sold by Martha Gurney, had achieved widespread influence among abolitionists by early 1792.[55] Martha Gurney printed several favorable responses to the *Address*, including *A Vindication of the Address to the People of Great Britain, on the Use of West India Produce*, which appeared in November 1791.[56] The author was Richard Hillier, formerly a sailor in the West India trade who had joined the congregation at Maze Pond by letter from Samuel Pearce's congregation at Cannon Street in Birmingham on 3 July 1791, just days before the

---

[54] Fox, *Address*, pp. 11, 12.

[55] During his travels around England in 1791-92, Clarkson observed 'that there was no town, through which I passed, in which there was not some one individual who had left off the use of sugar. In the smaller towns there were from ten to fifty by estimation, and in the larger from two to five hundred, who had made this sacrifice to virtue. These were of all ranks and parties. Rich and poor, churchmen and dissenters, had adopted the measure. Even grocers had left off trading in the article, in some places. In gentlemen's families, where the master had set the example, the servants had often voluntarily followed it; and even children, who were capable of understanding the history of the sufferings of the Africans excluded, with the most virtuous resolution, the sweets, to which they had been accustomed, from their lips. By the best computation I was able to make from notes taken down in my journey, no fewer than three hundred thousand persons had abandoned the use of sugar'. See Thomas Clarkson, *The History of the Rise, Progress, and Accomplishment of the Abolition of the African Slave-trade by the British Parliament* (2 vols; London: Longman, Hurst, Rees, and Orme, 1808), I, pp. 349-50.

[56] Besides the *Vindication* cited above, favorable responses printed or sold by Martha Gurney include *Considerations Addressed to Professors of Christianity of every Denomination, on the Impropriety of Consuming West-India Sugar and Rum as Produced by the Oppressive Labour of Slaves* (1792); *An Address to the People called Methodists, Concerning the Criminality of Encouraging Slavery* (1792), by the Methodist minister Samuel Bradburn; *A Second Address to the People of Great Britain; Containing a New and Most Powerful Argument to Abstain from the Use of West India Sugar* (1792), by Andrew Burn, the former naval commander and friend of the Baptist leader and mathematician, Olinthus Gregory; *The Duty of Abstaining from the Use of West India Produce, a Speech, Delivered at Coach-Maker's-Hall, Jan. 12, 1792* (1792), by William Allen; and *Cruelty the Natural and Inseparable Consequence of Slavery, and Both Diametrically Opposite to the Doctrine and Spirit of the Christian Religion: Represented in a Sermon, Preached on Sunday, March 11$^{th}$, 1792, at Hemel-Hempstead, Herts.* (1792), by the Baptist minister John Liddon.

Priestley riots.[57] Hillier arrived in London at the height of the slave trade controversy and joined the sugar boycott after reading Fox's *Address* 'in manuscript', which Martha Gurney was apparently circulating through the congregation at Maze Pond that summer.[58] Hillier's pamphlet was in response to *An Answer to a Pamphlet, Intituled An Address to the People of England, Against the Use of the West India Produce* (London: W. Moon, 1791), composed by an anonymous female apologist for the slave trade who had attacked Fox and the sugar boycott. She responded to Hillier in a second edition of her *Answer*,[59] berating him for not abstaining from sugar prior to the current debate, to which Hillier replied that his conscience had been 'asleep' until he read Fox's 'well-timed, and spirited Address, to the People of Great Britain'.[60] Hillier's antagonist, however, did not speak for all females when it came to the slave trade debate. One anonymous critic of Fox argued that the *Address* 'claims particular notice', not only for its 'fallacious reasoning and inconclusive arguments' but also for 'the rapid and extraordinary manner in which it has been circulated in all parts of the kingdom', a success the writer attributes to the fact that so many 'English ladies [had] patronized' Fox's *Address*.[61] 'The heaven-born daughters of our isle', the writer asserts, 'with all that delicate sensibility which is their distinguishing characteristic, were pierced to the heart with the sufferings of the

---

[57] Several entries in the *Maze Pond Church Book* note Hillier's arrival: 'The Church being stayed, M.ʳ Richard Hillier, a Member of the Baptized Church under the Pastoral care of M.ʳ Pearce at Birmingham, Warwickshire, was proposed for communion with us:--Resolved, that he be admitted a Member of this Church when the Church to which he now belongs, grant him a Letter of Dismission' (II, fol. 77); 'A Letter from the Baptized Church at Birmingham, under the Pastoral care of M.ʳ Pearce, honorably dismissing M.ʳ Richard Hillier, being read: Resolved, he be admitted into Fellowship with us at the Table the first opportunity' (f.78). Hillier was also present at the church meeting on 18 July 1791 (II, fol. 78). By September 1794, Hillier had emigrated to America, for that month he became a member of the Pennsylvania Society for Promoting the Abolition of Slavery, with his residence listed as Long Island, New York (*Act of Incorporation*, p. 23). He died in America on 1 September 1812 (*Maze Pond Church Book*, II, fol. 16). He may have been related to Thomas Hillier, pastor of the Baptist congregation at Tewkesbury, 1771-90 (see Robert W. Oliver, *The Strict Baptist Chapels of England: The Chapels of Wiltshire and the West* [London: Strict Baptist Historical Society and Fauconberg Press, 1968], p. 109).
[58] *A Vindication of the Address to the People of Great-Britain, on the Use of West India Produce. With Some Observations and Facts Relative to the Situation of Slaves. In Answer to A female Apologist for Slavery. The Second Edition, with Strictures on Her Reply to a Reply* (London: M. Gurney [and others], [1791]), p. 3.
[59] I have been unable to locate a copy of the second edition of this pamphlet. To my knowledge, this is the only *pro*-slave trade pamphlet written by a woman that appeared during this first phase of the abolitionist movement.
[60] Hillier, *Vindication*, 2nd ed., p. 3.
[61] *Strictures on an Address to the people of Great Britain, on the Propriety of Abstaining from West-India Sugar and Rum*, 2nd ed. (London: T. Boosey, 1792), p. 3.

oppressed Africans; and, with a fortitude which does them the highest honour, refused to enjoy those sweets, which they supposed to be the price of blood'.[62]

While the *Address* was circulating in massive numbers throughout Great Britain and America, Fox and Martha Gurney brought out another attack on the slave trade, this one titled *A Summary View of the Evidence Delivered before a Committee of the House of Commons, Relating to the Slave Trade*, which appeared early in 1792.[63] The *Summary* begins with a discussion of the natural resources and products of Africa that would be of commercial value to Europe and America. Fox then proceeds, based on the testimony before the Parliamentary Committee, to discuss the nature and capabilities of the African people. According to the testimony, the more virtuous Africans live inland; those who lived along the coasts, due to their intercourse with Europeans, had become 'adepts in roguery', having been taught 'to plunder, and pick up one another to sell'.[64] The most baneful effect of the slave trade was the constant state of war

---

[62] Anon, *Strictures on an Address*, p. 4. Some went to great lengths to mock Fox and the sugar boycott. In a letter to the editor of the *European Magazine* (March 1792), purportedly written by a six-year-old boy who had made a promise to a Lady L— that he would not eat sugar, the boy wished to be relieved of his promise, for he had discovered that those promoting the boycott were 'great hypocrites', for they willingly partook of other commodities derived from slave labor but made no cry about them. He writes, 'I cannot think, dear Lady L---, how anybody who will not eat Sugar because it is eating Negro flesh, can handle gold or silver, or feed themselves with silver spoons or forks; for if eating sugar is eating Negroes flesh, sure every time anybody puts a fork or spoon in their mouths, it is putting a poor dead Negro's finger or toe there' (p. 185).

[63] The *Summary* went through at least six editions that year. On the title page of the 1st ed., the following note appeared (either by Fox or Gurney): 'The Address to the People of Great Britain having met with such an uncommon reception, as to have called for the printing, 50,000 in about four months, with a demand still greatly on the increase; the Author has been encouraged to publish this little piece with a view of making more generally known that dreadful traffic which has recently much engaged the public attention. To promote the circulation of both these pieces, they are published in a compendious form, and at a trivial price; notwithstanding which, editions, he understands, have been printed at Sheffield, Hull, Newcastle, Sunderland, Leeds, and other places; a circumstance rather disagreeable to an author, who, even though he may have abandoned any lucrative view in publishing, would, notwithstanding, wish to have the control over his work, and not have editions circulated subject to interpolation or mutilation, and which, at least must be destitute of those improvements, which are ever suggesting themselves to an author's mind'.

[64] William Fox, *A Summary View of the Evidence Delivered before a Committee of the House of Commons, Relating to the Slave Trade* (London: Sold by M. Gurney [and two others], 1792), p. 3. Elizabeth Donnan, in her massive four-volume work, *Documents Illustrative of the History of the Slave Trade to America* (New York: Octagon Books, 1965 [1931]), discusses Fox's *Summary View*, but confuses that pamphlet with another anonymous pamphlet of a similar title, A *Summary of the Evidence Produced before the Committee of the Privy Council, and before a Committee of the House of Commons:*

it produced along the coast, as the various kings vied for collecting the most slaves for the Europeans. Consequently, war in Africa had become nothing less than 'a piratical expedition for making slaves'.⁶⁵ After more review of the evidence, Fox concludes that the arguments of those who support the slave trade are disgusting, self-serving, and unworthy of serious consideration.⁶⁶ He deeply regrets the failure of the House of Commons to abolish the slave trade, but the evidence from the hearings is nevertheless before the public at last. Fox trusts that the day will come when the English will once again restore 'the rights of humanity' to the slaves, and no longer allow them 'to be stolen, degraded, insulted, and murdered by us'.⁶⁷ Given the horrid consequences of the slave trade upon the African, Fox fears that the slave can 'justly say, that the injuries he receives at the hands of his murderous oppressors; must be placed to our account; and that the blood of him, and his unhappy posterity, will be required at our hands'.⁶⁸

### William Fox, Tom Paine, and War in Europe

As Martha Gurney continued to print and sell pamphlets devoted to the slave trade controversy during 1792-93, William Fox turned his attention to other issues.⁶⁹ In *The Interest of Great Britain, Respecting the French War*, published by Gurney and two other booksellers early in 1793, just prior to Eng-

---

*Relating to the Slave Trade* (London: J. Bell, 1791) (Documents, II, p. 597, n. 4). Donnan apparently did not read the latter pamphlet, which takes a decidedly pro-slave trade position and was no doubt one of the many pamphlets Fox was attempting to counter in his own Summary.

⁶⁵ Fox, *Summary View*, p. 4.

⁶⁶ 'But surely we shall not ask them', Fox surmises, 'whether the loss of 2,000 seamen yearly, in the African Trade, be an injury or benefit to the English nation; or take their opinions as to the advantage resulting to us, from converting our wheat into a poisonous spirit, to be poured out on the coast of Africa, in exchange for the blood of its inhabitants, merely for the pleasure of glutting our savage minds, by murdering a part of them ourselves, and delivering over the residue to be murdered by others (*Summary View*, p. 11).

⁶⁷ Fox, *Summary View*, p. 12.

⁶⁸ Fox, *Summary View*, p. 12.

⁶⁹ Besides those mentioned above (n. 56), Gurney also printed or sold *A Short Sketch of the Evidence, Delivered before a Committee of the House of Commons, for the Abolition of the Slave-Trade; to which is added, a Recommendation of the Subject to the Serious Attention of People in General* (1792), by William Crafton Bell; *Considerations Addressed to Professors of Christianity of Every Denomination, on the Impropriety of Consuming West-India Sugar and Rum as Produced by the Oppressive Labour of Slaves* (1792); *The Negro: a Tale. Addressed to the Consideration of the Humane and Just* (1793); and *Slavery Inconsistent with Justice and Good Policy; Proved by a Speech Delivered in the Convention, held at Danville, Kentucky* (1793), by the American Presbyterian minister, David Rice.

land's declaration of war with France, Fox took a strong anti-war stance, blaming the threat of war more on English resistance to French principles, inflamed by Edmund Burke, than on French aggression. Fox argued that 'had the French King appeared cordially disposed to support the new order of things; and had the sovereigns of Europe, manifested the same disposition; there is no ground to suppose, the recent events would have taken place. All these events . . . may far more justly be attributed to Mr *Burke* than to the people of France'. Since Burke had been allowed 'to stigmatize [the French] with impunity', the English people should not 'wonder at the rage of the French populace, or its consequences'. The demise of the Royal Family of France, for whatever reason, was hardly 'a sufficient cause, for deluging Europe in blood'.[70] To Fox, however, it was natural that the European monarchs would seek to destroy the new French Republic, for 'Revolution principles, whether French, English, or Polish, are certainly dangerous to them, in proportion as they are beneficial to their subjects'.[71]

In *Thoughts on the Death of the King of France*, published shortly after Louis XVI's execution in January 1793, Fox argues that efforts by the British government to inflict its own view of justice on those responsible for killing the King of France cannot be supported by the law of nations or even English history. The English would never have tolerated French interference in the Glorious Revolution, and neither should England interfere in the proceedings of the National Convention. Besides, Fox satirically argues,

> admitting the British court to be actuated by the purest motives;—admitting that Africa, the West-indies, the East-indies, and our Sister Kingdom were to bear a united testimony to the rectitude and beneficence of our conduct, that we never interfere in the concerns of other countries, but to promote their happiness, and secure their rights;—that our sword is the sword of justice, and not of outrage; and, that it never was unsheathed but to protect the innocent, and to punish the aggressor: yet, still might the propriety of our avenging the death of the king of France be doubted, because we have hardly the means of discriminating the guilty, or ascertaining their proportionate share in the guilt.[72]

Fox claims that England is largely to blame for the war by failing to mediate between France and the other kingdoms of Europe.[73] Going to war against

---

[70] William Fox, *The Interest of Great Britain, Respecting the French War*, 3$^{rd}$. ed. (London: T. Whieldon and Butterworth, W. Richardson, and M. Gurney, 1793), p. 2.

[71] Fox, *The Interest of Great Britain*, p. 10.

[72] William Fox, *Thoughts on the Death of the King of France* (London: J. Ridgway, W. Richardson, T. Whieldon and Butterworth, and M. Gurney, 1793), p. 6.

[73] Fox writes: 'When the French nation proffered us the office of mediator, we could without violating the law of nations, without insulting the independency of a great nation, have then pointed out the defects in the new established government . . . The friends of the then existing government would, doubtless, have been desirous to have

France over the killing of the King only 'manifests the absurdity of attempting to punish crimes by a war, and proves that such a war must in its nature be unjust'.[74] It is also hypocritical, he believes, that Parliament should be outraged at the killing of the king of France yet unable 'to prosecute the inquiry any farther on the Slave Trade', for not even the murder of a King is more significant than 'those murders which occur every hour of the day in our West-india islands, and in the holds of our Corsairs'.[75] Fox closes with a daring critique (given the growing paranoia of the Pitt administration in 1793) of monarchical government:

> If then those experiments in government, which are going forward in the world, should at length prove that the government of nations, the preservation of property, the benefit of society, do not absolutely require a *regal order*. If no great injury would result to mankind from its abolition, it might then possibly become a question, not unworthy consideration; *whether it be compatable with humanity, to dress out the gaudy trappings of a throne, to ensnare our fellow creatures; thus tempting them to ascend a dangerous eminence, from whence to be precipitated, must be calamitous, in proportion to the extent of the power they possessed, and the splendor and the adulation with which they had been surrounded.*[76]

In his next pamphlet, *An Examination of Mr Paine's Writings*, Fox found himself, like many reformers of the 1790s, at odds with some of the more radical views of Thomas Paine, especially those espoused in Part 2 of his *Rights of Man* (1792). Though not afraid to criticize the idea of monarchy, as his previous pamphlet demonstrated, Fox nevertheless believed that a radical redistribution of private property and a leveling of all social distinctions were not required for political reform. To Fox, echoing the views of the Commonwealthmen from earlier in the century, the landed interest was essential to the continued prosperity and security of England.[77] Though Fox was not afraid to join

---

listened to our friendly council, and then have guarded the state from those threatened dangers [of anarchy], and themselves from Prussian prisons'. But England refused 'to interfere', and instead made 'this anarchy, which we refused to prevent, a pretence for joining in the hostile attack, and thereby perpetuate[d] the evils we ought to have prevented; and now avenge the death of the king of France, though we declined taking any measure for his preservation' (Fox, *Thoughts*, pp. 11-12).

[74] Fox, *Thoughts*, p. 14.

[75] Fox, *Thoughts*, p. 18.

[76] Fox, *Thoughts*, p. 19 (emphasis Fox).

[77] William Fox, *An Examination of Mr Paine's Writings* (London: T. Whieldon and Butterworth, W. Richardson, and M. Gurney, 1793), p. 12. Fox argued that this 'state of a landed property which Mr *Paine* stigmatizes, appears to be of the most sacred nature, it must have a collateral existence with the increase of man, and to shake it, is to terminate that increase . . . if society innovate on this species of property, it violates that confidence which was reposed in it, and a confidence from whence it derives the most essential benefits' (*Examination*, pp. 12-13).

with many radicals in criticizing the hypocrisy of the British government in the early 1790s, he was conservative enough to realize that since 'a permanent and exclusive property in land is that which will render the earth fit to sustain the greatest number of inhabitants, it follows that to preserve that permanent and exclusive property must be a principal object of laws and government, and in proportion as any system of government tends to weaken the possession of land, in that proportion it is unfit to be adopted in that advanced stage of civil society where the increase of man calls for an increasing means of support'.[78]

In *A Discourse on National Fasts, Particularly in Reference to that of April 19, 1793, on Occasion of the War against France*, Fox criticized the hypocrisy of the King and his ministers in asking God's blessing upon what many Dissenters believed to be an unjust and unnecessary war. As a Dissenter, Fox could not overlook the blatant irony between England's professed religion and its political reality. 'To promulgate amongst the people', he writes,

> a religion against which every national act militates; to be continually at war, yet profess the gospel of peace; to be ranging round the world to spread misery, desolation, famine and war; yet to place before us for an example him who went about doing good. To have the same government and legislature, who are perpetrating those deeds, enacting penal laws to compel us to profess a belief in the very religion that condemns them, are certainly admirable contrivances to destroy every religious, and every moral principle. Nor, is it less observable that, because *Jesus* has declared that his kingdom is not of this world, it is determined that it shall be of this world; because he has told us, that his disciples shall be hated for his name sake, they therefore enact penalties to compel them to profess their belief in him; as we are informed by him, that his church shall consist of a remnant, chosen out of all nations, and tongues, and people, with infinite propriety, it is made to consist of whole nations; and, to finish the picture, because *Jesus* has proclaimed himself to be the head over all things to his church, the *king* is proclaimed to be the head of it.[79]

If subjects are commanded to pray for the 'success' of its nation's armies', Fox argues, then they have a right to ask 'how they are to be employed, and what consequences are to result from the success we are to ask'. If those reasons and consequences are not biblically correct, then, he argues, it 'becomes our duty, not only to decline affirming it ourselves, but to urge others to make a similar inquiry, that they may thereby avoid the guilt of asserting a falsehood to God'.[80] Fox believes the Fast Days are mainly used by the church and state for

---

[78] Fox, *Examination*, p. 15.

[79] William Fox, *A Discourse on National Fasts, Particularly in Reference to that of April 19, 1793, on Occasion of the War against France* (London: J. Ridgway, W. Richardson, T. Whieldon and Butterworth, and M. Gurney, 1793), pp. 2-3.

[80] Fox, *Discourse on National Fasts*, p. 11. Not all Dissenters agreed with Fox's position on Fast Days. Robert Winter, at that time the morning preacher at Salter's Hall in London, in *The Reasonableness of National Humiliation: A Sermon Addressed to a*

purposes of propaganda, manufacturing opportunities to warn the people about the 'danger from republicans and levellers, from french daggers and french principles, of king-killing, and atheism'. With obvious disgust, Fox notes that 'the night passes in praising the constitution, damning dissenters and execrating the French, interlarded with cursing, swearing, quarrelling, and obscenity'.[81] The public peace would be less 'endangered', he contends, if the authorities would allow 'the Revolution Society to drink the Rights of Man, and send the most splendid embassy to their friends the Jacobins'.[82] Peace is far more threatened by England's refusal to recognize the new French government, a meaningless gesture, according to Fox, for France 'is as much recognized by a war, as by a treaty'.[83]

A year later Fox developed the same topic even further in *A Discourse, Occasioned by the National Fast, February 28, 1794*. Here he lays out a simple principle concerning war, one remarkably applicable to our own age: 'That a community, as well as an individual, ought to defend themselves when *actually* attacked, will not be disputed; but to go abroad in quest of blood and slaughter, under pretence of guarding against *future* and *supposed* dangers, is certainly incompatible with every moral principle even as recognized by the common practice of civil life'.[84] Fox believes that Christians are to submit to those in authority over them, but submission was never meant to be 'unlimited'.[85] Yet it is this very idea of submission that Fox believes makes Christianity so popular with monarchs and slave-owners, who rely on this alliance of church and state as their chief ally in all their crimes. Unfortunately, many people, especially Dissenters like Fox, understand Christianity in far different terms, holding the virtues of kindness, patience, and meekness in much greater esteem than violence, hatred, and revenge. Thus, when they see Christian kings and ministers 'trampling' on these virtues', they are apt, as Fox does, 'to look with horror on their conduct'.[86] Once again, Fox cannot resist comparing the actions of the King of England towards France and those of the English regarding the slave trade and colonization:

---

*Congregation of Protestant Dissenters, at Hammersmith; on the General Fast, April 19, 1793* (London: [n.d.], 1793), argued that on Fast Days Dissenting ministers should say nothing that 'borders on rudeness to that government, under which they live quiet and peaceable lives. On a day which if at all proper, is soon a religious account, it is totally unsuitable to drop even an expression, tending to foment that wretched party-spirit, which social devotion is most adapted to destroy' (p. 30).

[81] Fox, *Discourse on National Fasts*, p. 13.
[82] Fox, *Discourse on National Fasts*, p. 13.
[83] Fox, *Discourse on National Fasts*, p. 16.
[84] William Fox, *A Discourse, Occasioned by the National Fast, February 28, 1794* (London: M. Gurney, [1794]), p. 3.
[85] Fox, *A Discourse, Occasioned by the National Fast*, p. 6.
[86] Fox, *A Discourse, Occasioned by the National Fast*, pp. 7-8.

Will it be said, that the parent, the Head of this family, residing in this Island, has any right as such, to send one of his sons to extirpate the family in a West India Island? . . . Will it be said, that he has a right to send another of his sons to the East Indies, under pretence of trading with the Asiatic family for the produce of their industry, and quarelling with another foreigner who had come there under the same pretext, make that quarrel a foundation not only for possessing their houses and their lands, but spreading famine and death among them, by seizing their very food; and shall the English parent grant a charter to his son, authorising him *thus* to *govern* the Asiatic family, on condition of his sending part of the money to England, which has been so obtained in Asia, to enable him to pay his debts: and lastly, suppose he were to send another of his sons to the Irish family, harrassing them from age to age, without the shadow of a pretext, but that they had the misfortune to be neighbours, and therefore exposed to their inroads; and less powerful, consequently unable to retaliate the injury; should he compel them to contribute a tenth of the produce of their labour to support an English clergy, whose religion they abhored, and the greater part of the rents of their land to aggrandise and enrich their neighbour? Let us ask, whether there be any principle which could justify this conduct? would any one presume to apologise for it? would not the voice of reason and justice, call on mankind to abhor it?[87]

Monarchs patronize Christianity out of perverseness, Fox concludes, 'because it is peculiarly hostile to their conduct'. Wicked people will favor such rulers, for they reflect their own evil character, but truly Christian people will 'abhor those who assume his name to disgrace it, and to trample on his authority'.[88]

### *A Defence of the Decree of the National Convention of France, for Emancipating the Slaves in the West Indies* (1794)

In 1794, Fox returned once again to his favorite subject in *A Defence of the Decree of the National Convention of France, for Emancipating the Slaves in the West Indies* (1794).[89] He proposes, with obvious irony, that England should be happy with France's decision to emancipate the slaves of West India, for now England can see firsthand the results of a decision it has been incapable of making. According to the proponents of the slave trade, anarchy should break out everywhere and the French economy become bankrupt, forcing the French

---

[87] Fox, *A Discourse, Occasioned by the National Fast*, pp. 8-9.
[88] Fox, *A Discourse, Occasioned by the National Fast*, p. 15.
[89] The French Assembly first debated the subject of abolition in 1790, an account of which was published in *Proceedings of the National Assembly of France, upon the Proposed Abolition of the Slave Trade in that Kingdom* (London, 1790). Though Fox's *Defence* is undated, some bibliographic citations have dated the *Defence* as 1790, most likely basing that date upon the *Proceedings*; however, on the title pages to several of Fox's 1794 pamphlets are notices alerting the reader to the recent publication of the *Defence*.

slaves to seek asylum in the English colonies, where they can once again enjoy the benefits of slavery.[90] With biting sarcasm, Fox ridicules both the proponents and opponents of the slave trade bills of 1791 and 1792, especially Pitt, arguing that, in many cases, the only difference between the two groups was how best to perpetuate slavery in the West Indies.[91] To Fox, the hypocrisy of many members of Parliament was self-evident: 'The Abolitionists and the Anti-abolitionists, indeed, both talked, and with equal propriety, about justice and humanity, but it was merely to lengthen, diversify and ornament their speeches. The most eligible mode of increasing the Slaves was the sole question, and so far was the Abolition of slavery from being intended, that Mr Pitt's principal argument in favour of his plan was, that, it secured Slavery from impending dangers'.[92] The outcome of the issue was easily predicted: 'That liberty and happiness are to be confined to his foggy Island, is an Englishman's favourite idea, to spread mischief and desolation through the earth, is his most luxurious enjoyment'.[93] Fox is amazed that Pitt could refer to this act of emancipation by the French as 'absurd, weak and improvident', a comment that brings another Swiftian effusion from Fox:

Let us contrast it [the French decision to emancipate] with *our* conduct, which is, to be sure, as *laudable* as that of the *French* is *detestable*. The French have resolved, that a million of fellow-creatures shall be restored to the benefit of society, and the protection of the laws. This is it seems, *weak* and *foolish*. We say they shall be considered as chattels, remain out of the protection of the law, subject to the will of their fellow subjects, to be treated as brutes; this it seems quite *wise* and *laudable*. The French, having obtained liberty for themselves, are desirous of communicating its happiness to others; this is *absurd*. We make use of the power we derive from the liberty we enjoy to enslave others; this is perfectly *rational*. The French refer the subject to a Committee, to adopt *prudent* measures; this is *improvident*. We are for years agitating the subject of the West India Slavery, bringing the enormities of it before the public, without having the least intention of interfering in it; and even suffer the Planters to insult the Legislature, by declaring that it had no right to interfere between them and their Slaves, and that, if even it presumes to endeavour to prevent additional importations, they will set our

---

[90] William Fox, *A Defence of the Decree of the National Convention of France* (London: M. Gurney ... and D. I. Eaton, [1794]), p. 2.

[91] 'Mr *Pitt* and the other Abolitionists', he writes, 'contend that our Colonial Slavery was endangered by introducing Negroes from *Africa*, who, bred in the enjoyment of Freedom, disdaining the yoke of Slavery, would be ever attempting to subvert the venerable fabric, and wickedly endeavouring to obtain their freedom; he therefore proposed, that the importation of such dangerous Negroes should be prohibited, and that the Colonist, should be confined to the home manufacture of Slaves, and these being born and bred Slaves would more patiently submit to chains and whips, to incessant labour and extreme hunger' (Fox, *Defence of the Decree*, pp. 3-4).

[92] Fox, *Defence of the Decree*, pp. 4-5.

[93] Fox, *Defence of the Decree*, p. 5.

laws at defiance, and the Colonial Judicatures shall trample them under foot. All this is perfectly *prudent*.[94]

Fox repudiates the notion that abolition harms the slave and the slaveholder as well as the belief that slavery is somehow 'benevolent'. He also rejects Pitt's claim that a '*Black* government is an idea sufficient to excite our horror'. A true Englishman, he argues, will 'deliver [the slaves] from their oppressors' and restore the slaves 'to the protection of the law, and subject them to its control'.[95]

## The Jacobin Threat

Fox returned to the ever-worsening war with France in his next pamphlet, *Thoughts on the Impending Invasion of England* (1794), chastising England for spurning France's offer of mediation and castigating the monarchs of Europe for their dislike of liberty and self-determination for the French people. 'If we in attempting to subvert other governments', he writes, 'should be in danger of producing the destruction of our own. If in spreading the flames of war through the world, they should be on the point of reverberating on ourselves, we may then possibly contemplate the present war through a less pleasing medium, and may possibly be willing to return into the bosom of peace with less reluctance'.[96] Fox can only lament that since the English 'have brought such horrors and desolation on other countries', they should not complain if they are forced 'to partake of the bitter cup' themselves. 'If a powerful enemy should invade our land, and banish from it happiness and peace, let us recollect how many nations we have involved in those calamities of war, which we are at length destined to experience'.[97]

In his next pamphlet, *On Jacobinism*, Fox explored one of the most politically charged words of the 1790s. Given the history of such words as 'Puritan', 'Papist', 'Pretender', 'Tory', 'Court and Country', and 'Rights of Man', applying deceptive meanings to religious and political terms was nothing new for the 1790s.[98] He argues that these words, by means of their arbitrary usage, cur-

---

[94] Fox, *Defence of the Decree*, pp. 6-7.
[95] Fox, *Defence of the Decree*, p. 16.
[96] Fox, *Defence of the Decree*, p. 12.
[97] Fox, *Defence of the Decree*, p. 16.
[98] William Fox, *On Jacobinism* (London: M. Gurney, 1794), p. 3. In 1805, the Baptist preacher and essayist, John Foster, who was exposed to radical politics during his days at Bristol Baptist College in 1791-92, commented on the power and persistence of the epithet 'Jacobin'. Politicians, Foster argues, know that a clear, rational presentation of the facts rarely moves the populace. 'But if a single word, devised in hatred and defamation of political liberty, can be made the symbol of all that is absurd and execrable, so that the very sound of it shall irritate the passions of this ignorant and scorned multitude, as dogs have been taught to bark at the name of a neighbouring tyrant, it is a commodi-

rently 'bear no definite sense, and thereby appear to be well adapted to enable a party to stigmatise their adversaries; for in such proportion as these terms are equivocal and destitute of meaning, are they adapted to this purpose'.[99] In light of the Jacobin scare, with its supposed threat of anarchy and dissolution of property, Fox is unmoved. 'If it appears that anarchy is so abhorrent to our nature,' he asks, 'as that the political body has as an invariable tendency to counteract it, as the natural body has to discharge the morbid matter with which it may be loaded, shall any one dare to tell us that *Jacobinism* will break up civil society, destroy social order, and introduce perpetual anarchy and ruin?'[100] If Jacobinism is, as Burke, Pitt, and other conservatives contended, 'a principle operating to the subversion of the general order of Europe', then the monarchies and aristocracies of Europe have for centuries operated under an even worse principle of subversion.[101] Jacobinism is hostile to the present system, Fox asserts, precisely because the present system is in need of 'innovation', and Jacobinism will 'prevail' in correcting that system because it is not really a 'form of government' at all.[102]

In some countries the convulsion will be great, but in England, the least corrupted of the European systems, the innovations need not be all that convulsive. He argues that the principle of innovation has been present in England and Europe for centuries, and is basically a principle of nature.[103] 'If Jacobinism be the progress of human knowledge subverting ancient systems founded on ignorance and superstition', Fox argues, 'can it be destroyed by imprisoning or hanging a few noisy demagogues'. 'No!' he insists, 'The English, the American, and the French Revolutions, are merely the channels in which Jacobinism has flowed: had they never taken place, had those countries never had existence, the mighty torrent would have rolled, its course only would have been varied'. Not even Burke's 'lamentation on modern innovation' will stop its progress.[104]

---

ous expedient for rendering these passions available and subservient to the interests of those who despise, while they cajole, their duped auxiliaries' (*Essays, in a Series of Letters* [London: Bell and Daldy, 1872], p. 131).

[99] Fox, *Jacobinism*, pp. 3-4.

[100] Fox, *Jacobinism*, pp. 6-7.

[101] 'The privileged orders', Fox declares, 'have uniformly exerted the power, derived from the property they possess, to overawe and control the existing government, whatever may be its form; to obtain privileges, and exemptions incompatible with every idea of good government; and to throw the burden of the state upon those who are destitute of the means of supporting it. And it has been only in proportion to the subversion of this system, that the governments of any of the countries of Europe have been able to exercise their proper functions' (*Jacobinism*, p. 11).

[102] Fox, *Jacobinism*, p. 13.

[103] Fox, *Jacobinism*, p. 14.

[104] Fox, *Jacobinism*, p. 15.

## On the Renewal of the East India Charter

Just like his pamphlets on the war with France, Fox's *On the Renewal of the East India Charter*, in its stinging critique of British colonialism, expresses sentiments more common to the present day than the 1790s. According to Fox, the British government, through the work of the East India Company, had attained new heights of arrogance; not content with determining 'how the inhabitants of the immense continent of Africa ought to be disposed of', it has now granted itself the right to subdue another continent for its own gain.[105] To Fox, these 'piratical adventures' are nothing less than kingdom stealing.[106] If the English really believe they can occupy and govern such a vast land, they must never have learned 'that important truth, which peculiarly distinguishes the civilized from barbarous ages, that the value of the earth depends on its quiet enjoyment, and is destroyed by violence and outrage'.[107] Fox is bewildered by the East India Company's idea of governance, for 'if it be deemed expedient to *murder* half the inhabitants of India, and *rob* the remainder, surely it is not requisite to call it *governing* them. If we choose to seize, and carry off the inhabitants of Africa, what is the use of terming it a *trade*. And if we convert our West India Islands into jails to confine them, why, in the name of common sense, must they be called *colonies*?'[108] After the renewal of the East India Company's charter in 1793, an unwarranted assumption of power occurred on the part of the English in India, resulting in 'rapacity, treachery, and cruelty', and for those actions the English are now viewed with 'horror and detestation', not 'reverence'.[109] 'Experience will warrant no intercourse between nations', Fox concludes, 'but the intercourse of fair and legitimate commerce; experience testifies that all other is ruinous as it is wicked'.[110]

## 'Patriotism', National Defence, and the French War

The progress of England's war with France during 1794 provoked Fox's most ironic pamphlet, *Defence of the War against France*. With a tone and style reminiscent of Swift's *A Modest Proposal*, Fox mocks the government's justifications for the war by suggesting that

---

[105] William Fox, *On the Renewal of the East India Charter* (London: M. Gurney, 1794), p. 2.
[106] Fox, *Renewal*, p. 6. In fact, Fox believes the King's ministers may never be satisfied until they 'range the planetary system, dispose of the moon by a royal charter, catch Mercury in the budget, and share out the *Georgium Sidus* in Change Alley' (*Renewal*, p. 3).
[107] Fox, *Renewal*, p. 7.
[108] Fox, *Renewal*, p. 8.
[109] Fox, *Renewal*, p. 13.
[110] Fox, *Renewal*, p. 15.

it is highly becoming this nation, to exert all the energy of the state, to prevent France, Poland, or any other considerable nation in Europe, from adopting any alternative in their Government, or Laws, which may meliorate and improve the circumstances of the people, or remove those defects in their Governments, which impede their Manufactures, Trade, Agriculture, and General Happiness—That on our preventing the removal of those defects in their Governments, and our subverting their rising happiness, depends the very existence of every thing which peculiarly distinguishes us amongst Nations.—That it becomes us to persevere, with a zeal proportioned to the importance of the cause, assured that in abandoning it we expose our religion, the administration of our laws, the great system of our commerce, nay our well balanced government, the wonder and the admiration of the world! to certain and irreparable ruin.[111]

As the numerous Fast Day sermons made clear, God was on the side of the English. Thus, Fox surmises, the most efficient way of eliminating the French would be to ask God for a natural calamity, such as a famine, much like the English procured in India, 'by which notable contrivance we have not only the pleasure of destroying our fellow creatures, but the additional satisfaction of imputing our deeds to heaven, or, if it suits our purpose, to those whom we destroy'. Fox is forced to admit that 'where ever the English have gone, whether into Ireland, Asia, or the West Indies, famine constantly follows their footsteps', a reality he finds most difficult to stomach.[112] Fox is aware that Jacobinism might spread to England, Scotland, Poland, and other places, so it may be necessary, he ironically suggests, for the government to resort to famine in those countries as well; for the sword, he contends,

is little adapted to root out Jacobinism. Its progress, in destruction, is too slow. It rouses to resistance, inflames the passions, promotes disquisition, and invigorates the mind. Pestilence and famine produce the contrary effects. Their havoc is not only more rapid, and extensive, than the most destructive war, but the survivors naturally sink into an abject state, well fitted to receive any yoke that may be imposed.[113]

Consequently, 'MR BURKE'S wishes may be gratified, in carrying us back to the state of those past ages, whose ignorance and whose barbarism we are now called to look on with envy'.[114] The English government has learned the true lesson of the French Revolution, so much so that future Kings and Prime Ministers will 'be careful not to grant their subjects any degree of liberty . . . '. Instead, 'they will restrict commerce and manufactures within the narrowest bounds', 'subject Agriculture to the most barbarous system', and, for certain, 'annihilate the press', all because of one overriding principle---that to make

---

[111] William Fox, *Defence of the War against France* (London: M. Gurney, 1794), p. 5.
[112] Fox, *Defence of the War*, p. 13.
[113] Fox, *Defence of the War*, p. 14.
[114] Fox, *Defence of the War*, p. 15.

man 'servile', he must be rendered 'miserable'.[115] Fox concludes his pamphlet with a *reductio ad absurdum* reminiscent of the political satires of Benjamin Franklin:[116]

> As, then, the object for which this war was undertaken cannot possibly be attained without extirpating the French, and as we have been uniformly told, that on the attainment of the object of the war, depended every thing that was dear to us, nay our very existence; it then follows, that to sign a peace with France on any terms whatever, must be signing nothing less than our own destruction, and annihilation, nor can any man propose peace with them without acknowledging the falsehood of those reasons which have been assigned for the prosecution of the war, which must be pursued on the magnificent plan of MR BURKE, that if we fail to extirpate the French the war must be continued until they extirpate us.[117]

Similar attacks on the Pitt administration and the war with France surfaced in Fox's next pamphlet, *On Peace*. Since Burke had declared that the war against France and its Jacobin principles would, if necessary, be an 'eternal war', fought to the last man, Fox concludes that, should England endure such a fate, the government would be taken over by England's women, who were fortunately excluded from Burke's 'bloody proscription'. Even though 'no partizan of liberty and equality has ever yet condescended to consider Woman as a part of the Human Race, although all their principles and systems of government, founded on the Rights of *Man*, have left the *Women* unnoticed, as though they had no existence, yet surely, when the last *Man* has fallen, on them the Government must devolve...'.[118] The English can only hope, if they do not want to face such an end, to utterly destroy France, and then they shall be known to posterity, 'not merely as the Desolators and Oppressors of Ireland, the plunderers of Asia, the Kidnappers of Africa, and the base Slave-holders of the West', but as conquerors 'crowned with Glory, eclipsing the triumphs of ancient Rome...'.[119] Should the English lose the war (a reality Fox takes quite seriously), he proposes that the French could simply imitate the English by employing 'Liverpool ships to convey all the young men, women, and children [of England], and sell them to the people of France ... In such a case, they might find plenty of evidence, produced before a committee of the House of Commons by Lords, and Knights, and Squires, proving the miserable situation of the people of England, and how much they would be benefited by being

---

[115] Fox, *Defence of the War*, p. 15.

[116] Martha Gurney, like many Dissenters, highly esteemed Franklin's political writings, especially his views on religious toleration. She reprinted and sold two of his works, *A Parable against Persecution*, 2nd ed. [1793], and *Information to Those Who Would Remove to America* (1794).

[117] Fox, *Defence of the Decree*, p. 16.

[118] William Fox, *On Peace* (London: M. Gurney, 1794), pp. 2, 4-5.

[119] Fox, *Peace*, p. 11.

made slaves'.[120] In a comment that a year later could have landed Fox in prison, he suggests that if the French were to dispose of the English according to French principles, it would actually prove to be a blessing, for

> should the War terminate in depriving us of all our foreign dependencies, should the plunder of India no longer deluge our land, should our mart of slavery no longer exist, and should our Ministers be delivered from the thraldom of governing a neighbouring Island, should we behold in our Sovereign merely a King of Great Britain, and our House of Commons cease to be crouded with the representatives of West India Slavery or an East India Squad, it is possible that the change produced on our Government, our Laws, and general Polity may not prove extremely calamitous.[121]

In the second half of 1794, Fox collaborated with Martha Gurney in a series of anonymous pamphlets in imitation of Benjamin Franklin, entitled *Poor Richard's Scraps*. These pamphlets were separately numbered, with each pamphlet containing two numbers that formed a continuous argument under one title. In numbers one and two (of which only number one survives), Fox created a French Poor Richard who had recently read a Manifesto by the English government concerning its intent to form a Confederation of European powers for the purpose of invading France and restoring the rightful heirs to the throne, even if against the wishes of the French people. The speaker is pleased that England is finally recognizing France's 'national existence', but he 'cannot help but wonder if such recognition should not have come *before* the invasion rather than after it!'[122] The manifesto gives the French no option other than surrender and a return to the former system. England, the speaker believes, has made her intentions clear, that 'she abhors the thought that any other nation should taste the sweets of freedom; and if a younger brother dares but to glance a look at the throne of liberty, behold, she prepares the bowstring'.[123] As far as Fox's Frenchman is concerned, he sees nothing but treachery and duplicity in England's actions toward France since the Revolution of 1789.

The second issue (numbers three and four) of *Poor Richard's Scraps*, another ironic piece entitled *On the Excellence of the British Government*, most likely appeared in November 1794, about the time of the annual celebrations of the Glorious Revolution. Here Fox takes his reader on a history of 'innovations' in the British Constitution since Magna Charta. The current power held by the House of Commons, he argues, is itself an innovation, having been wrested over several centuries from the power once held by the monarch.[124]

---

[120] Fox, *Peace*, p. 15.
[121] Fox, *Peace*, p. 16.
[122] William Fox, *Poor Richard's Scraps, No. 1* (London: M. Gurney, [1794]), pp. 2-3.
[123] Fox, *Poor Richard's Scraps, No. 1*, p. 10.
[124] Fox writes, 'The House of Commons obtained, and have ever since retained their power, not from any antient or natural right to the Government, but because, from the

Obviously frustrated by the lack of integrity he sees in the current system, especially the House of Commons, Fox lashes out at a legislative body bent on accumulating even greater power for itself, only now that power is being taken from the people, not the Crown.[125] The Glorious Revolution merely replaced an absolute sovereignty with a ruling aristocracy, with democracy rejected as unworkable and wrong-headed. Consequently, the House of Commons, deriving its power and wealth from colonial conquests and slavery, found themselves in need of a puppet King, 'a foreign Prince, remotely allied to the Crown, who could have no hope but through them of ever possessing it' and who would 'become a tool in their hands, or an accomplice in their designs'.[126] According to Fox, 'innovation' has always been the norm in English history, not the aberration.[127]

As 1794 came to a close, Fox could not fail but notice the growing climate of fear fostered by the Pitt administration's efforts to prosecute a number of leading reformers on charges of sedition and treason. It was during some of the celebrated treason trials of 1794-1796 that Martha Gurney's nephew, John

---

nature of its constitution, men of wealth, influence, and ability, obtained seats in it, and when thus congregated together, were enabled to wrest from the King, Nobles, and Clergy, the small remnant of their power, and were equally enabled to assume it themselves. No scruples did they entertain as to the lawfulness of thus assuming power; nor do they appear to have entertained a thought of forming any rational system of Government, but grasped the whole of it themselves' (pp. 12-13). Thus, he contends, 'to what period then of the British history do the advocates for the antiquity of our Government wish to refer us? In what age are we to find . . . the standard of perfection, for any one of the branches of our excellent government?' (*Poor Richard's Scraps, No. 1*, p. 14).

[125] 'In this view', he writes, 'it is evident, that the sole contest, both in the reigns of *Charles* I. and II. was, whether the lower House of Parliament should exercise the whole authority of the state? Imitating the stile of the ancient Barons, and our piratical invaders, they dared to call *themselves* the people of England; and, under the *guise* of that appellation, artfully advanced their own power, and undermined that of the crown; and, amidst all the disputes to which these contests have given rise, it is extraordinary that no one has ever yet condescended to undertake to prove, either that this body of men had a right to wrest from the crown the government of the country, or that such a transfer of it would have been beneficial to the people' (*Poor Richard's Scraps, No. 1*, pp. 21-22).

[126] Fox, *Poor Richard's Scraps, No. 1*, p. 27.

[127] 'In this extended range of our history', he writes, 'from its earliest period until the Revolution in 1688, it does not, then, appear that any particular form, or principle, of Government can be stated as its characteristic.---We see nothing but a series of events, producing a vast variety of changes in the Government, so important, and so sudden, as, so far from suggesting the shadow of a pretext of there existing a regular permanent, well formed Government, it does not appear that such an one had ever even a momentary existence, as to which we can look back with regret, as having passed away, which can be referred to for our imitation, or as to which we can boast of our ancestors forming by their wisdom, or transmitting to us by their heroism' (*Poor Richard's Scraps, No. 1*, p. 30).

Gurney, rose to prominence as a defense attorney. In a pamphlet arising from the arrests for treason of Thomas Hardy, Horne Tooke, John Thelwall and others in 1794, Fox argues that the definition of treason being used in these trials is a clear 'innovation', altered now to protect the ministers, not the King, for 'to whatever extent our discontents may prevail, yet never was there a period in which they had so little relation to *Treason*'.[128] A new definition of treason was being designed by the authorities 'to make 'terror the order of the day', for the suppression of speculation on improvements in Government, which our Ministers suppose to be peculiarly dangerous',[129] especially when coming from the various societies organized for the purpose of political reform. For the government to charge the members of these reform societies with sedition and treason simply because they were criticizing the House of Commons, implying that such criticism was an attack upon the King himself, is ludicrous to Fox, for throughout English history the House had rarely seen itself as indissolubly connected to the Throne.[130] The greatest danger to English freedoms, Fox argues, resides in an elite group of legislators, and not the King. Otherwise, there is no reason that a proposed 'Convention, which should have for its object the obtaining a *Parliamentary Reform*, and that object only . . . would be High Treason in all the actors in it', except that it sought to do so 'without the authority of Parliament'.[131] To Fox, this new 'Law of Treason' is nothing less than an 'absurdity' that flies in the face of all 'principles of common sense'.[132]

## The Politics of Fear and Attempts to Silence the Radical Voice

By the end of 1794, William Fox's brief career as a political writer was over.[133]

---

[128] William Fox, *On Trials for Treason* [London: M. Gurney, 1794], p. 1. This pamphlet is bound in Elizabeth Gurney's volume at the University of Michigan, but is missing the title page; the title was provided by Miss Gurney in her MS. 'Table of Contents'. The pamphlet may have appeared anonymously.

[129] Fox, *Trials for Treason*, p. 4.

[130] Pitt's power as Prime Minister, Fox argues, is in fact derived from previous eruptions of the House against the King, some occurring as recently as the end of the war with America (Fox, *Trials for Treason*, pp. 10-12).

[131] Fox, *Trials for Treason*, pp. 14-15. Thomas Muir, Thomas Fyshe Palmer, William Skirving, and Maurice Margarot were tried for sedition as a result of activities related to the Edinburgh Convention on constitutional reform in October 1793. They were convicted and sentenced to deportation, sailing to Botany Bay in March 1794. When members of the London Corresponding Society planned a similar convention for summer 1794 in London, its leaders—Thomas Hardy, Horne Tooke, John Thelwall, Jeremiah Joyce, and others—were arrested, held for six months in the Tower, and then tried for treason. All were acquitted by early 1795.

[132] Fox, *Trials for Treason*, p. 16.

[133] Despite his prolific political pamphleteering, Fox has never received a prominent place in studies of the British anti-slavery and political reform movement of the early

His political ideals were now embodied in the magnificent speeches of Thomas Erskine and John Gurney recorded in the transcripts of numerous state trials held during the mid- to late 1790s, taken in shorthand by Joseph Gurney and printed and sold in Martha Gurney's bookshop in Holborn.[134] We should not be surprised at Fox's cessation of political activity. The climate in England at that time was anything but conducive to writing and distributing radical political pamphlets. After the passage of the Royal Proclamation in May 1792 against 'seditious' writings and speech and the formation of John Reeves's Association for the Preservation of Liberty and Property against Republicans and Levellers in November 1792, mechanisms were put in place for clamping down on radical printers, booksellers, and writers. Thomas Paine was convicted in *absentia* in December 1792, and some of his chief promoters, H. D. Symonds and James Ridgeway, London printers and booksellers, and Daniel Holt, publisher of the radical *Newark Herald*, were all found guilty of distributing seditious material, mostly related to Paine's *Rights of Man*.[135] The suspension of *habeas corpus* in May 1794 and the series of state trials that followed in its wake set off an even

---

1790s. Scholars have primarily focused on Fox's *Address*. Examples include Lewis Patton, in his edition of Samuel Taylor Coleridge's *The Watchman* (London: Routledge and Kegan Paul; Princeton: Princeton University Press, 1970), p. 138, n. 2; Jack Gratus, *The Great White Lie: Slavery, Emancipation and Changing Racial Attitudes* (New York: Monthly Review Press, 1973), p. 74; Clare Midgley, *Women Against Slavery: The British Campaigns, 1780-1870* (London: Routledge, 1992), p. 35; Coleman, 'Conspicuous Consumption', pp. 348-49; J. R. Oldfield, *Popular Politics and British Anti-Slavery: The Mobilisation of Public Opinion against the Slave Trade, 1787-1807* (Manchester: Manchester University Press, 1995), pp. 56-57; David Brion Davis, *The Problem of Slavery in the Age of Revolution 1770-1823* (New York and Oxford: Oxford University Press, 1999), p. 381; John Barrell, *Imagining the King's Death: Figurative Treason, Fantasies of Regicide 1793-1796* (Oxford: Oxford University Press, 2000), pp. 1, 81; Charlotte Sussman, *Consuming Anxieties: Consumer Protest, Gender, and British Slavery, 1713-1833* (Stanford, CA: Stanford University Press, 2000), pp. 38-44, 114-15; Keith Sandiford, *The Cultural Politics of Sugar: Caribbean Slavery and Narratives of Colonialism* (Cambridge: Cambridge University Press, 2000), p. 124; and John Oldfield, ed., *The Abolitionist Struggle: Opponents of the Slave Trade*, vol. III of *The British Transatlantic Slave Trade*, gen. ed. Kenneth Morgan (4 vols; London: Pickering & Chatto, 2003), pp. xvi, 321-2.

[134] These include *The Trial of Thomas Hardy for High Treason, at the Sessions House in the Old Bailey* . . . 4 vols. (1794-95); *The Trial of John Horne Tooke for High Treason at the Sessions House in the Old Bailey* . . . (1795); *The Trial of Robert Thomas Crossfield, for High Treason, at the Sessions House in the Old Bailey* (1796); and *The Trial of William Stone, for High Treason, at the Bar of the Court of King's Bench, on Thursday the Twenty-Eighth, and Friday the Twenty-Ninth of January, 1796* (1796); and *The Trial of James O'Coigly ... Arthur O'Connor, Esq., John Binns, John Allen, and Jeremiah Leary for High Treason, under a Special Commission, at Maidstone, in Kent, on Monday the Twenty-Dirst, and Tuesday the Twenty-Second days of May, 1798* (1798).

[135] Goodwin, *Friends of Liberty*, p. 272.

further wave of fear within the radical press. With the passage of the Pitt and Grenville Acts in December 1795, the government's efforts to silence the radical press became virtually complete, forcing many out of the reform movement altogether, some into clandestine rebellion, and others into a considerably muted, though still critical, form of public resistance.

By 1800, many radical reformers of the early 1790s had become pro-government conservatives due to their fear of the ongoing war with France, the possibility of a French invasion, and, for some, the even greater threat of French infidelity. A few, however, remained true to the principles of reform. William H.G. Salter relates how his grandfather, W.B. Gurney, filled 'his table-talk' for more than fifty years with all the leading 'events of the day—public affairs and public men—and, in the second place, of Missions and other religious work. Sometimes there was an echo to be heard of the great antislavery agitation in which he had taken part'.[136] Gurney told his grandson that he became a liberal 'Democrat' in 1795, 'which meant one opposed to the arbitrary power then attempted to be assumed by Pitt and his colleagues', and for the rest of his life he exemplified the finest ideals of political reform and Christian activism.[137] We should not be surprised at this, for W.B. Gurney, his older brother John, and his sister, Elizabeth, could not have escaped the struggle for abolition and reform being carried on around them by their family, their church, and their friends. With William Fox and Martha Gurney as their mentors in this war against political corruption and religious hypocrisy, the Gurney children learned their lessons well. During three glorious years in the 1790s, Fox and Gurney produced a series of pamphlets that extolled the virtues of equality among men, integrity in government, and consistency in religion, virtues they believed the British nation sorely needed at that time. Though historians have largely ignored their efforts, history has proved their sentiments remarkably correct. Despite two hundred years of neglect and obscurity, the works of these two London Dissenters remain a testimony to a political and moral idealism that would later be a hallmark of many Baptists and nonconformists of the nineteenth and twentieth centuries, an idealism grounded in a Christian faith that dared to challenge the accepted practices of the government of their day, regardless of the consequences.

---

[136] Salter (ed.), *Some Particulars*, p. 97.
[137] Salter (ed.), *Some Particulars*, p. 66.

# Index

\* All congregations designated by place of meeting are in London unless otherwise stated.

Abolition, 9, 24, 153, 154, 156, 159-63, 167, 168, 172-83, 185, 187, 190-92, 200, 201
Act of Toleration, 1, 16
Act of Uniformity, 27
Adams, Richard, 5
Allen, Richard, 5
Anne (Queen), 17
Antinomianism, 4, 130
Anti-trinitarianism, 5
Arian, 5, 7, 44, 45, 47, 48, 49, 52, 54, 55, 56, 76
Arianism, 44, 45, 55, 76
Arminian, 7, 24, 27, 28, 34, 42, 51, 53-55, 75, 76, 136, 138, 139, 143, 149, 150, 168
Ash, John, 106
Ashworth, Caleb, 50, 55
Ashworth, John, 50, 52
Atkins, Abraham, 15, 113
Ball, John, 45
Bampfields, 1
Baptism, 6, 15, 16, 21, 24, 27, 29, 43, 45, 47, 49, 52, 53, 55, 65, 75-92, 98, 104, 112, 115, 120-27, 154, 155, 158
Baptist Missionary Society (BMS), 8, 11, 22, 128, 129, 146, 160, 167, 170
Barbican, 17, 22, 23, 43, 45-47, 49
Barron, Richard, 52
Bath, 3, 21, 22, 161, 181
Baxter, Richard, 29, 32, 39, 54, 55
Beatson, John, 167
Beddome, Benjamin, 24, 93-111

Bedfordshire, 7, 15, 25, 168
Berkshire, 7, 58, 67, 113, 117, 132
Betjeman, John, 10
Billingsley, Nicholas, 44-49, 54
Blackfriars, 21
Booth, Abraham, 7, 13, 15, 123, 127, 143, 167, 171
Bosher, John, 48
Bourton on the Water, 10, 24, 94-96, 99-104
Bowen, Emmanuel, 23
Bowyer, Robert, 22
Boyce, Gilbert, 24, 27, 75-92
Bradburn, Samuel, 171, 182
Brine, John, 4, 51, 54, 129, 148, 150
Bristol, 3, 5, 7, 12, 15, 16, 18, 19, 22-24, 67, 95, 97, 102, 112, 131, 132, 136, 138, 147, 152, 153, 154, 156-64, 167, 192
Bristol Academy, 3, 22, 23, 95, 102, 131, 132, 138, 147, 167
Broadmead, 24, 97, 152, 154-60, 164, 167
Broughton, 58, 60-62, 64, 65, 67
Brown, John, 122-24
Brown, Thomas, 20
Buckinghamshire, 5, 7, 25, 27, 31, 41
Bulkeley [Bulkley], Charles, 50-55, 126
Bull, Frederick, 16
Bull, John, 158
Bunyan, John, 15, 25, 26, 42, 94, 101, 115, 124, 135

Burke, Edmund, 162, 166, 180, 186, 193, 195, 196
Burroughs, Joseph, 22, 45, 46
Caffyn, Matthew, 5
Calvinism, 1, 3, 7, 15, 19, 36, 37, 40, 42, 53, 55, 95, 96, 99, 101-103, 128-32, 134, 135, 138, 140, 145, 147-50, 155, 157, 167
Calvinism - high, 15, 55, 128-32, 135, 147, 149, 150
Calvinism - hyper, 1, 3-4, 36, 37, 129, 150
Calvinism - moderate, 148
Calvinism - strict, 19, 140, 145, 149, 150, 155
Calvinists, 3-5, 18, 24, 28, 36, 40, 51, 54, 87, 131-37, 141-44, 148-50, 155, 168
Calvinistic, 3, 27, 28, 32, 34, 38, 68, 69, 73, 94-97, 101, 106, 109, 112, 118, 125, 128, 129, 131, 136, 141, 143, 148-50, 175
Cambridge, 3, 7, 44, 128, 136, 155, 156, 167, 177
Carey, William, 8, 25, 26, 42, 58, 99, 160
Carter's Lane, 8, 9, 20, 22
Caswell, Sir George, 16
Catechism, 82, 85, 86, 91, 101, 102
Chamberlains, 1
Charles II, 27, 28
Chevalier, Thomas, 22
Christology, 1, 5, 24, 50, 55,
Church and King Riots, 2
Clark, James, 78
Clark, John, 46
Clark, Samuel, 32
Clarke, Samuel, 44, 50
Clarkson, Thomas, 19, 153, 159, 160, 174, 177, 179-82
Closed communion, 15, 89
Coade, Eleanor, 21
Coleman, Thomas, 52

Collett, John, 159
Collins, Hercules, 101
Collins, William, 101
Communion, 10, 11, 15, 24, 53, 55, 89, 112, 113, 115-27, 142, 149, 169, 183
Congregational singing; hymn singing, 4, 8, 12, 24, 26, 38, 88, 96
Congregationalists, 77, 94, 117
Cottle, Joseph, 23
Covenant, 10, 24, 28, 32, 34-36, 39, 63, 112, 113, 124, 126, 136, 137
Cripplegate, 103
Crisp, Dr Tobias, 3
Cromwell, Oliver, 18, 27, 94
Crosby, Thomas, 26, 28, 38, 39
Cruger, Henry, 161, 162, 163
Curriers' Hall, 4
Dale, R.W., 11
David, Rees, 18
De Fleury, Maria, 171
Despard, Edward, 171
Devon, 7, 44, 45
Doddridge, Philip, 49, 50, 52, 53, 55
Dolben, William, 161
Dore, James, 13, 14, 18, 109, 167, 169, 171, 173, 176, 177
Dossey, John, 75
Drapers' Company, 3
East India Company, 194,
East Midlands, 7
Ecclesiology, 15, 16, 109, 114, 121, 126, 130
Edwards, Jonathan, 4, 7, 99, 128-30, 137-41, 145-47, 150
Emlyn, Thomas, 49, 51, 55
Erskine, Thomas, 137, 141
Essex, 7
Evangelical Revival, 6, 10, 11, 23, 24, 54, 66, 99, 129, 136, 137
Evans, Allen, 17

*Index* 205

Evans, Caleb, 5, 18, 58, 95, 106, 132, 152-64, 167
Evans, Hugh, 158
Evans, John, 54, 131
Eve, John, 130, 135
Exeter, 21, 43, 44, 45, 48, 49, 51, 62, 102
Fanch, James, 24, 58-74
Fifth Monarchists, 18
*First London Baptist Confession*, 116, 120
Fisher, Samuel, 171
Fleming, Caleb, 49-51
Foskett, Bernard, 95, 97, 98, 105, 131, 157
Foster, James, 22, 23, 43-57, 126
Foster, John, 23, 192
Fox, William, 24, 165-201
Fry, Samuel, 48
Fuller, Andrew, 4, 7, 8, 15, 24, 58, 128-51, 155, 156
Fullerism, 11, 129, 135, 140, 150
Gainsford Street, 20
Gale, John, 22, 23, 45, 46, 49
Gandy, Harry, 153, 160
General Baptist Assembly, 5, 20, 56, 76, 91, 119
General Baptists, 1, 4-8, 17, 20, 22, 24, 27, 28, 45, 46, 48, 50, 52-57, 75-92, 119, 125, 126, 143, 148, 170
General Baptists - New Connexion, *See New Connexion of General Baptists*
General Baptists - Old Connexion, 7, 24, 76, 88
George II, 23
George III, 23, 157
Gibbs, Philip, 19
Gibson, Edmund, 76
Gill, John, 4, 6, 8, 19, 23, 26, 58, 59, 119, 129-131, 133, 148, 150, 168
Grafton Street, 22

Grantham, Thomas, 5, 8
Griffith, John, 5
Gurney, John, 169, 170, 173, 200
Gurney, Joseph, 169, 171, 173, 178, 200
Gurney, Martha, 24, 165-201
Guy, Thomas, 16
Hackney, 22, 176
Hall, Robert (elder), 7, 128, 136, 138, 140, 147
Hall, Robert Jr, 14, 15, 23, 101, 106, 107, 120, 122, 124, 154-56, 158, 164, 167
Hallett, Joseph III, 43, 44, 48
Hampshire, 52, 58, 59, 61, 65-67, 131
Hann, Isaac, 132
Hardy, Thomas, 169, 171, 199, 200
Harris, John, 154-61
Hertfordshire, 7, 60
Hillier, Richard, 182, 183
Hoffman, Melchior, 5
Hogg Hill Independent Church, Cambridge, 3
Holborn Hill, 170, 172, 173
Hollis Family, 2
Hollis, Thomas III, 3
Horselydown (Horsleydown), 25, 26, 28, 37, 39, 48, 95, 119
Horton/Rawdon, 12
Hughes, Joseph, 23
Hussey, Joseph, 3, 129
Independents, 17, 27, 42, 43, 44, 50, 52, 55, 64, 87, 117, 154, 181
Indulgence, 28
Itinerant Society, 12, 175
Jacobin/Jacobinism, 166, 172, 189, 192, 193, 195, 196
James, John, 155
Jeffries, Joseph, 76
Justification, 32, 35, 39, 42
Keach, Benjamin, 5, 10, 24, 25-42, 95, 96, 102

Kent, 4, 7, 56, 200
Keppel Street, 22
Kettering, 4, 122, 133, 142, 147, 148
Key, Mark, 5
Killingworth, Grantham, 53, 126
Kimber, Isaac, 23
King's Heath, Birmingham, 2
Kinghorn, Joseph, 15, 122, 147
Kingsbury, Benjamin, 171
Kitchin, Thomas, 23
Knollys, Hanserd, 28
Lacy, John, 63, 64, 67
Laying on of hands, 4, 29, 85
Liddon, John, 167, 182
Lincolnshire, 7, 24, 56, 75, 76, 91
Little Prescot Street, 7, 20, 21, 95, 98, 100-104, 158, 175
Little Wild Street, 17, 20, 62, 157
Liverpool, 19, 22, 196
Locke, John, 45, 54, 141
Lockerley, 58, 59, 65-68
Lyme Regis, 21
Marlow, Isaac, 96
Maze Pond, 13, 18, 20, 24, 96, 167, 169, 173, 176, 177, 182, 183
Mead, Matthew, 26
Medley, Samuel, 19-22
Mennonite, 4, 9, 53
Merchants Hall, 161
Methodist, 6, 75, 77, 78, 80, 81, 86, 91, 92, 112, 136, 162, 170, 181, 182
Methodist Revival, 6, 24, 75, 76, 86, 92
Mixed communion, 53, 113, 115, 120, 149
Monk, Thomas, 5
Moore, John Jr, 45
Morgan, Thomas, 45
Morris, Joseph, 46
Neonomian, 29, 32, 39
New Connexion of General Baptists, 5, 7, 24, 56, 75, 76, 88, 143
New Park Street, 26
New Road, Oxford, 2, 10, 112, 113, 124
Newcastle upon Tyne, 7
Newton, James, 23, 154
Newton, John, 93, 94, 99, 107
Northampton, 7, 15, 52, 150
Northampton Academy, 57
Northamptonshire, 7, 11, 25, 52, 148, 150
Northamptonshire Association, 7, 11, 135-36, 148
Old Jewry, 49, 51, 53
Open communion, 15, 24, 120-27
Open membership, 3, 15, 24, 50
Original Sin, 51, 83, 87
Owen, John, 103, 135, 144
Oxford, 2, 10, 112-14, 117
Paine, Thomas, 171, 180, 185, 187, 200
Palmer, Anthony, 94, 95
Parsons, Robert, 21, 22
Particular Baptist, 3-8, 12, 24-26, 28, 31, 36, 38, 42, 62, 75, 86, 94, 115-20, 126, 128-34, 142, 143, 147-50, 157, 166, 171, 176
Particular Baptist Board, 62
Particular Baptist Fund, 3, 48, 61, 63, 65
Particular Baptist Missionary Society, 8
Paul's Alley, 45, 46, 49, 50, 55
Pearce, Samuel, 167, 182, 183
Peirce, James, 44-53
Pelagian, 52, 87
Petty France, 101
Pine, William, 156, 161, 162
Pinners Hall, 3, 49-51
Plymouth, 19
Pope, Alexander, 49
Pope, Andrew, 157
Pope, Michael, 157

*Index* 207

Portsmouth, 20, 64, 177
Presbyterians, 4, 16, 17, 38, 43, 44, 48, 49, 53-55, 77, 102, 112, 117, 131
Prescot Street, *See Little Prescot Street*
Priestly, Joseph, 2
Quakers, 4, 27, 29, 39, 78, 82, 153, 160, 177, 178, 181
Red Cross Street, 169, 173
Religious Tract Society, 170
Reynolds, John, 103
Rider, William, 27
Rippon, John, 8, 9, 22, 26, 58, 65, 100, 101, 105, 106, 112, 131, 148, 149, 175
Robinson, Robert, 115, 122, 155, 167, 177
Romsey, 24, 58-68
Ryland, John Sr, 15, 99, 102, 103, 122, 123, 130
Ryland, John Jr, 6, 58, 128-30, 133, 136-38, 141, 147, 148, 154-56
Sabbatarian Baptists, 1, 48
Sacheverell riots, 2
Salters Hall, 44-46, 55
*Savoy Declaration*, 38
Scott, Daniel, 52-53
Scott, Joseph Nicoll, 52-53
Scott, Thomas, 52-53
*Second London Baptist Confession of Faith*, 28, 35, 38, 68, 70, 149
Serampore, 8, 167
Seventh Day Baptists, *See Sabbatarian Baptists*
Sharp, Granville, 153, 159, 167, 176, 178
Shepton Mallett, 45
Sheraton, Thomas, 21
Sierra Leone, 9
Skepp, John, 3, 4
Slavery, 9, 13, 14, 16, 18, 19, 24, 152-64, 165,-201

Socinianism, 7, 39, 49, 52-56, 76, 125, 126, 155, 156
Somerset (place), 7, 44, 48
Somerset (person), 159
Somerset Street, Bath, 3
Southampton, 63-65
Southwark, 18, 20, 26, 27, 33, 37, 95, 167, 169, 171
Spurgeon, Charles, 26, 41, 58, 150
Stamp Act, 162
Steele, Anne, 23, 58, 59, 61, 62, 65, 66
Steele, Henry, 64
Steele, William, 62, 64-67
Stennett, Joseph, 62, 63
Stennett, Samuel, 132, 157
Stepney College, 170
Stinton, Benjamin, 26, 28
Stogdon, Hubert, 43-57
Stone, William, 171, 200
Stony Stratford, 10
Strict Baptist, 149, 150, 183
Strict Baptist Historical Society, 25, 103
Sunday School Society, 175
Sunday School Union, 170
Sussex, 4, 7, 56
Sutcliff, John, 7, 106, 110, 129, 131, 136, 138
Swain, Joseph, 171
Taylor, Dan, 24, 56, 75, 76, 88, 123, 143-45
Test and Corporation Acts, 16, 153, 165
*The Baptist Annual Register*, 8, 9, 65, 100, 148, 149, 175
Thompson, Joshua, 117
Thompson, William, 75
Thorverton, 43
Tooke, Horne, 169, 171, 199, 200
Tooley Street, 27, 28
Toulmin, Joshua, 53
Towgood, Matthew, 45
Tozer, Arthur, 155, 156

Triangular Trade, 171
Trinitarianism, 5, 44, 46, 47, 53, See also Anti-Trinitarianism
Trinity, 4, 5, 35, 36, 44-53
Turner, Daniel, 15, 58-68, 105, 112-27, 132
Unicorn Yard, 157
Unitarianism, 2, 23, 46-48, 54-56, 76, 166, 170, 174
Upton, James, 21
Wallin, Benjamin, 132
Ward, William, 167, 181
Warwick, 6, 100, 103
Watts, Isaac, 8, 46, 47, 52, 53, 59, 98, 108, 109
Wesley, John, 24, 55, 75-92, 136, 162, 167, 168, 173
Western Baptist Association, 132, 153, 154
*Westminster Confession of Faith*, 38
Whiston, William, 44, 45, 50, 51
Whitefield, George, 6, 7, 94, 99, 110, 128, 137, 157, 168
Wickham Market, 2
Wilberforce, William, 161-63, 179
William III, 32
Williams, Daniel, 32
Wiltshire, 3, 7, 50, 52, 59, 103, 131, 183
Winterbotham, William, 19
Withers, John, 44
Wookey, 45, 48
Worship Street, 5
Wright, Joseph, 5
Yorkshire, 7, 12, 75, 76

www.ingramcontent.com/pod-product-compliance
Lightning Source LLC
Chambersburg PA
CBHW070321230426
43663CB00011B/2187